# JONESY™

### HUMPHRIES · BOYLE · QUINN

## VOLUME ONE

**JONESY Volume One, August 2016.** Published by BOOM! Box, a division of Boom Entertainment, Inc., 5670 Wilshire Boulevard, Suite 450, Los Angeles, CA 90036-5679. Jonesy is ™ & © 2016 Sam Humphries & Caitlin Rose Boyle. Originally published in single magazine form as JONESY No. 1-4. ™ & © 2016 Sam Humphries & Caitlin Rose Boyle. All rights reserved. BOOM! Box™ and the BOOM! Box logo are trademarks of Boom Entertainment, Inc., registered in various countries and categories. All characters, events, and institutions depicted herein are fictional. Any similarity between any of the names, characters, persons, events, and/or institutions in this publication to actual names, characters, and persons, whether living or dead, events, and/or institutions is unintended and purely coincidental. BOOM! Box does not read or accept unsolicited submissions of ideas, stories, or artwork.

A catalog record of this book is available from OCLC and from the BOOM! Studios website, www.boom-studios.com, on the Librarians page.

BOOM! Studios, 5670 Wilshire Boulevard, Suite 450, Los Angeles, CA 90036-5679. Printed in China. First Printing.

ISBN: 978-1-60886-883-4, eISBN: 978-1-61398-554-0

DEDICATED TO

EMILY & KRISTEN

♥ ♥ ♥ SAM & CAITLIN

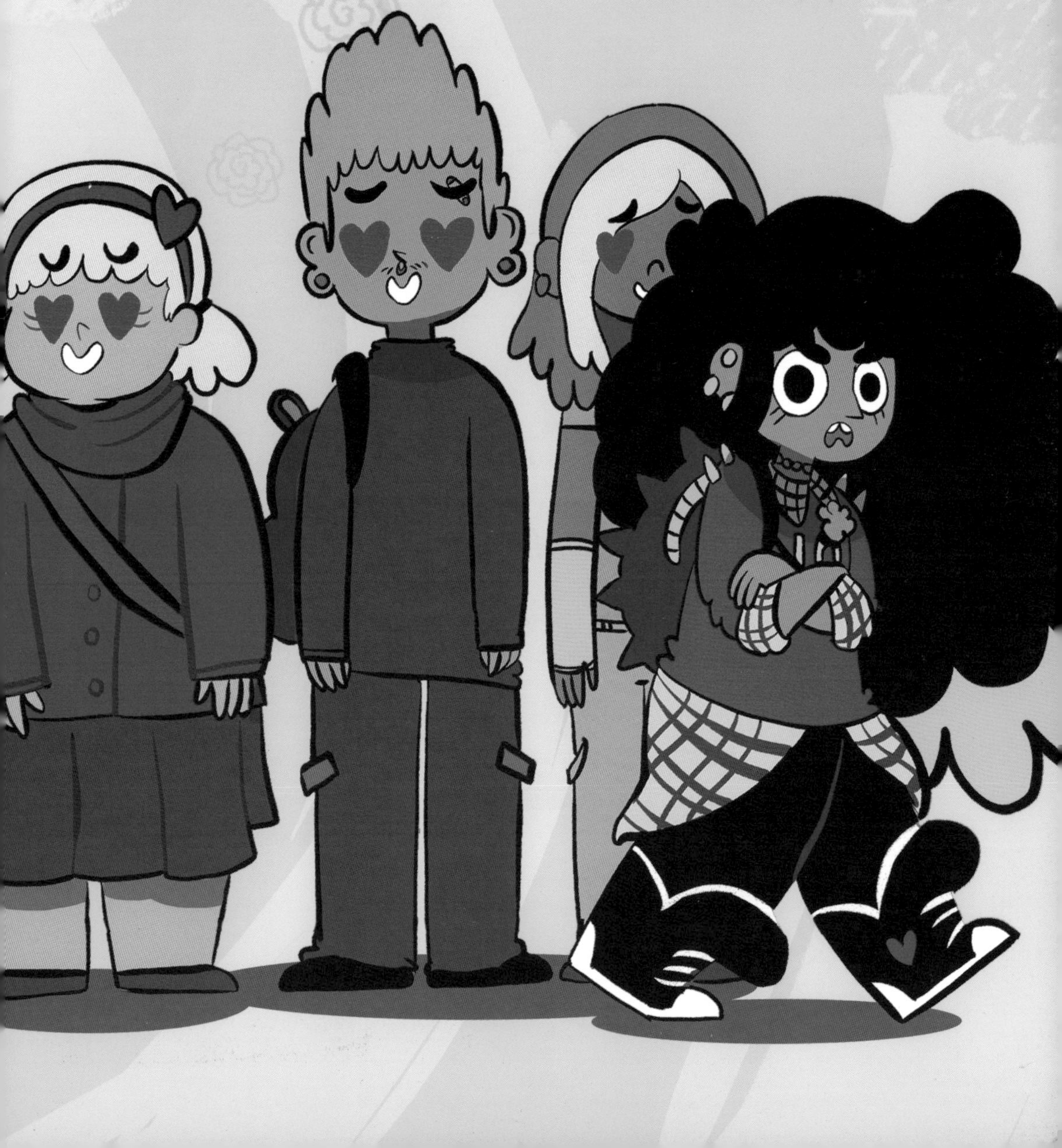

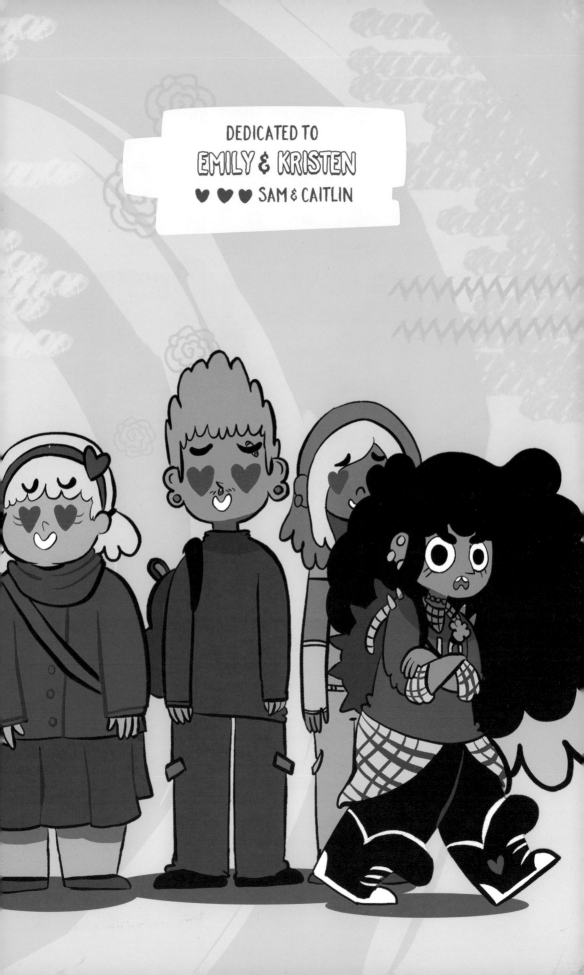

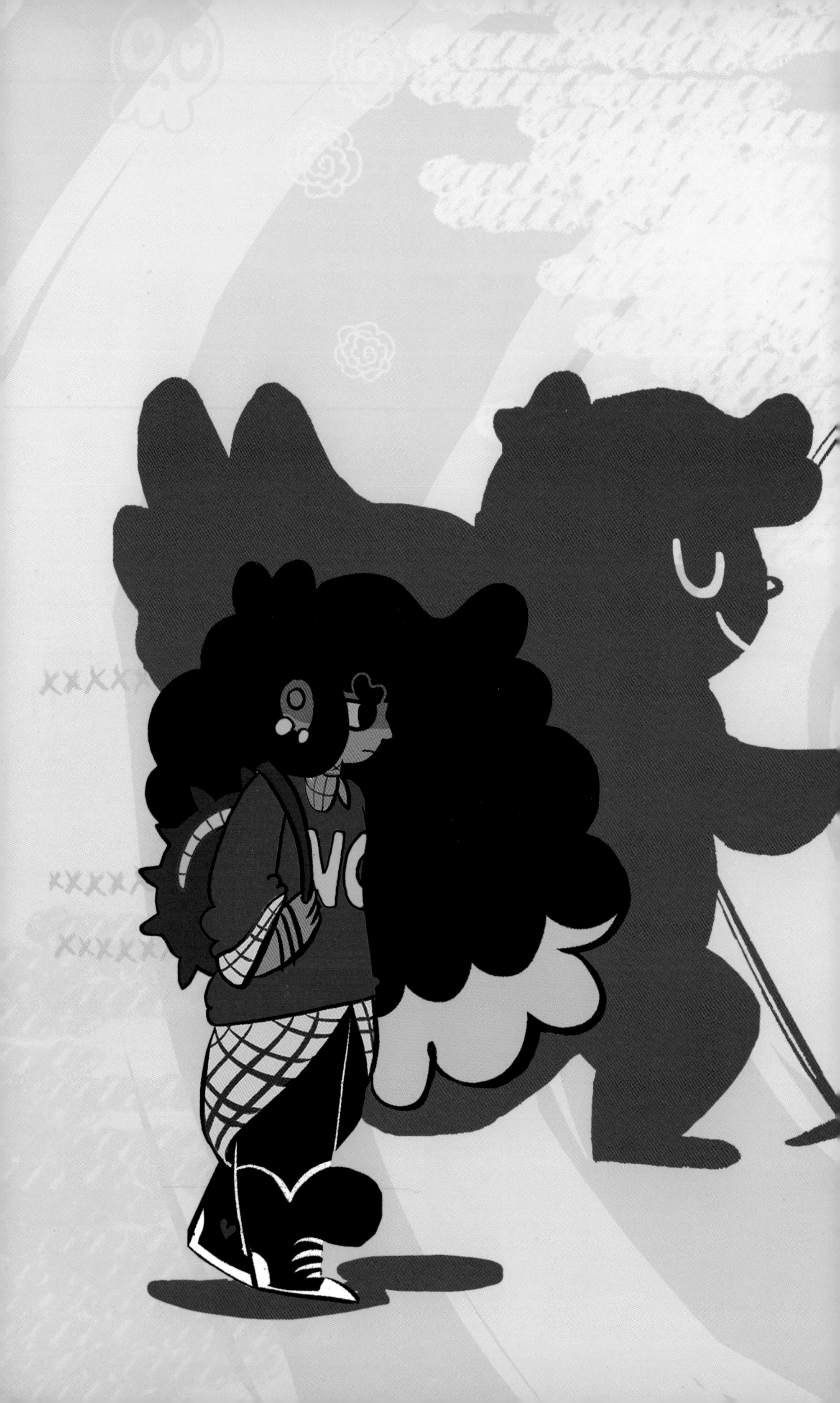

BY
## SAM HUMPHRIES &
## CAITLIN ROSE BOYLE

COLORS BY
## MICKEY QUINN

LETTERS BY
## COREY BREEN

COVER BY
## CAITLIN ROSE BOYLE

DESIGNER
## KELSEY DIETERICH

EDITORS
## JEANINE SCHAEFER &
## SHANNON WATTERS

# CHAPTER ONE

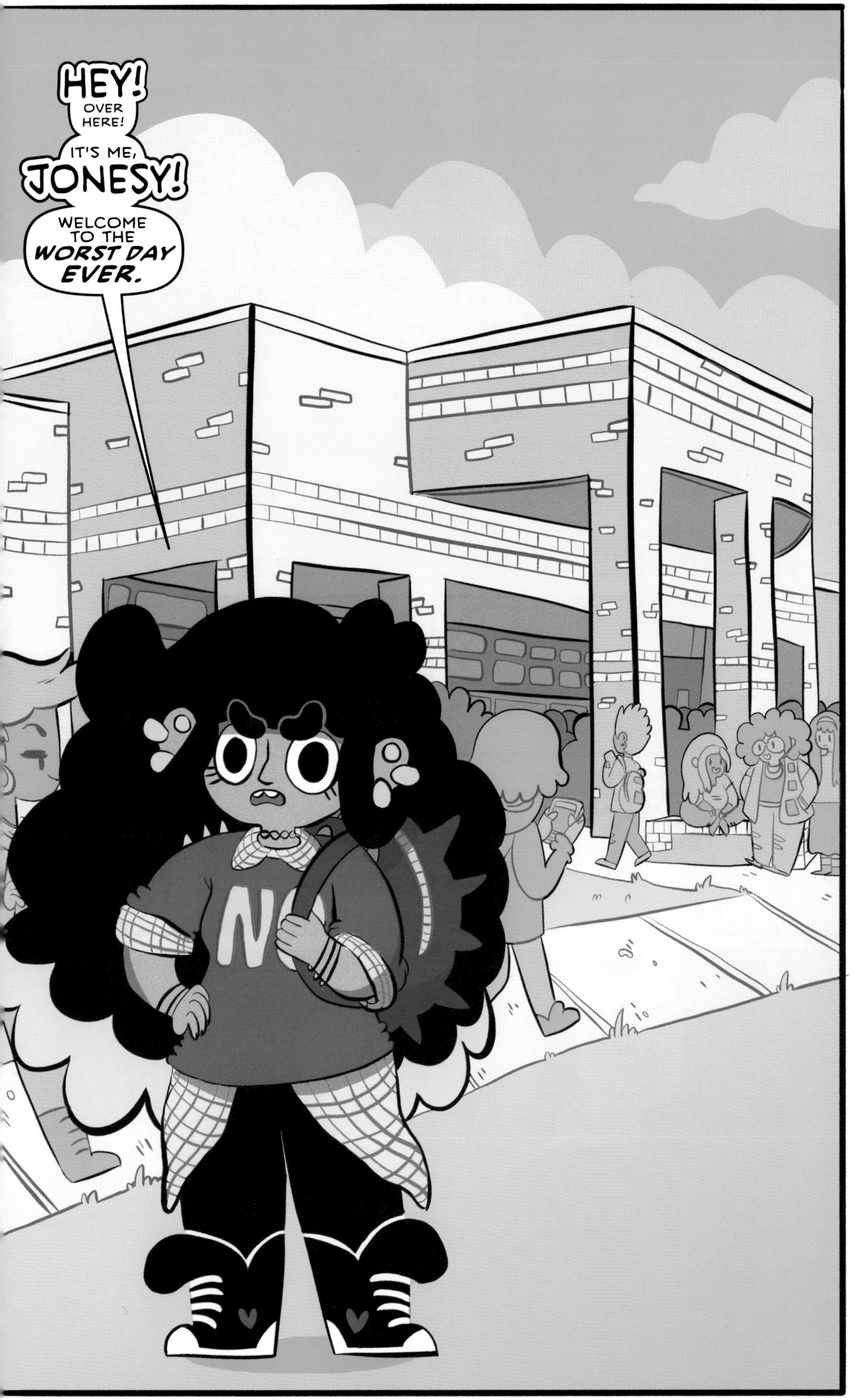
HEY! OVER HERE!
IT'S ME, JONESY!
WELCOME TO THE WORST DAY EVER.
NO

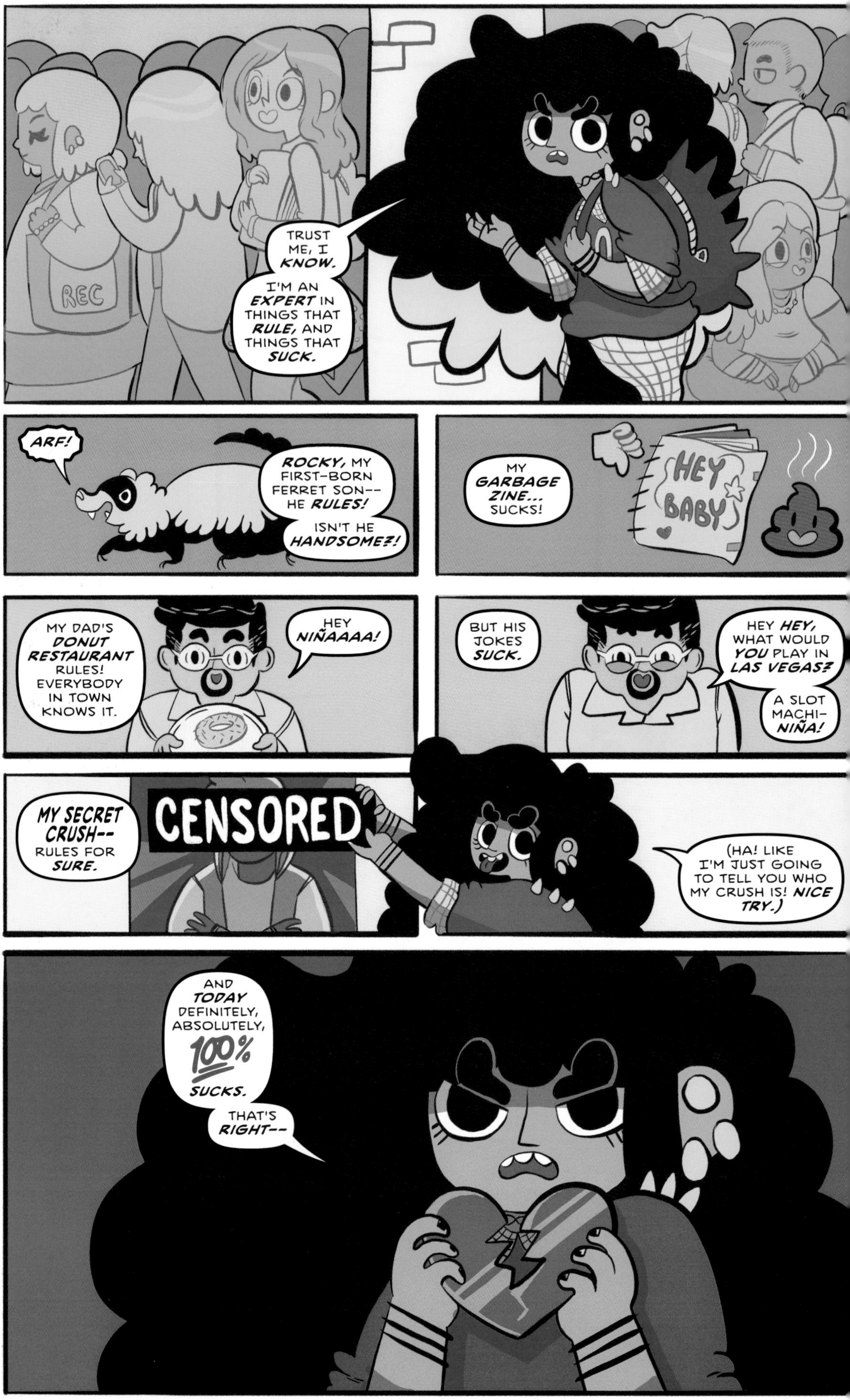

TRUST ME, I KNOW.
I'M AN EXPERT IN THINGS THAT RULE, AND THINGS THAT SUCK.
REC
ARF!
ROCKY, MY FIRST-BORN FERRET SON-- HE RULES!
ISN'T HE HANDSOME?!
MY GARBAGE ZINE... SUCKS!
HEY BABY
MY DAD'S DONUT RESTAURANT RULES! EVERYBODY IN TOWN KNOWS IT.
HEY NIÑAAAAA!
BUT HIS JOKES SUCK.
HEY HEY, WHAT WOULD YOU PLAY IN LAS VEGAS?
A SLOT MACHI-NIÑA!
MY SECRET CRUSH-- RULES FOR SURE.
CENSORED
(HA! LIKE I'M JUST GOING TO TELL YOU WHO MY CRUSH IS! NICE TRY.)
AND TODAY DEFINITELY, ABSOLUTELY, 100% SUCKS.
THAT'S RIGHT--

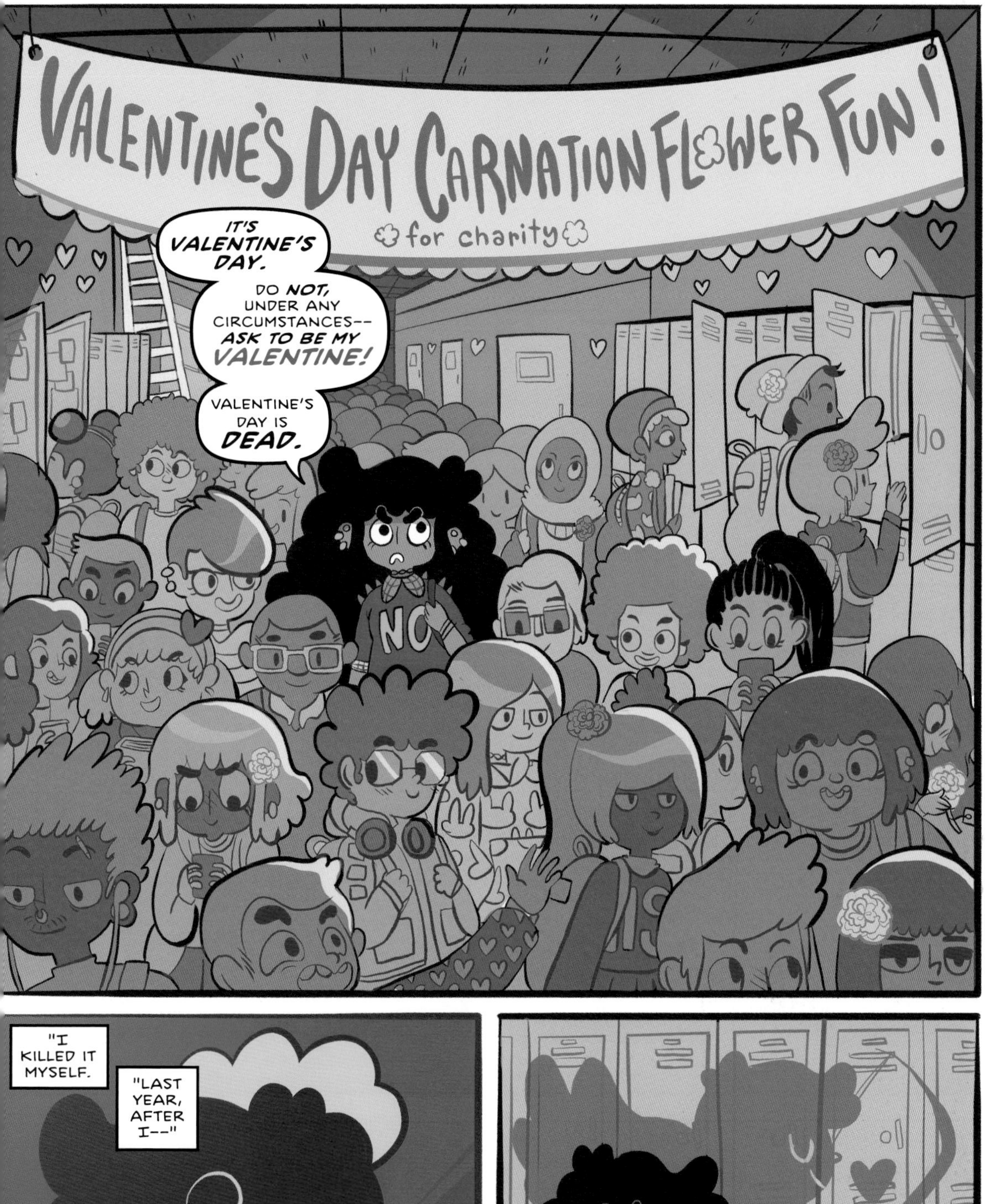

VALENTINE'S DAY CARNATION FLOWER FUN!
for charity
IT'S VALENTINE'S DAY.
DO NOT, UNDER ANY CIRCUMSTANCES-- ASK TO BE MY VALENTINE!
VALENTINE'S DAY IS DEAD.
NO


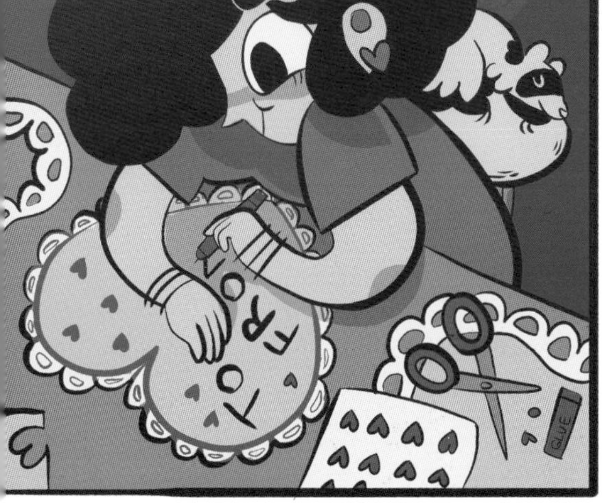

"I KILLED IT MYSELF.
"LAST YEAR, AFTER I--"


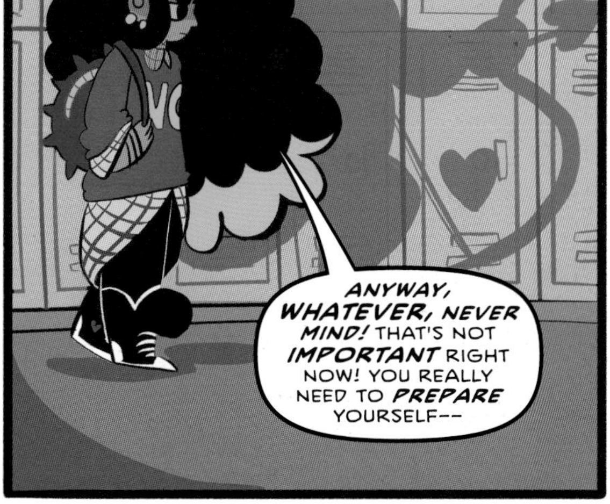

ANYWAY, WHATEVER, NEVER MIND! THAT'S NOT IMPORTANT RIGHT NOW! YOU REALLY NEED TO PREPARE YOURSELF--

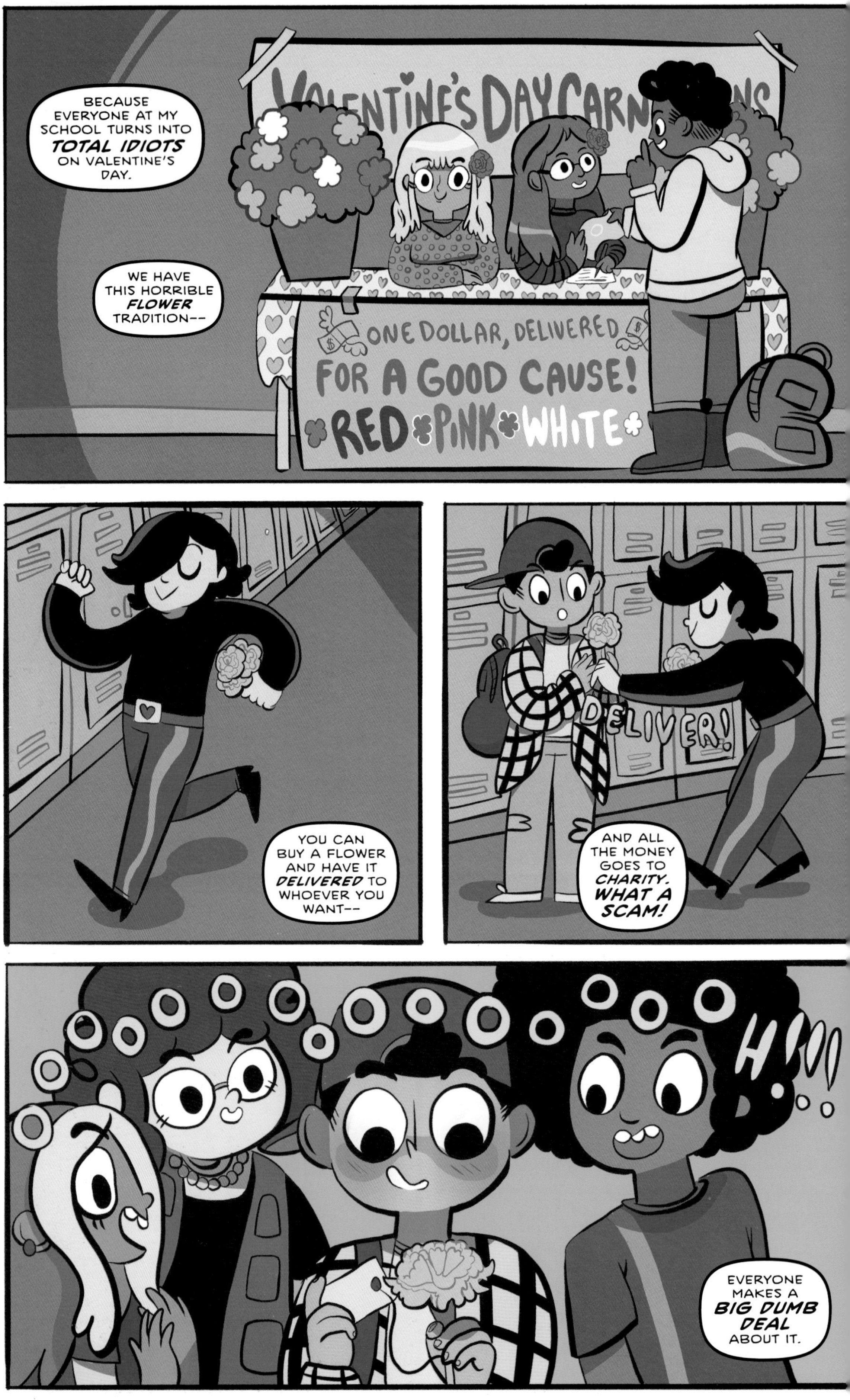
BECAUSE EVERYONE AT MY SCHOOL TURNS INTO TOTAL IDIOTS ON VALENTINE'S DAY.
WE HAVE THIS HORRIBLE FLOWER TRADITION--
ONE DOLLAR, DELIVERED
FOR A GOOD CAUSE!
RED PINK WHITE
YOU CAN BUY A FLOWER AND HAVE IT DELIVERED TO WHOEVER YOU WANT--
DELIVER!
AND ALL THE MONEY GOES TO CHARITY. WHAT A SCAM!
EVERYONE MAKES A BIG DUMB DEAL ABOUT IT.

"WHO GOT A FLOWER?"

"WHO SENT IT?"

"WHAT COLOR IS IT?"

WHO CAAAAARES.

NEEDLESS TO SAY, I HAVE *UNSUBSCRIBED* FROM THE WHOLE MESS.

# CARNATION STATUS BREAKDOWN

RED     PINK     WHITE

THE CODE BEHIND THE CARNATIONS IS ARBITRARY, YET LOADED WITH *IDIOTIC SIGNIFICANCE.*

THE *RED FLOWERS* ARE FOR YOUR BOYFRIEND AND GIRLFRIEND *ONLY. NO EXCEPTIONS!*

THE *PINK FLOWERS* ARE FOR YOUR CRUSHES.

THE *WHITE FLOWERS* NEVER SELL. EVERYONE LOOKS AT THEM LIKE THEY'RE *GARBAGE,* BUT--

HMM JONESY, IF YOU COULD TAKE YOUR SEAT *PLEEEEASE*--

NO

CARNATION DE-LIV-ER-EEE.

UH, WE GOT LARRY, SUSAN, GEMINI, *JONESY*--

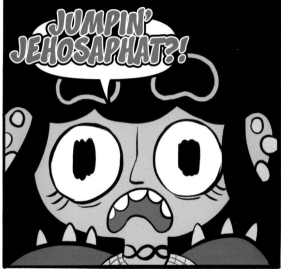

JUMPIN' JEHOSAPHAT?!

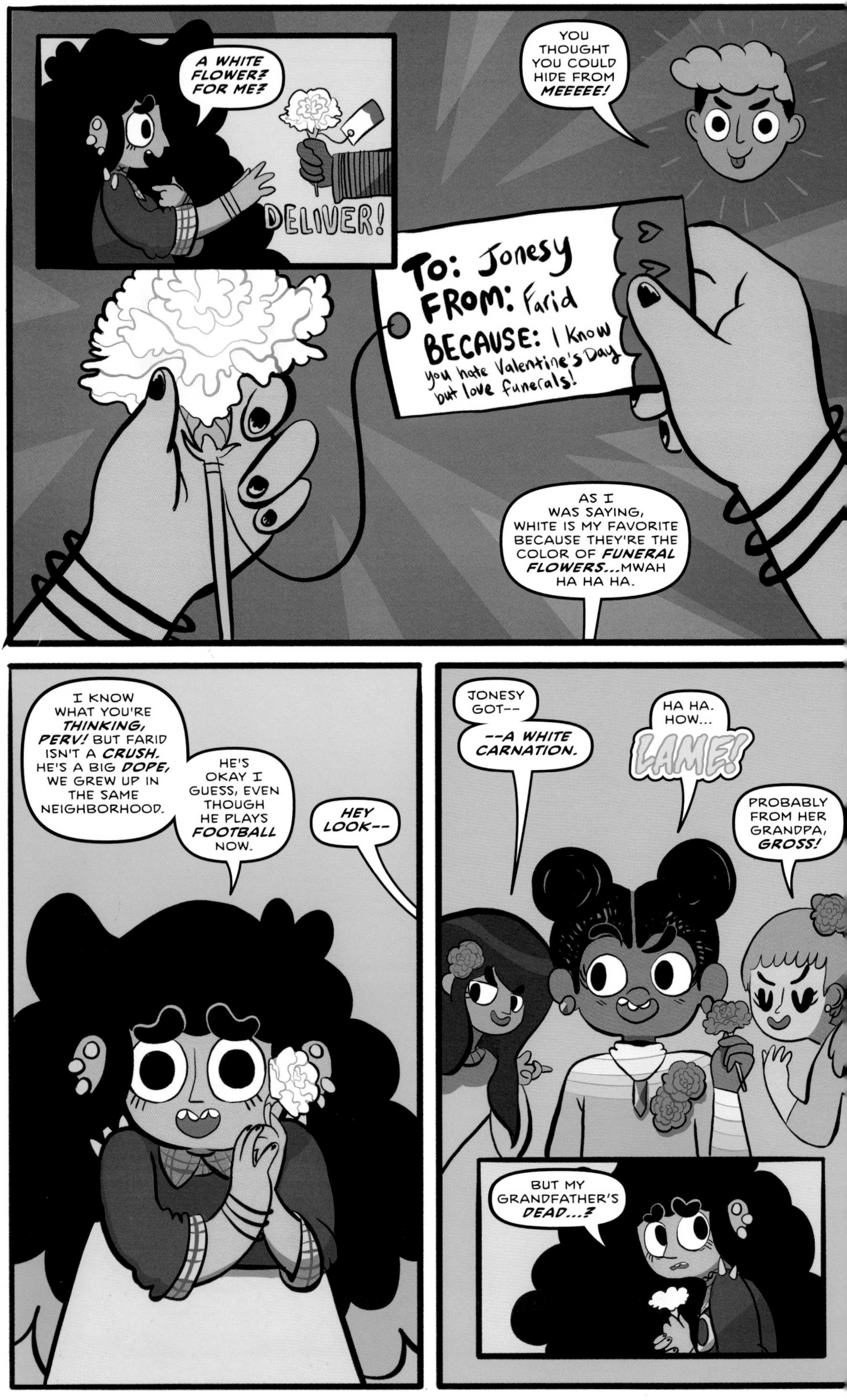
A WHITE FLOWER? FOR ME?
DELIVER!
YOU THOUGHT YOU COULD HIDE FROM MEEEEE!
To: Jonesy
FROM: Farid
BECAUSE: I know you hate Valentine's Day but love funerals!
AS I WAS SAYING, WHITE IS MY FAVORITE BECAUSE THEY'RE THE COLOR OF FUNERAL FLOWERS...MWAH HA HA HA.
I KNOW WHAT YOU'RE THINKING, PERV! BUT FARID ISN'T A CRUSH. HE'S A BIG DOPE, WE GREW UP IN THE SAME NEIGHBORHOOD.
HE'S OKAY I GUESS, EVEN THOUGH HE PLAYS FOOTBALL NOW.
HEY LOOK--
JONESY GOT--
--A WHITE CARNATION.
HA HA. HOW...
LAME!
PROBABLY FROM HER GRANDPA, GROSS!
BUT MY GRANDFATHER'S DEAD...?

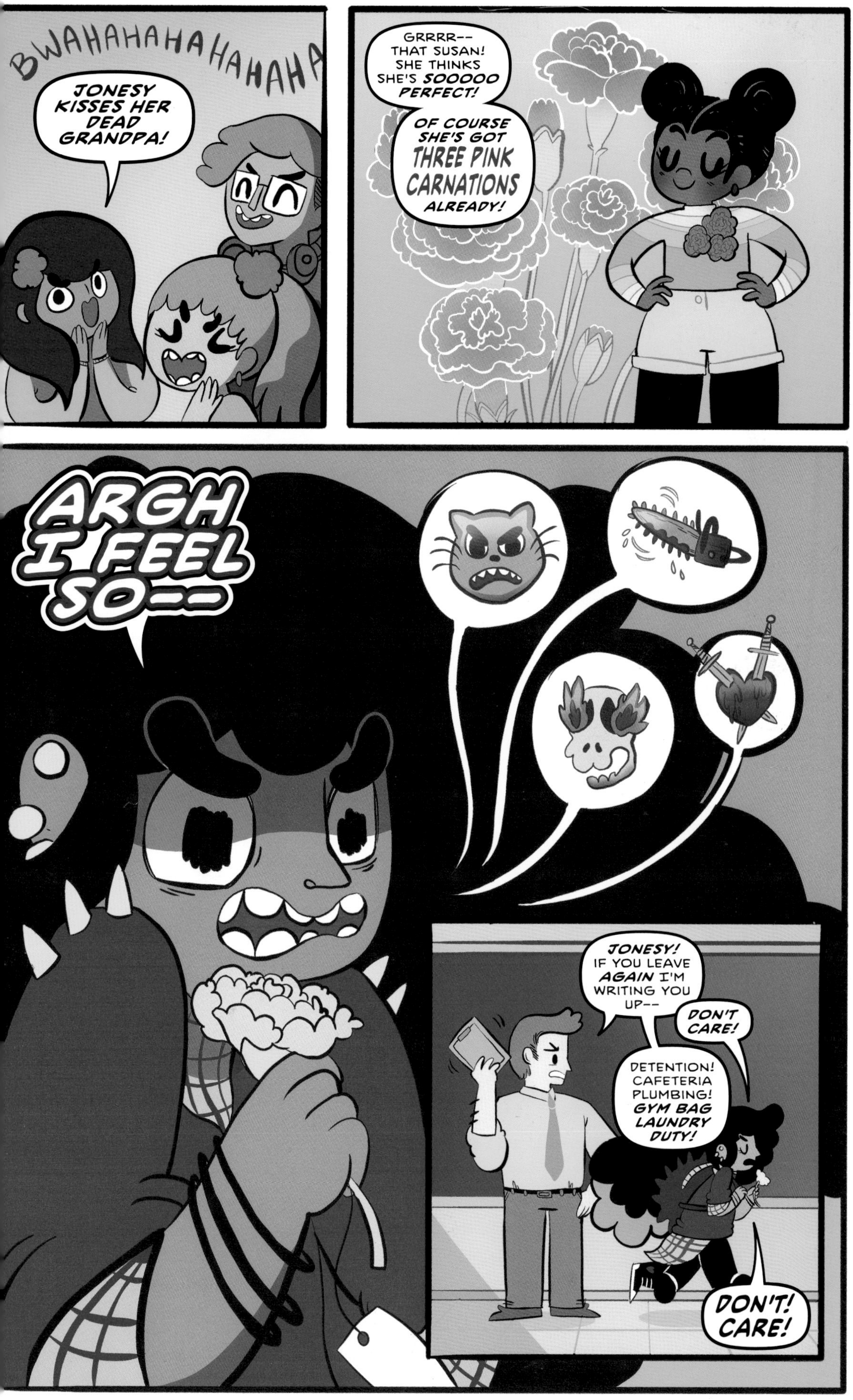
BWAHAHAHAHAHAHAHA
JONESY KISSES HER DEAD GRANDPA!
GRRRR-- THAT SUSAN! SHE THINKS SHE'S SOOOOO PERFECT!
OF COURSE SHE'S GOT THREE PINK CARNATIONS ALREADY!
ARGH I FEEL SO--
JONESY! IF YOU LEAVE AGAIN I'M WRITING YOU UP--
DON'T CARE!
DETENTION! CAFETERIA PLUMBING! GYM BAG LAUNDRY DUTY!
DON'T! CARE!

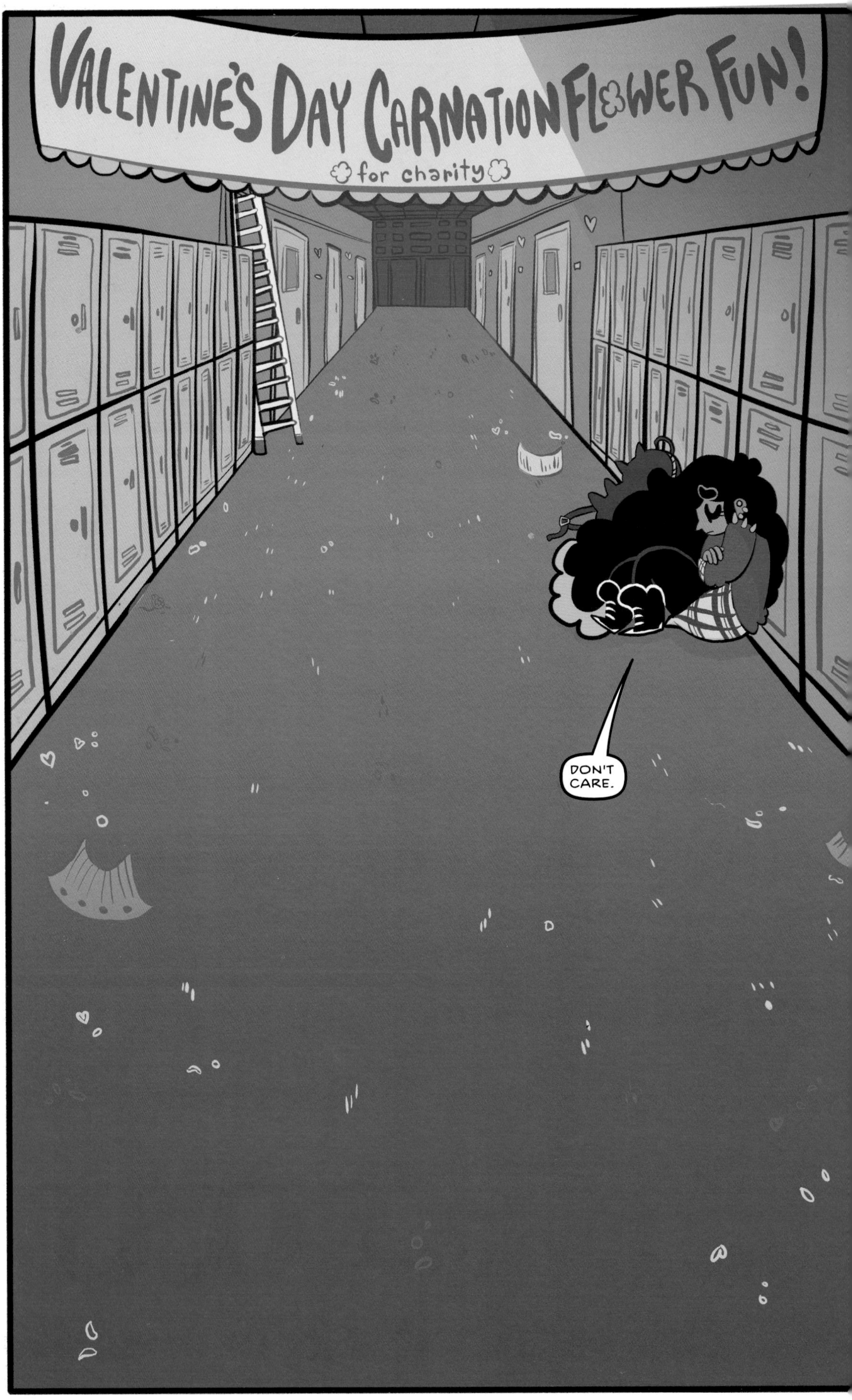
VALENTINE'S DAY CARNATION FLOWER FUN!
for charity
DON'T CARE.

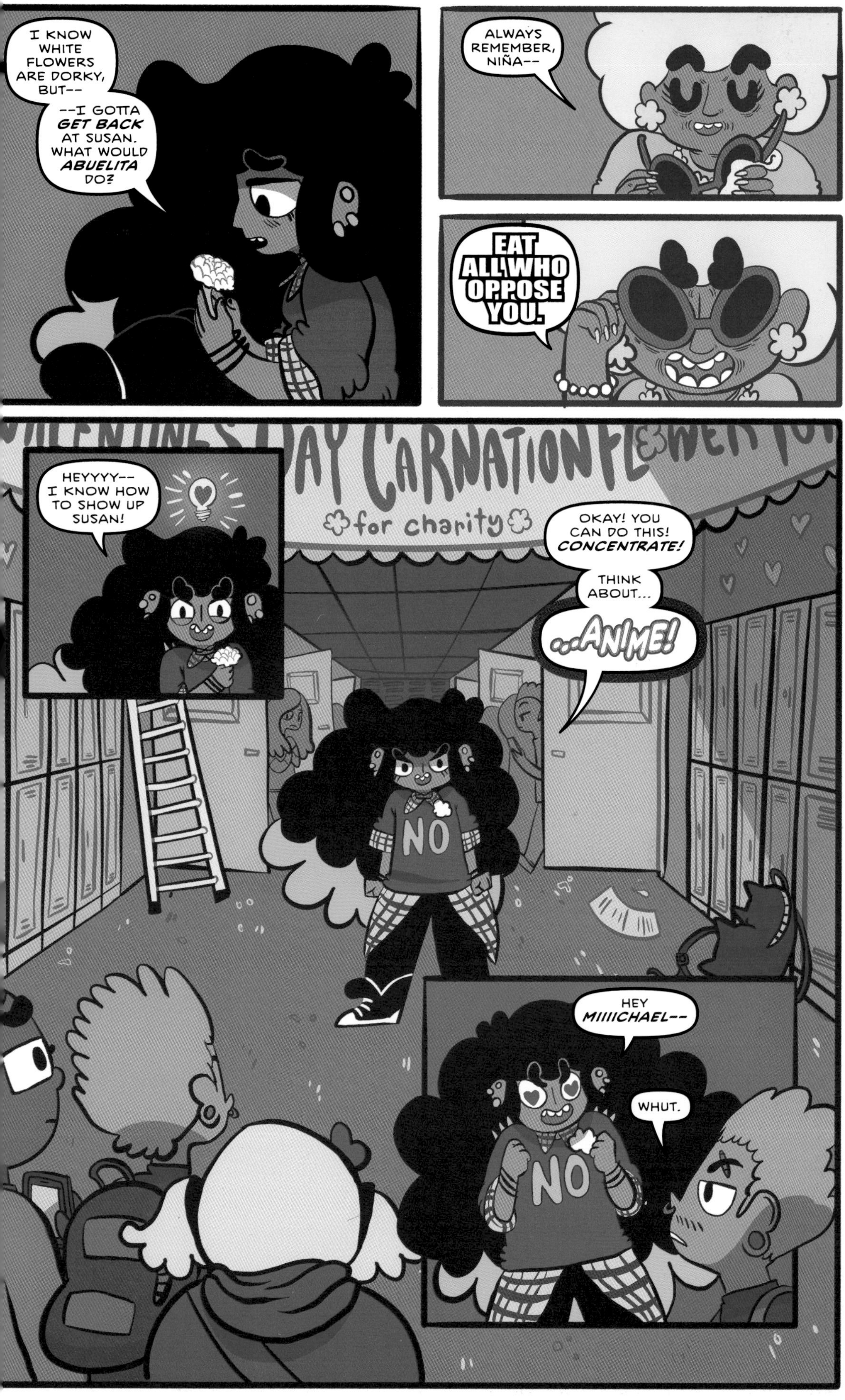
I KNOW WHITE FLOWERS ARE DORKY, BUT--
--I GOTTA GET BACK AT SUSAN. WHAT WOULD ABUELITA DO?
ALWAYS REMEMBER, NIÑA--
EAT ALL WHO OPPOSE YOU.
DAY CARNATION
for charity
HEYYYY-- I KNOW HOW TO SHOW UP SUSAN!
OKAY! YOU CAN DO THIS! CONCENTRATE!
THINK ABOUT...
...ANIME!
NO
HEY MIIIICHAEL--
WHUT.
NO

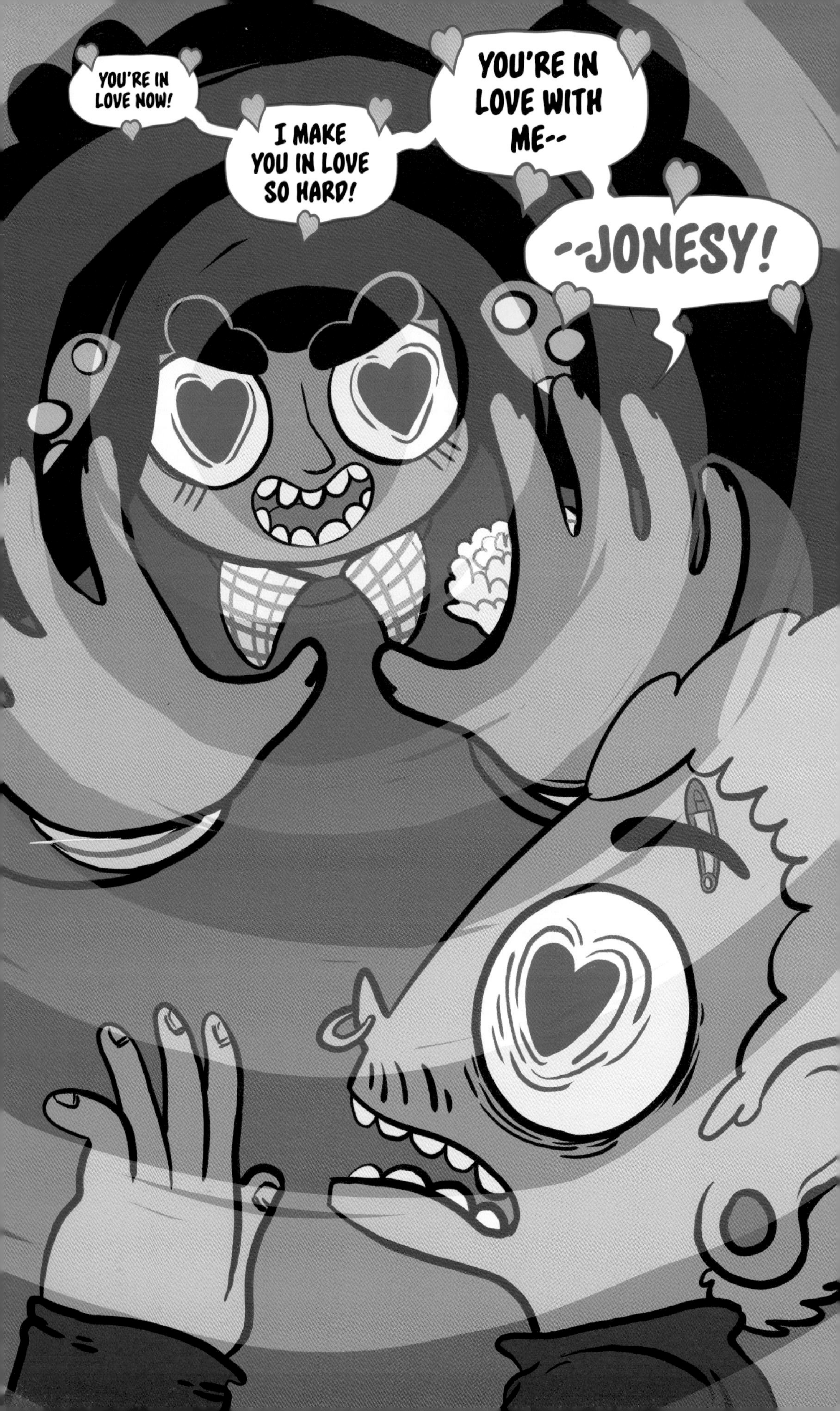
YOU'RE IN LOVE NOW!
I MAKE YOU IN LOVE SO HARD!
YOU'RE IN LOVE WITH ME--
--JONESY!

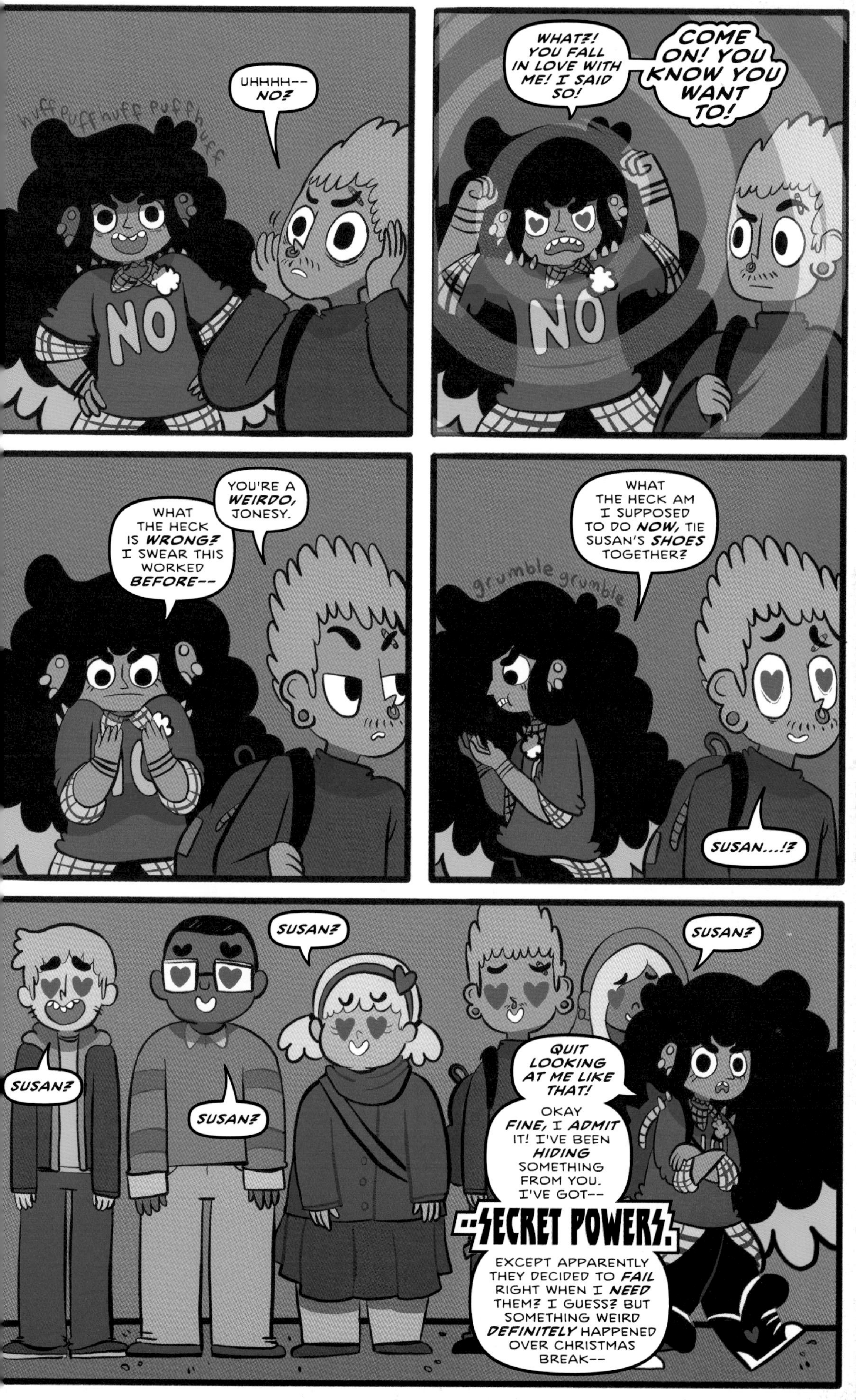
huff puff huff puff huff
UHHHH-- NO?
WHAT?! YOU FALL IN LOVE WITH ME! I SAID SO!
COME ON! YOU KNOW YOU WANT TO!
WHAT THE HECK IS WRONG? I SWEAR THIS WORKED BEFORE--
YOU'RE A WEIRDO, JONESY.
grumble grumble
WHAT THE HECK AM I SUPPOSED TO DO NOW, TIE SUSAN'S SHOES TOGETHER?
SUSAN...!?
SUSAN?
SUSAN?
SUSAN?
SUSAN?
QUIT LOOKING AT ME LIKE THAT!
OKAY FINE, I ADMIT IT! I'VE BEEN HIDING SOMETHING FROM YOU. I'VE GOT--
--SECRET POWERS.
EXCEPT APPARENTLY THEY DECIDED TO FAIL RIGHT WHEN I NEED THEM? I GUESS? BUT SOMETHING WEIRD DEFINITELY HAPPENED OVER CHRISTMAS BREAK--

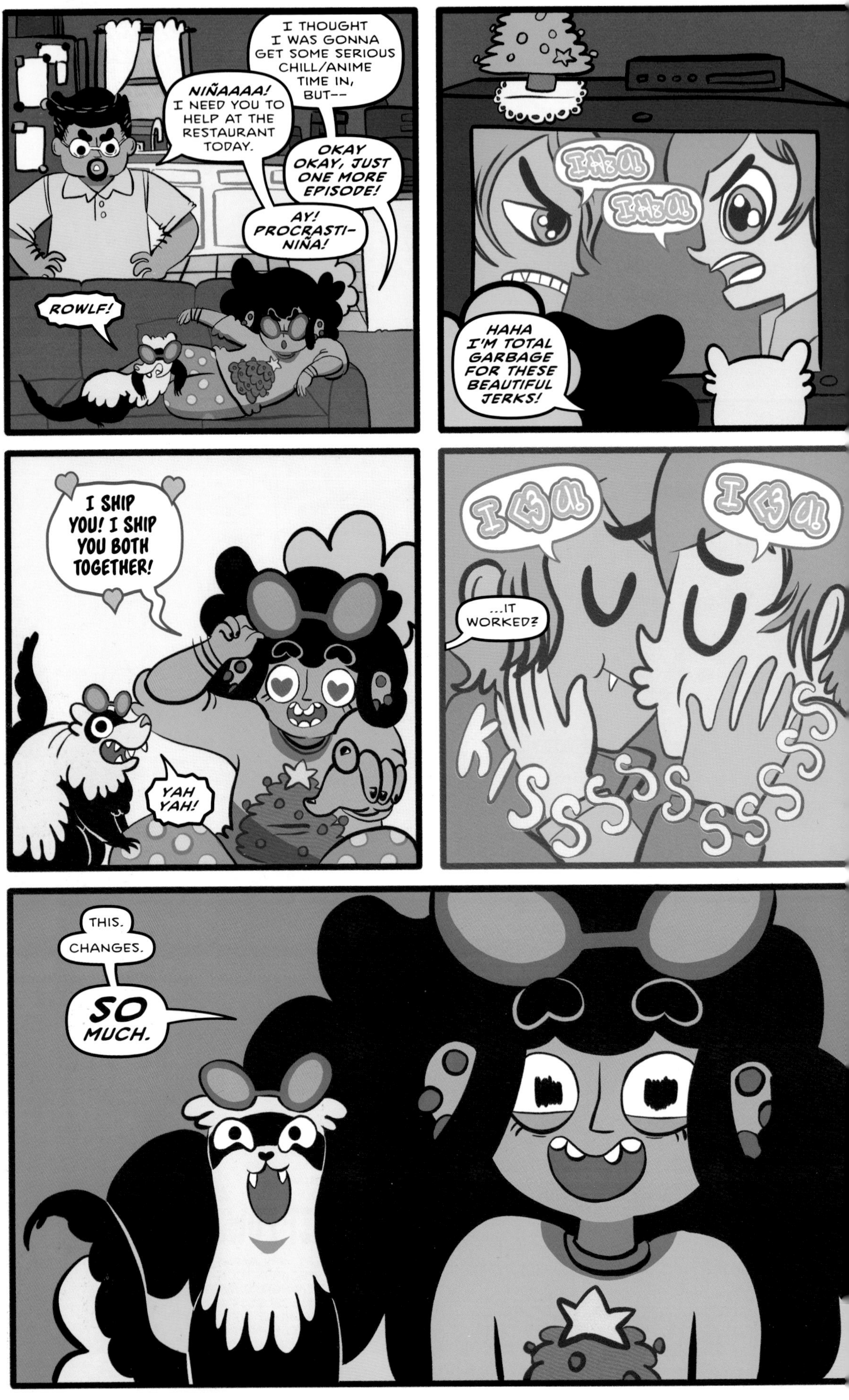
I THOUGHT I WAS GONNA GET SOME SERIOUS CHILL/ANIME TIME IN, BUT--
NIÑAAAA! I NEED YOU TO HELP AT THE RESTAURANT TODAY.
OKAY OKAY, JUST ONE MORE EPISODE!
AY! PROCRASTI-NIÑA!
ROWLF!
I H8 U!
I H8 U!
HAHA I'M TOTAL GARBAGE FOR THESE BEAUTIFUL JERKS!
I SHIP YOU! I SHIP YOU BOTH TOGETHER!
YAH YAH!
I <3 U!
I <3 U!
...IT WORKED?
KISSSSSSSSS
THIS.
CHANGES.
SO MUCH.

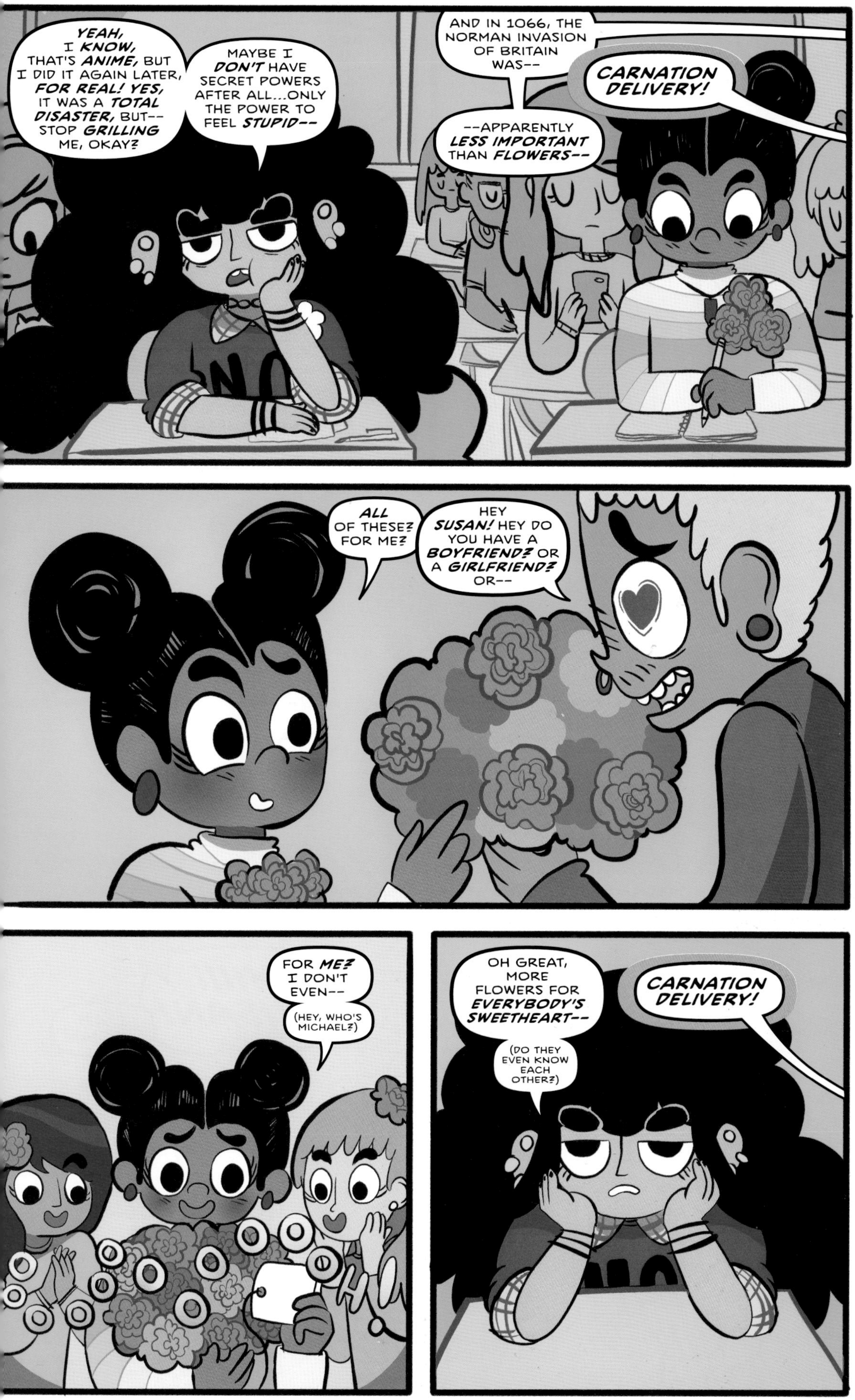

YEAH, I KNOW, THAT'S ANIME, BUT I DID IT AGAIN LATER, FOR REAL! YES, IT WAS A TOTAL DISASTER, BUT-- STOP GRILLING ME, OKAY?
MAYBE I DON'T HAVE SECRET POWERS AFTER ALL...ONLY THE POWER TO FEEL STUPID--
AND IN 1066, THE NORMAN INVASION OF BRITAIN WAS--
CARNATION DELIVERY!
--APPARENTLY LESS IMPORTANT THAN FLOWERS--
ALL OF THESE? FOR ME?
HEY SUSAN! HEY DO YOU HAVE A BOYFRIEND? OR A GIRLFRIEND? OR--
FOR ME? I DON'T EVEN--
(HEY, WHO'S MICHAEL?)
OH GREAT, MORE FLOWERS FOR EVERYBODY'S SWEETHEART--
(DO THEY EVEN KNOW EACH OTHER?)
CARNATION DELIVERY!

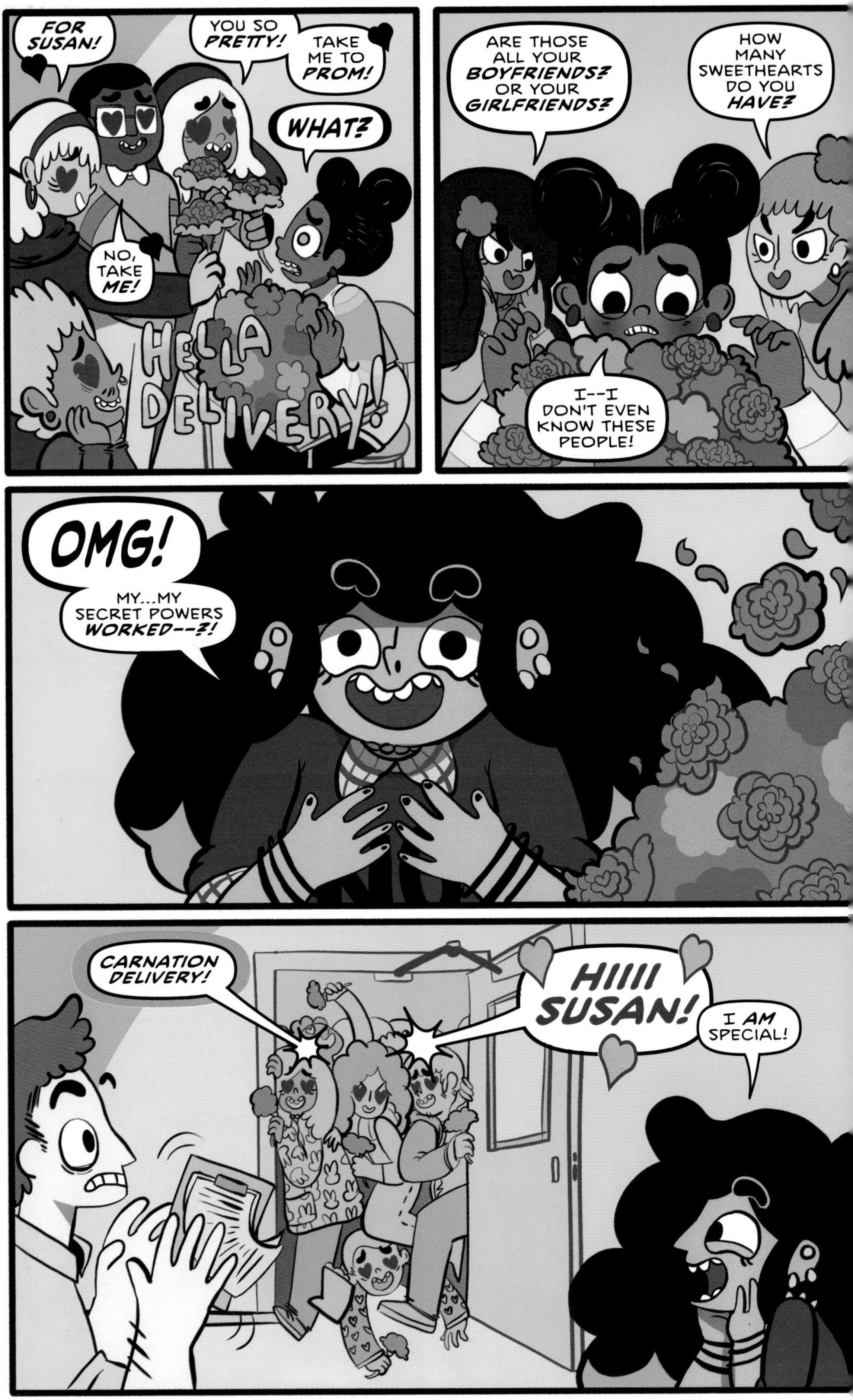

FOR SUSAN!
YOU SO PRETTY!
TAKE ME TO PROM!
WHAT?
NO, TAKE ME!
HELLA DELIVERY!
ARE THOSE ALL YOUR BOYFRIENDS? OR YOUR GIRLFRIENDS?
HOW MANY SWEETHEARTS DO YOU HAVE?
I--I DON'T EVEN KNOW THESE PEOPLE!
OMG!
MY...MY SECRET POWERS WORKED--?!
CARNATION DELIVERY!
HIIII SUSAN!
I AM SPECIAL!

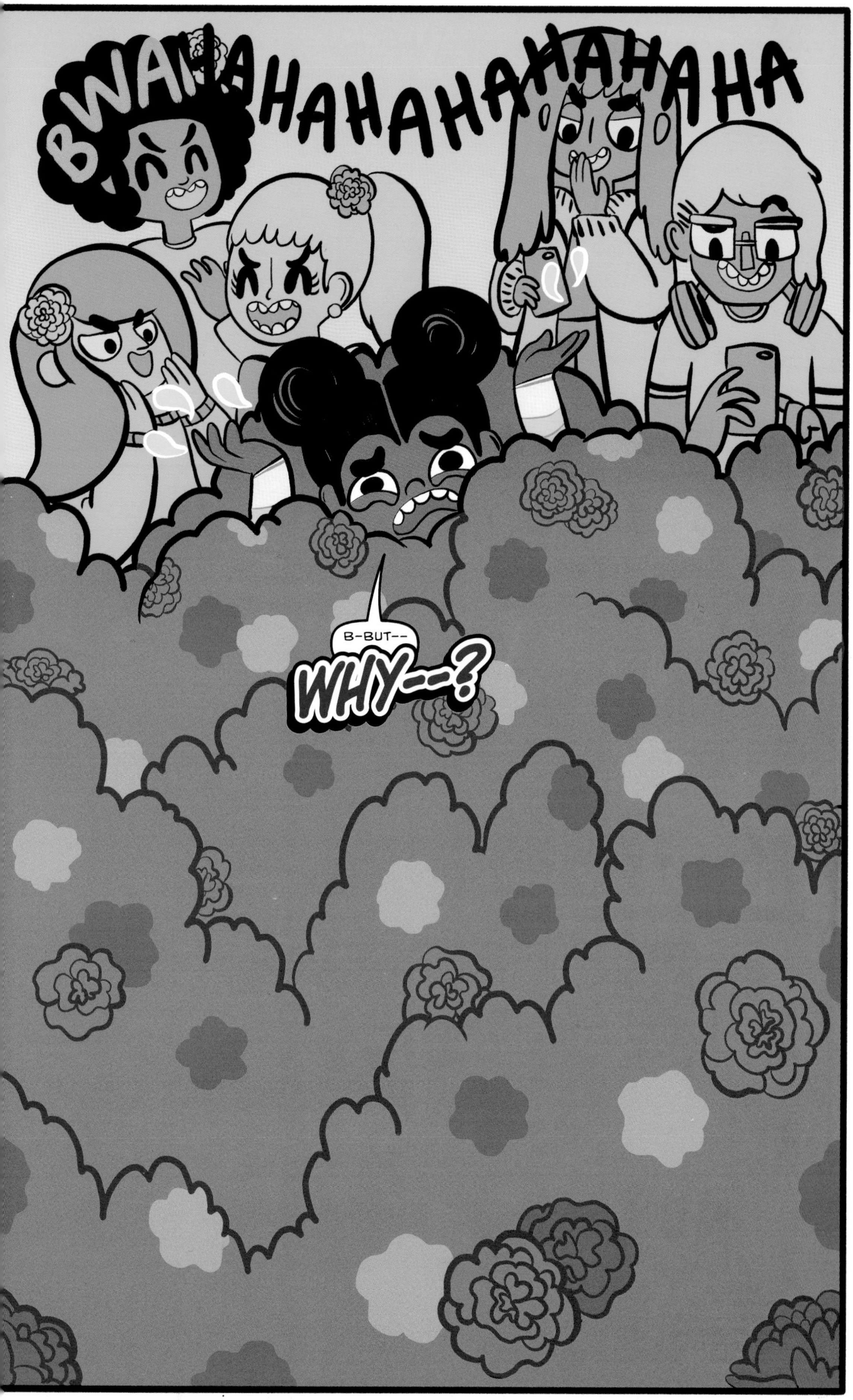
BWAHAHAHAHAHAHAHAHA
B-BUT--
WHY--?

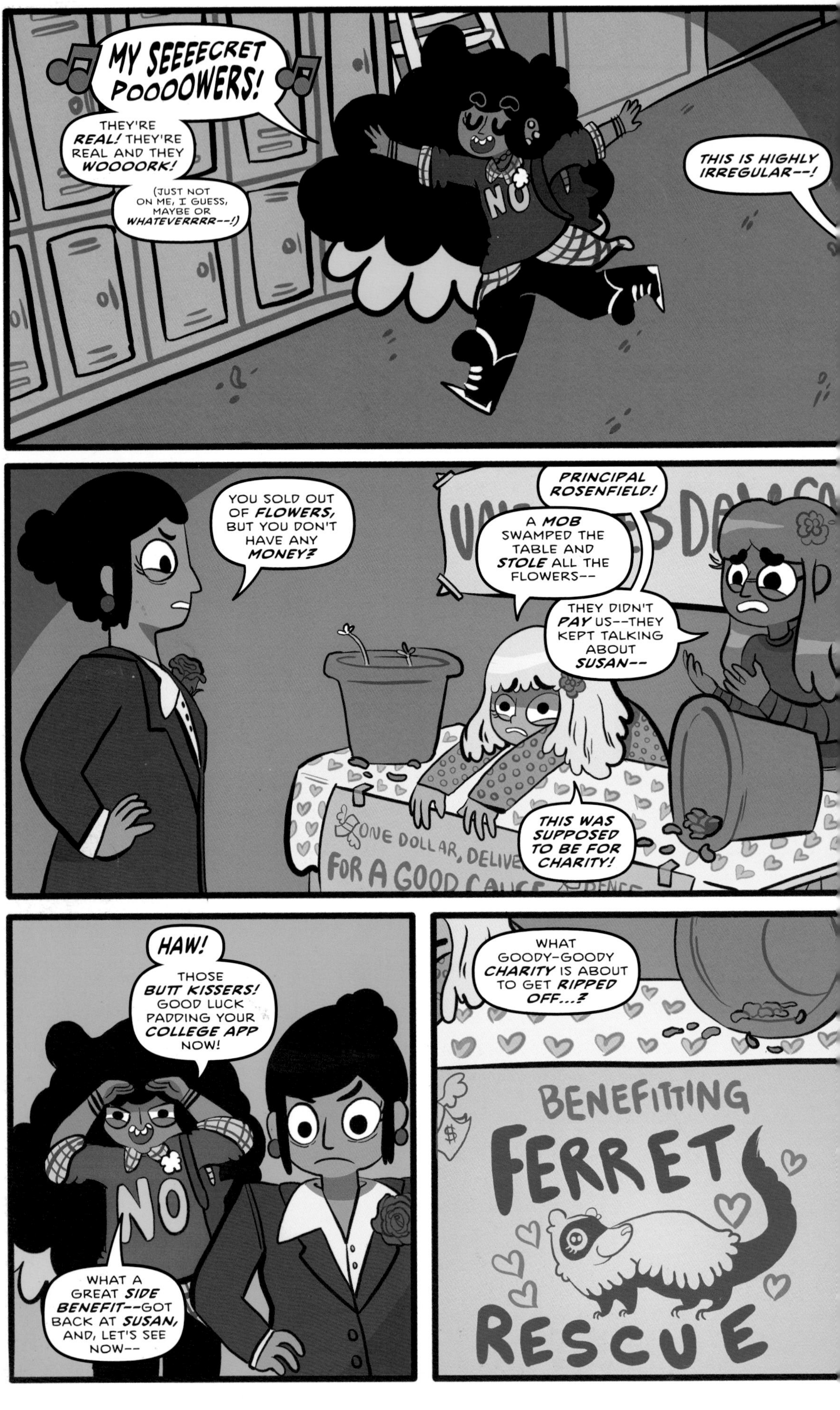
MY SEEEECRET POOOOWERS!
THEY'RE REAL! THEY'RE REAL AND THEY WOOOORK!
(JUST NOT ON ME, I GUESS, MAYBE OR WHATEVERRRR--!)
THIS IS HIGHLY IRREGULAR--!
YOU SOLD OUT OF FLOWERS, BUT YOU DON'T HAVE ANY MONEY?
PRINCIPAL ROSENFIELD!
A MOB SWAMPED THE TABLE AND STOLE ALL THE FLOWERS--
THEY DIDN'T PAY US--THEY KEPT TALKING ABOUT SUSAN--
THIS WAS SUPPOSED TO BE FOR CHARITY!
ONE DOLLAR, DELIVE
FOR A GOOD CAUSE
HAW!
THOSE BUTT KISSERS! GOOD LUCK PADDING YOUR COLLEGE APP NOW!
WHAT A GREAT SIDE BENEFIT--GOT BACK AT SUSAN, AND, LET'S SEE NOW--
WHAT GOODY-GOODY CHARITY IS ABOUT TO GET RIPPED OFF...?
BENEFITTING FERRET RESCUE

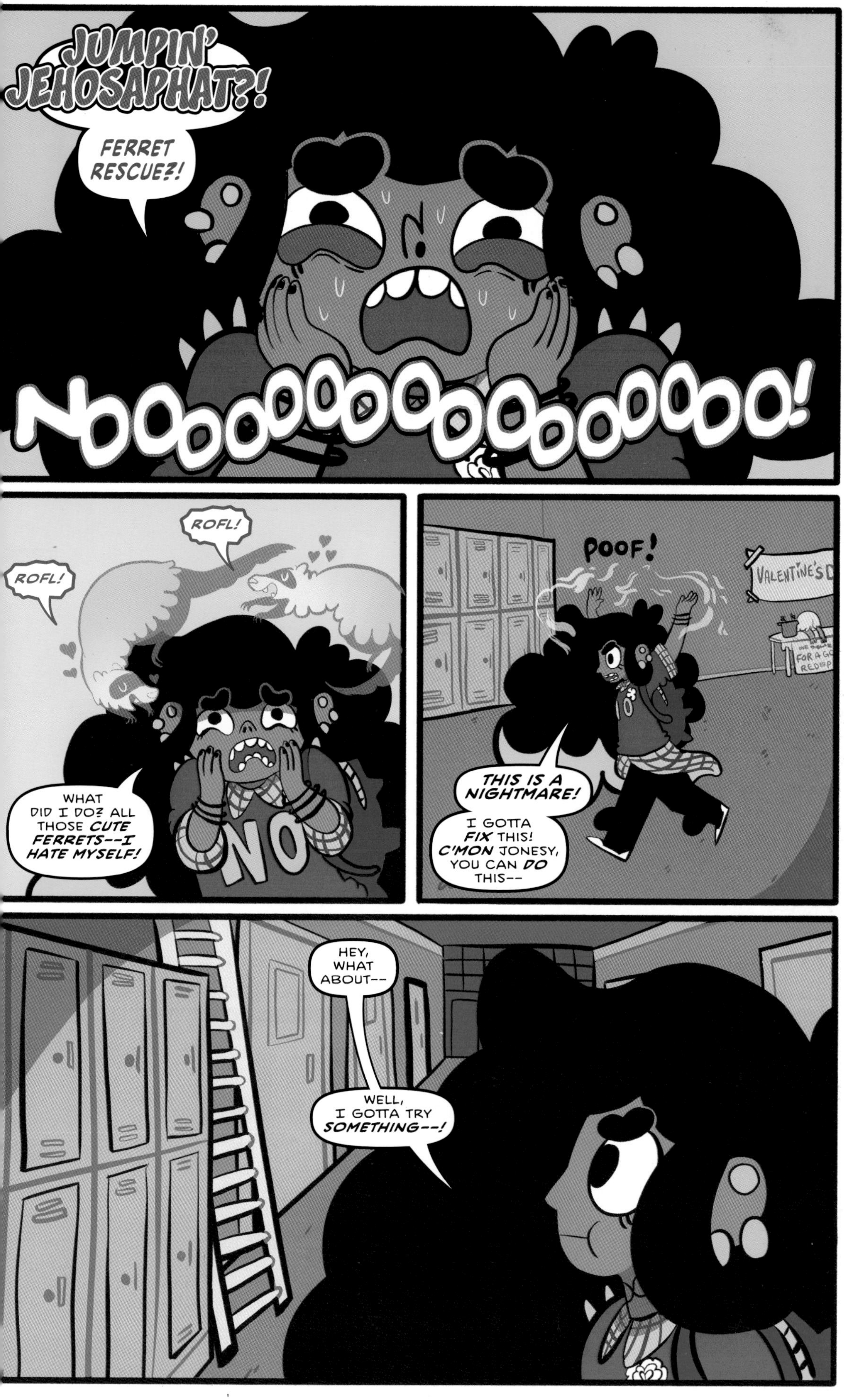
JUMPIN' JEHOSAPHAT?!
FERRET RESCUE?!
NOOOOOOOOOOOOOOOOO!
ROFL!
ROFL!
WHAT DID I DO? ALL THOSE *CUTE FERRETS--I HATE MYSELF!*
POOF!
*THIS IS A NIGHTMARE!*
I GOTTA *FIX* THIS! *C'MON* JONESY, YOU CAN *DO* THIS--
HEY, WHAT ABOUT--
WELL, I GOTTA TRY *SOMETHING--!*

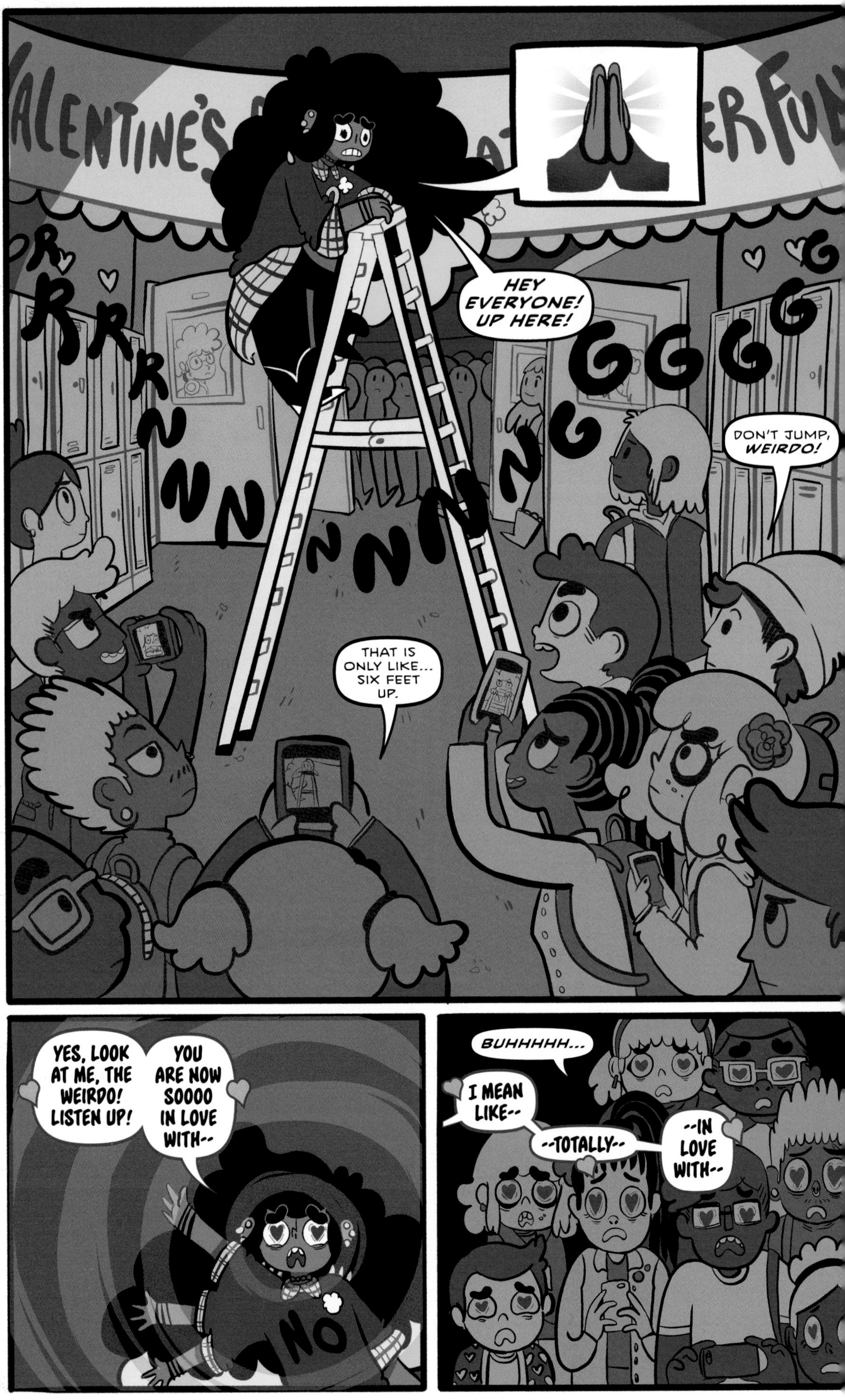
HEY EVERYONE! UP HERE!
DON'T JUMP, WEIRDO!
THAT IS ONLY LIKE... SIX FEET UP.
YES, LOOK AT ME, THE WEIRDO! LISTEN UP!
YOU ARE NOW SOOOO IN LOVE WITH--
NO
BUHHHHH...
I MEAN LIKE--
--TOTALLY--
--IN LOVE WITH--

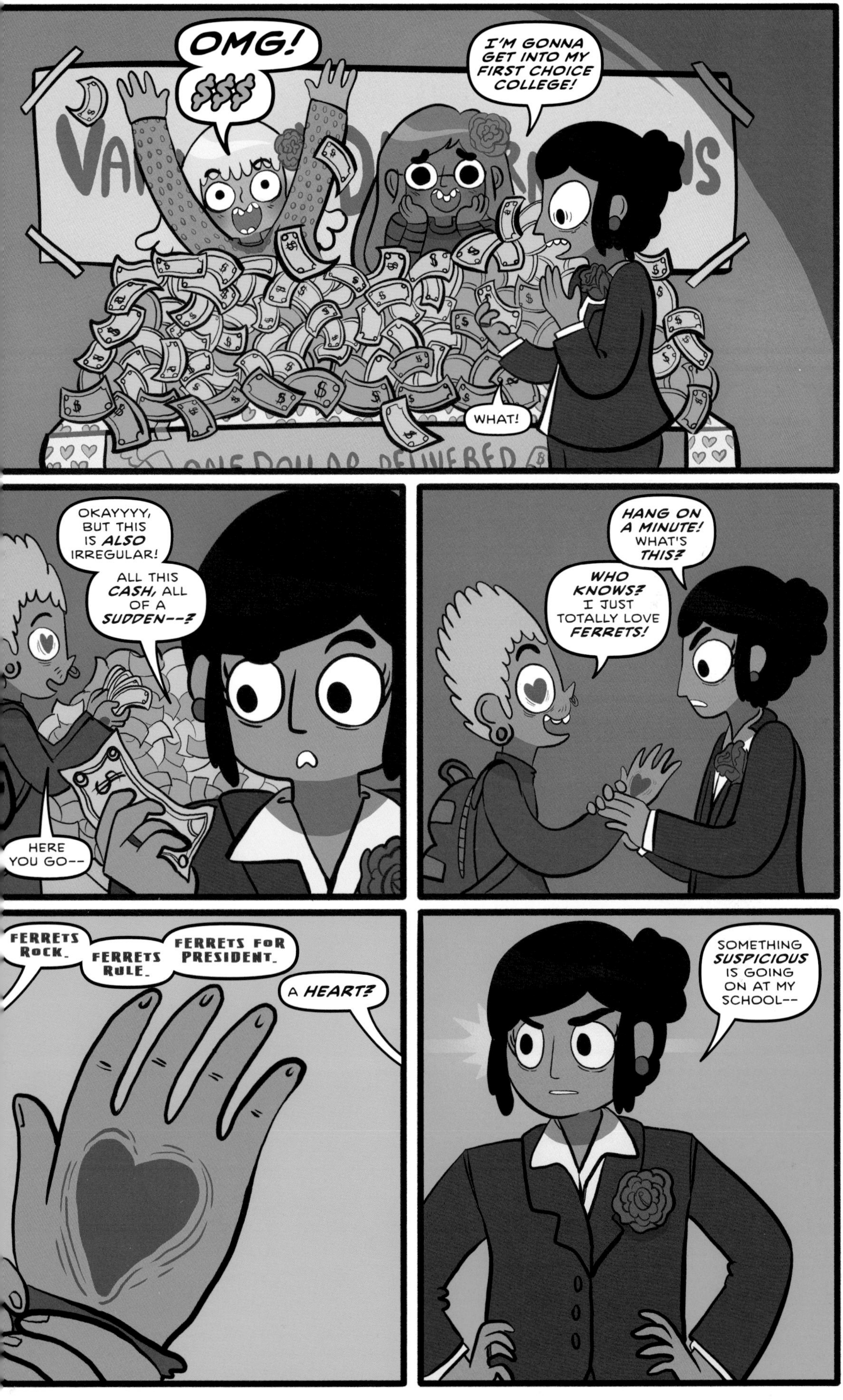

OMG!
$$$
I'M GONNA GET INTO MY FIRST CHOICE COLLEGE!
WHAT!
OKAYYYY, BUT THIS IS *ALSO* IRREGULAR!
ALL THIS *CASH*, ALL OF A *SUDDEN*--?
HERE YOU GO--
*HANG ON A MINUTE!* WHAT'S *THIS?*
*WHO KNOWS?* I JUST TOTALLY LOVE *FERRETS!*
FERRETS ROCK.
FERRETS RULE.
FERRETS FOR PRESIDENT.
A *HEART?*
SOMETHING *SUSPICIOUS* IS GOING ON AT MY SCHOOL--

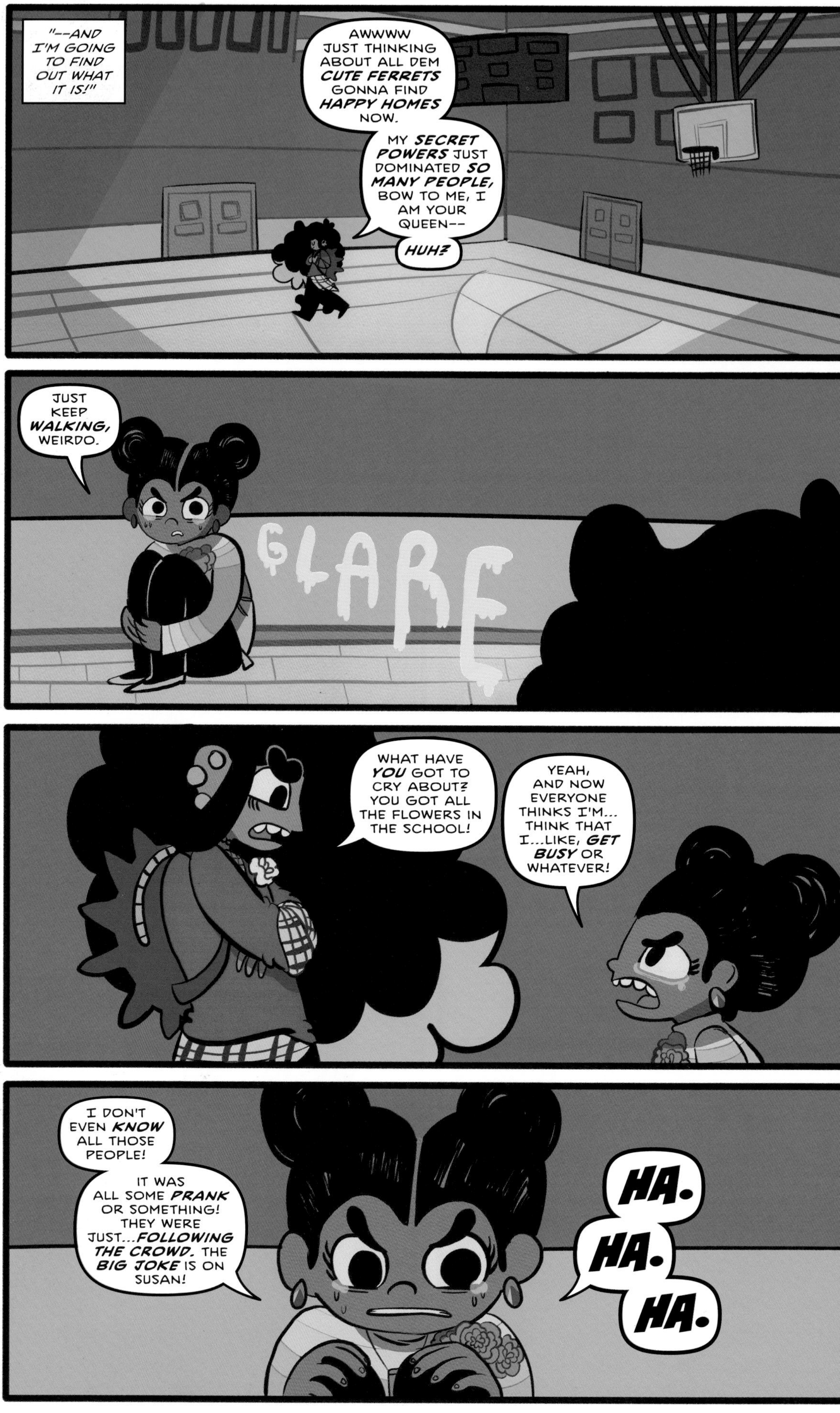
"--AND I'M GOING TO FIND OUT WHAT IT IS!"
AWWWW JUST THINKING ABOUT ALL DEM CUTE FERRETS GONNA FIND HAPPY HOMES NOW.
MY SECRET POWERS JUST DOMINATED SO MANY PEOPLE, BOW TO ME, I AM YOUR QUEEN--
HUH?
JUST KEEP WALKING, WEIRDO.
GLARE
WHAT HAVE YOU GOT TO CRY ABOUT? YOU GOT ALL THE FLOWERS IN THE SCHOOL!
YEAH, AND NOW EVERYONE THINKS I'M... THINK THAT I...LIKE, GET BUSY OR WHATEVER!
I DON'T EVEN KNOW ALL THOSE PEOPLE!
IT WAS ALL SOME PRANK OR SOMETHING! THEY WERE JUST...FOLLOWING THE CROWD. THE BIG JOKE IS ON SUSAN!
HA. HA. HA.

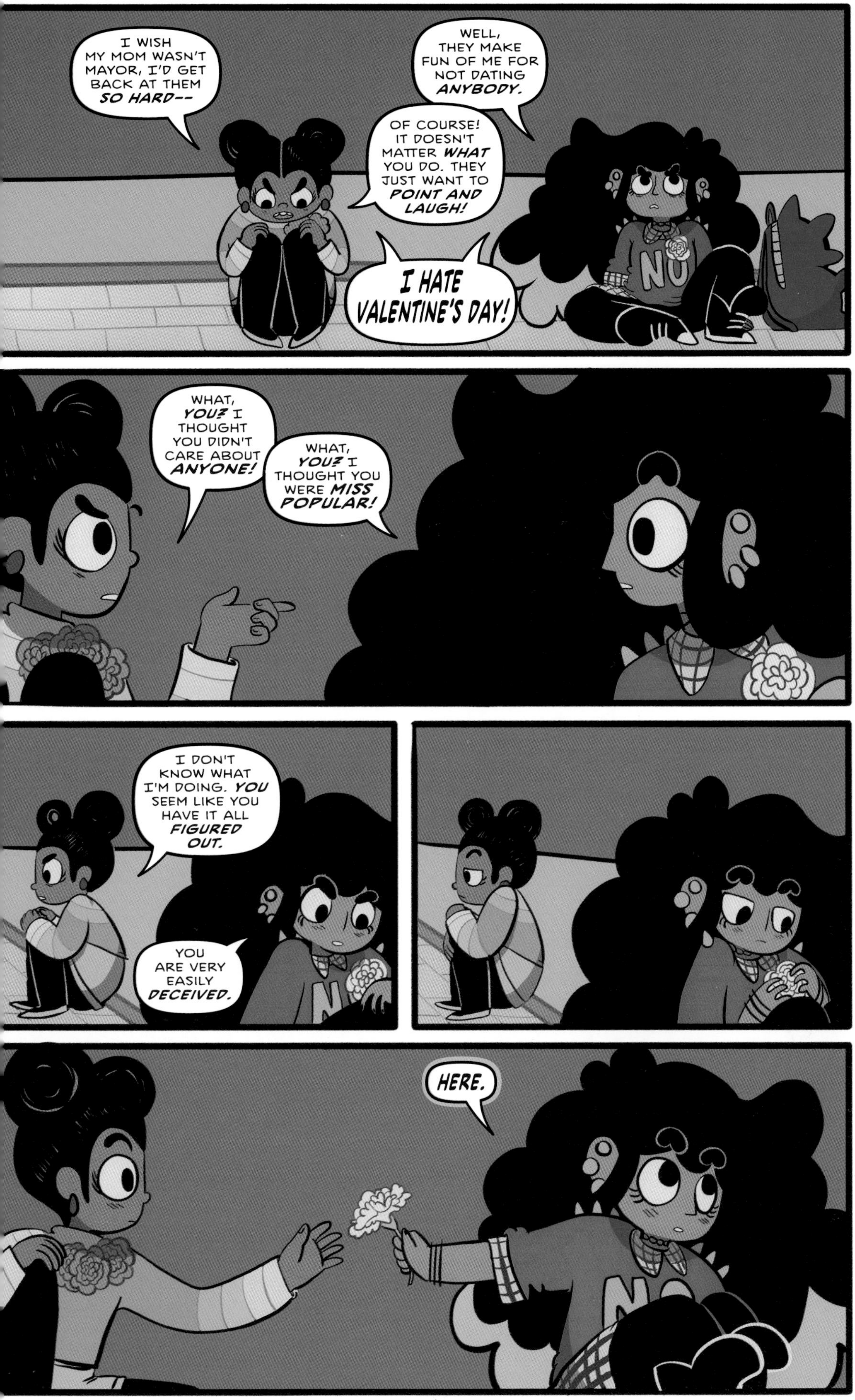
I WISH MY MOM WASN'T MAYOR, I'D GET BACK AT THEM SO HARD--
WELL, THEY MAKE FUN OF ME FOR NOT DATING ANYBODY.
OF COURSE! IT DOESN'T MATTER WHAT YOU DO. THEY JUST WANT TO POINT AND LAUGH!
I HATE VALENTINE'S DAY!
WHAT, YOU? I THOUGHT YOU DIDN'T CARE ABOUT ANYONE!
WHAT, YOU? I THOUGHT YOU WERE MISS POPULAR!
I DON'T KNOW WHAT I'M DOING. YOU SEEM LIKE YOU HAVE IT ALL FIGURED OUT.
YOU ARE VERY EASILY DECEIVED.
HERE.

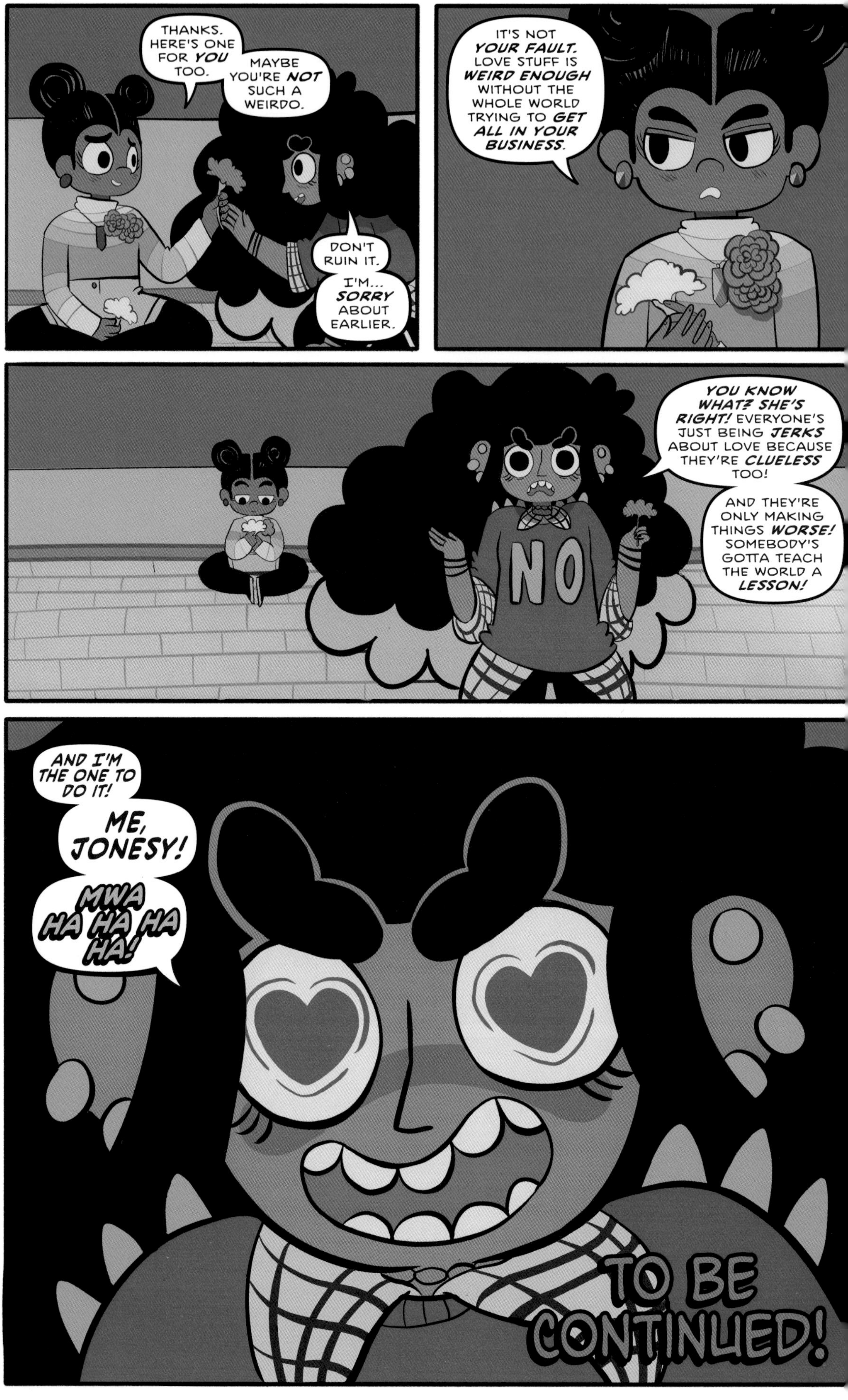
THANKS. HERE'S ONE FOR YOU TOO.
MAYBE YOU'RE NOT SUCH A WEIRDO.
DON'T RUIN IT.
I'M... SORRY ABOUT EARLIER.
IT'S NOT YOUR FAULT. LOVE STUFF IS WEIRD ENOUGH WITHOUT THE WHOLE WORLD TRYING TO GET ALL IN YOUR BUSINESS.
YOU KNOW WHAT? SHE'S RIGHT! EVERYONE'S JUST BEING JERKS ABOUT LOVE BECAUSE THEY'RE CLUELESS TOO!
AND THEY'RE ONLY MAKING THINGS WORSE! SOMEBODY'S GOTTA TEACH THE WORLD A LESSON!
NO
AND I'M THE ONE TO DO IT!
ME, JONESY!
MWA HA HA HA HA HA!
TO BE CONTINUED!

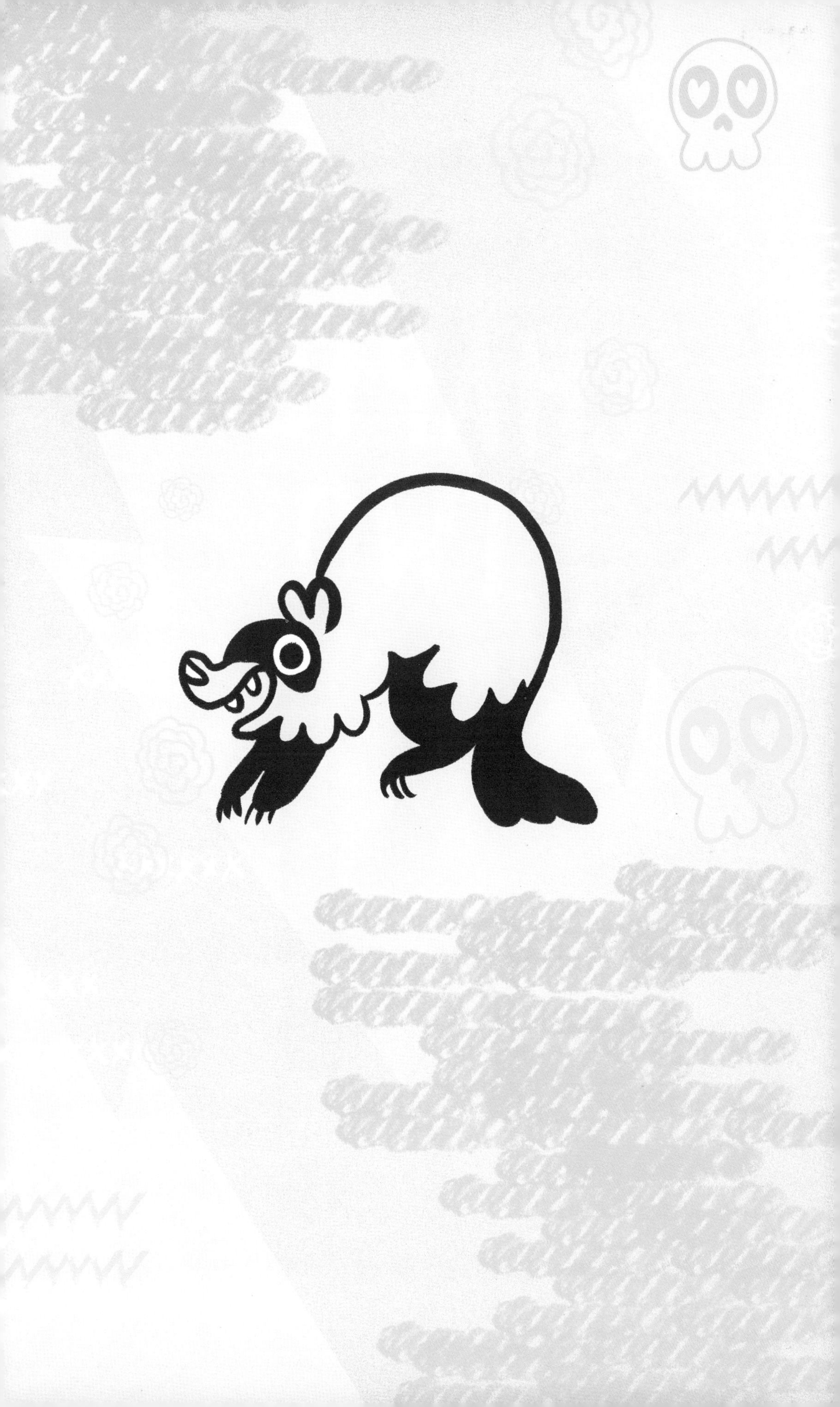

# CHAPTER TWO

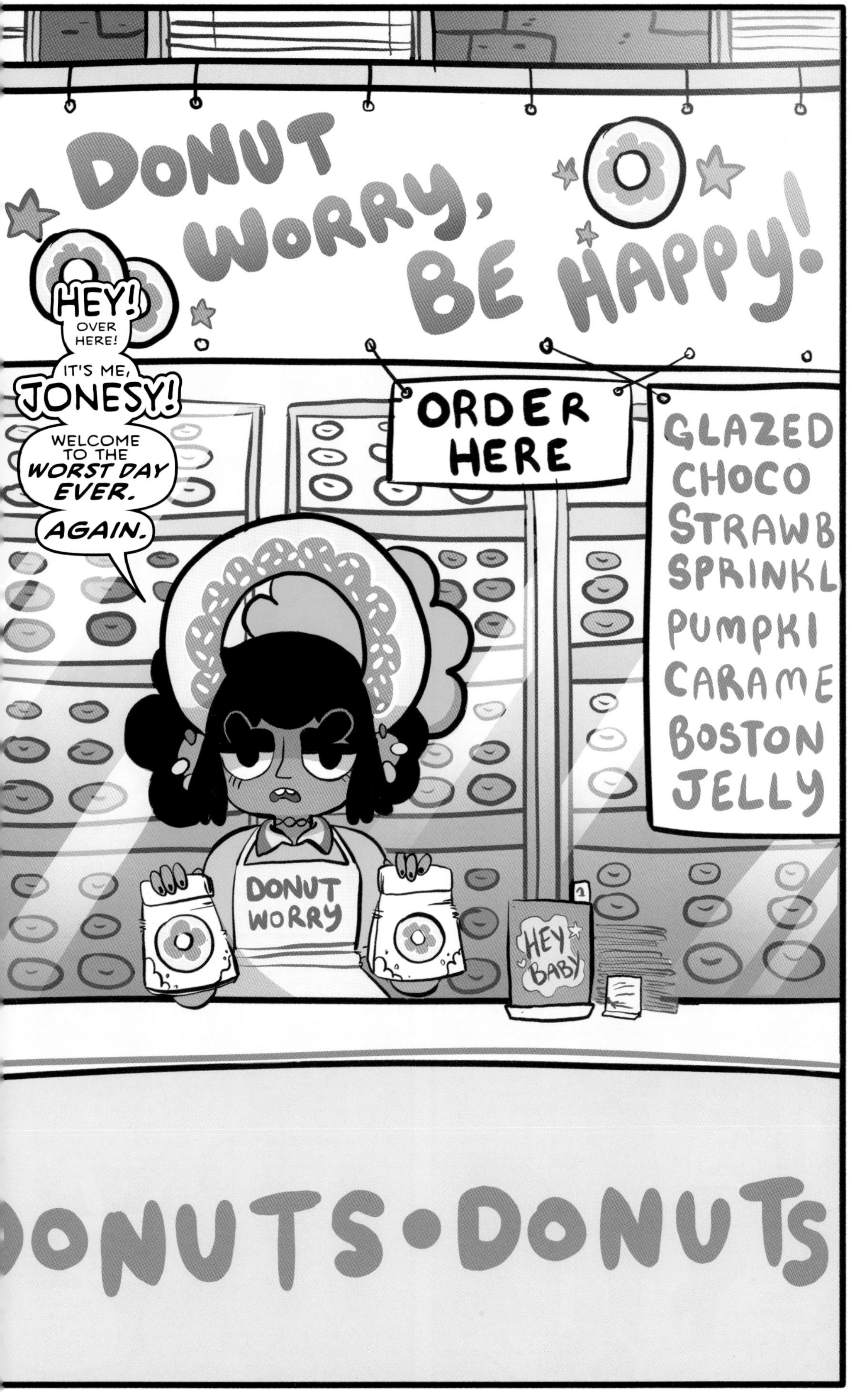
DONUT WORRY, BE HAPPY!
HEY! OVER HERE!
IT'S ME, JONESY!
WELCOME TO THE *WORST DAY EVER.*
*AGAIN.*
ORDER HERE
GLAZED
CHOCO
STRAWB
SPRINKL
PUMPKI
CARAME
BOSTON
JELLY
DONUT WORRY
HEY BABY
DONUTS•DONUTS

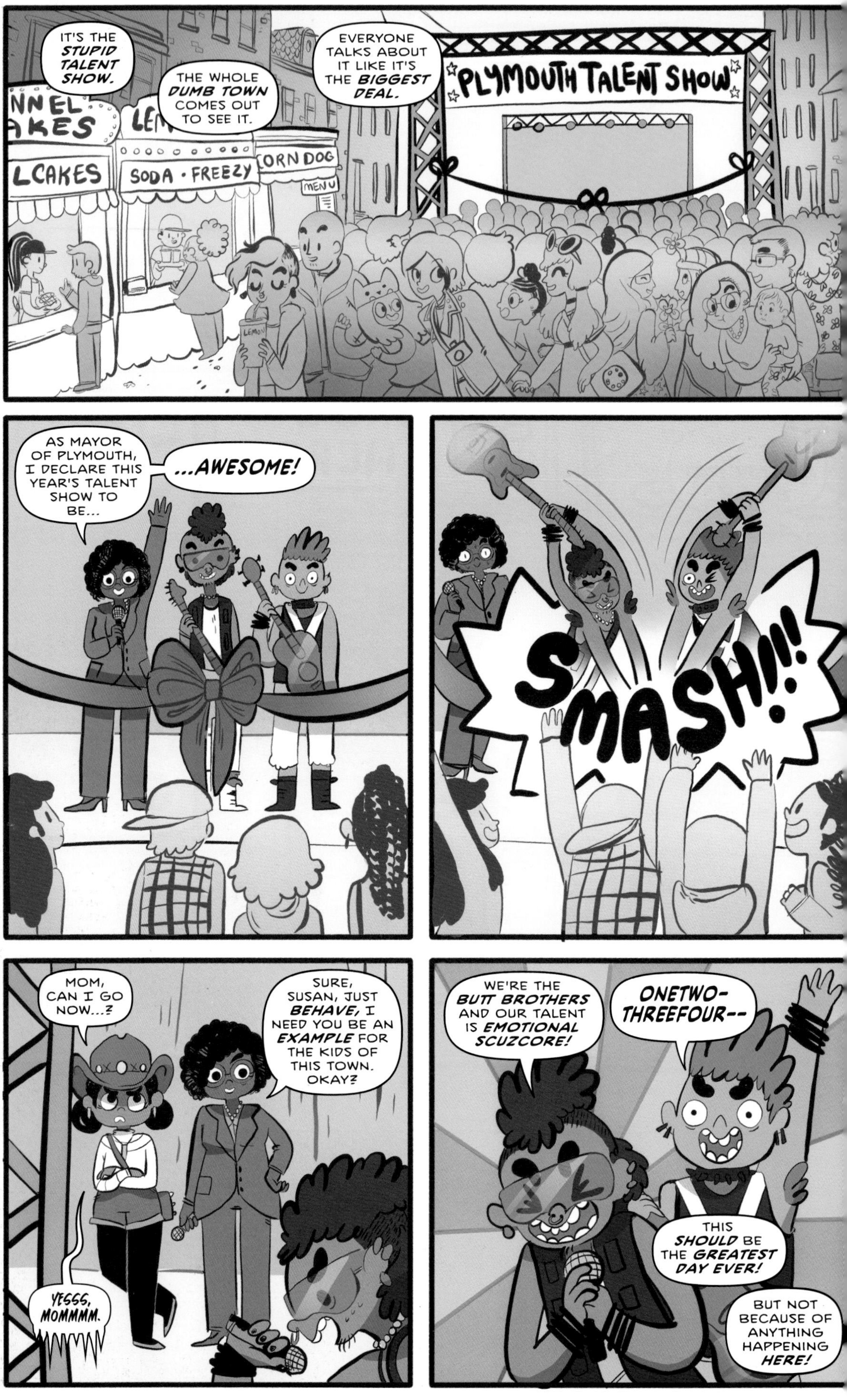
IT'S THE STUPID TALENT SHOW.
THE WHOLE DUMB TOWN COMES OUT TO SEE IT.
EVERYONE TALKS ABOUT IT LIKE IT'S THE BIGGEST DEAL.
PLYMOUTH TALENT SHOW
NNEL AKES
LEM
LCAKES
SODA · FREEZY
CORN DOG
MENU
LEMON
AS MAYOR OF PLYMOUTH, I DECLARE THIS YEAR'S TALENT SHOW TO BE...
...AWESOME!
SMASH!!!
MOM, CAN I GO NOW...?
SURE, SUSAN, JUST BEHAVE, I NEED YOU BE AN EXAMPLE FOR THE KIDS OF THIS TOWN. OKAY?
YESSS, MOMMMM.
WE'RE THE BUTT BROTHERS AND OUR TALENT IS EMOTIONAL SCUZCORE!
ONETWO-THREEFOUR--
THIS SHOULD BE THE GREATEST DAY EVER!
BUT NOT BECAUSE OF ANYTHING HAPPENING HERE!

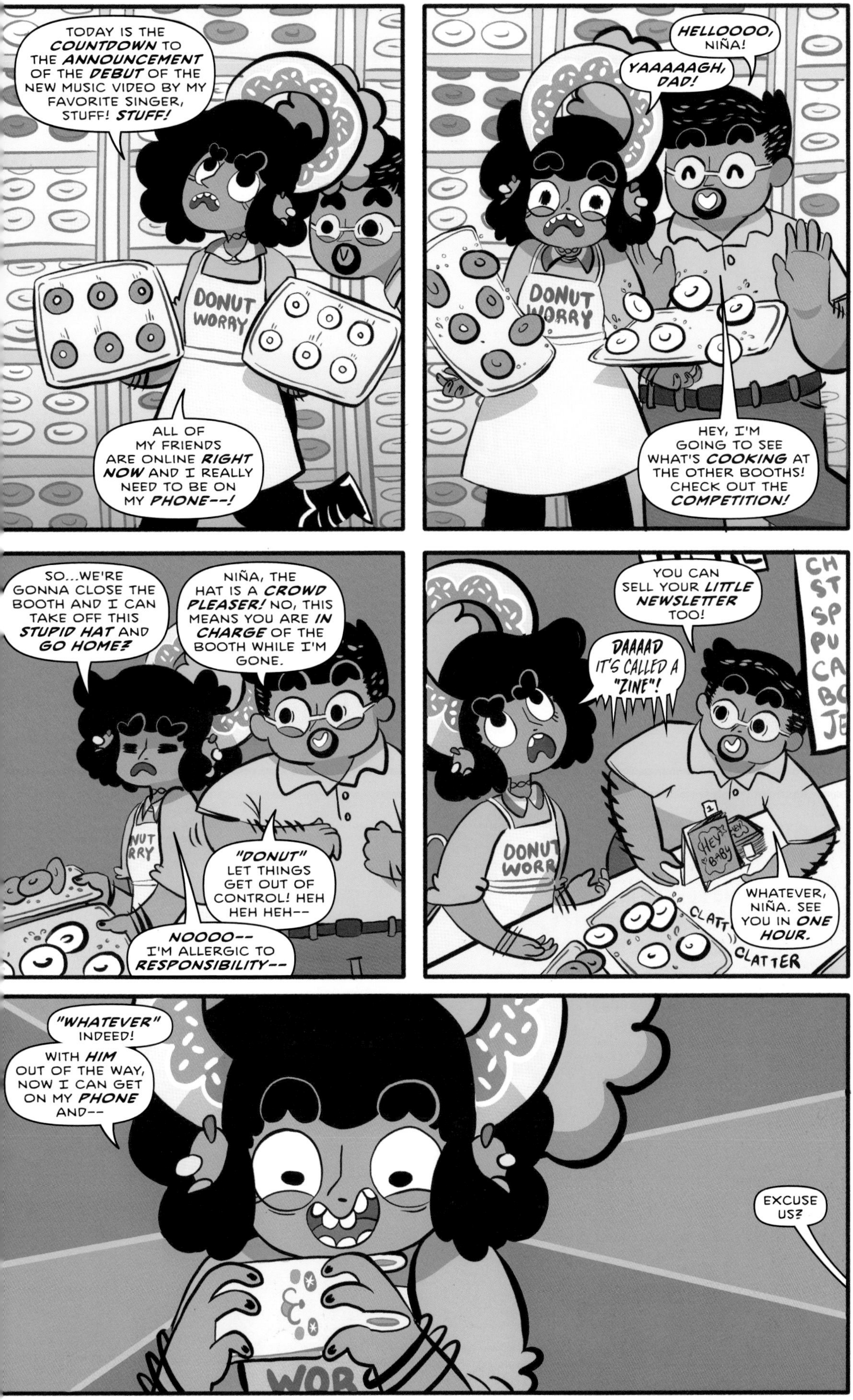
TODAY IS THE COUNTDOWN TO THE ANNOUNCEMENT OF THE DEBUT OF THE NEW MUSIC VIDEO BY MY FAVORITE SINGER, STUFF! STUFF!
ALL OF MY FRIENDS ARE ONLINE RIGHT NOW AND I REALLY NEED TO BE ON MY PHONE--!
HELLOOOO, NIÑA!
YAAAAAGH, DAD!
HEY, I'M GOING TO SEE WHAT'S COOKING AT THE OTHER BOOTHS! CHECK OUT THE COMPETITION!
SO...WE'RE GONNA CLOSE THE BOOTH AND I CAN TAKE OFF THIS STUPID HAT AND GO HOME?
NIÑA, THE HAT IS A CROWD PLEASER! NO, THIS MEANS YOU ARE IN CHARGE OF THE BOOTH WHILE I'M GONE.
"DONUT" LET THINGS GET OUT OF CONTROL! HEH HEH HEH--
NOOOO-- I'M ALLERGIC TO RESPONSIBILITY--
YOU CAN SELL YOUR LITTLE NEWSLETTER TOO!
DAAAAD IT'S CALLED A "ZINE"!
WHATEVER, NIÑA. SEE YOU IN ONE HOUR.
CLATT
CLATTER
"WHATEVER" INDEED!
WITH HIM OUT OF THE WAY, NOW I CAN GET ON MY PHONE AND--
EXCUSE US?

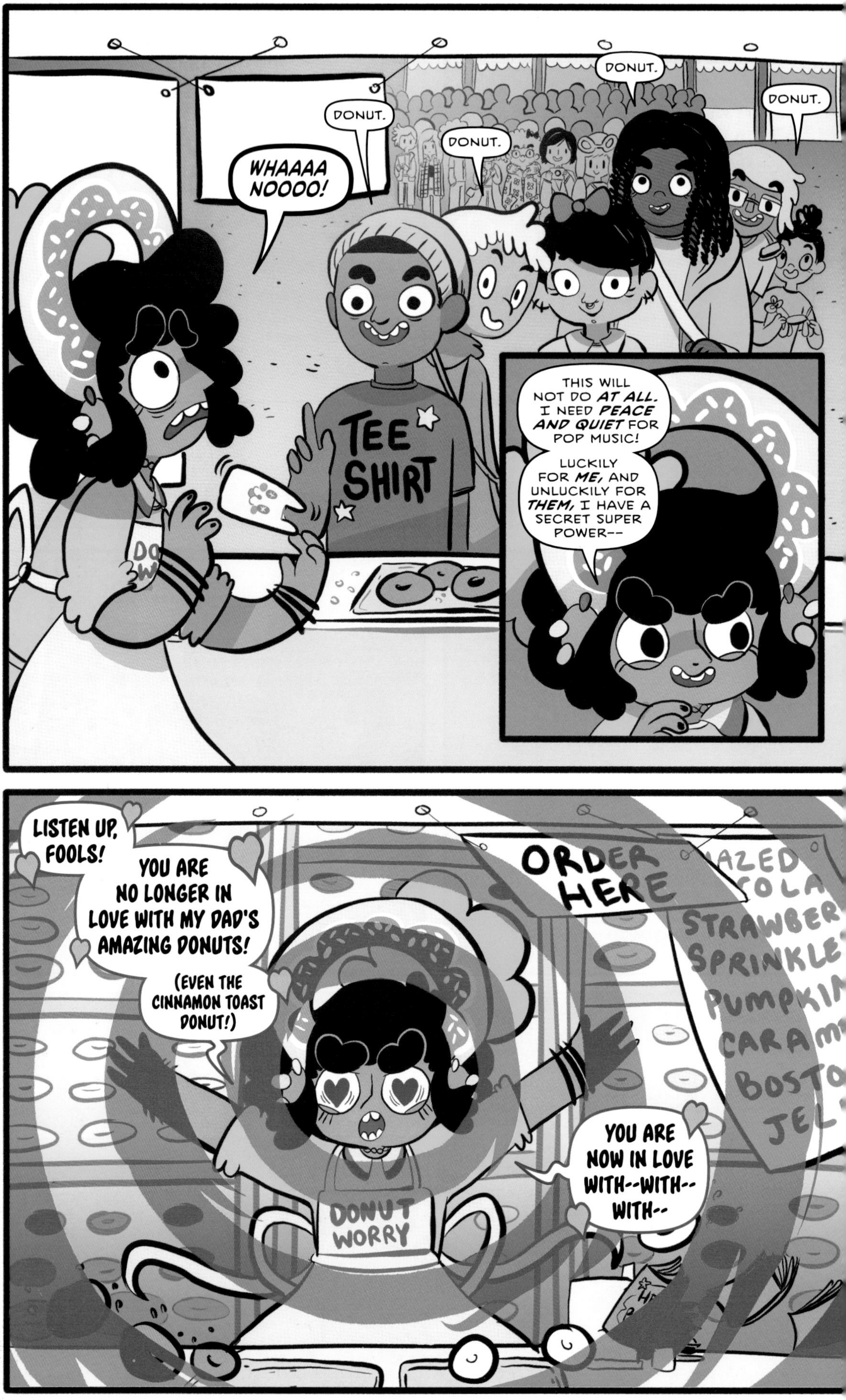

DONUT.
DONUT.
DONUT.
DONUT.
WHAAAA NOOOO!
TEE SHIRT
THIS WILL NOT DO *AT ALL.* I NEED *PEACE AND QUIET* FOR POP MUSIC!
LUCKILY FOR *ME,* AND UNLUCKILY FOR *THEM,* I HAVE A SECRET SUPER POWER--
LISTEN UP, FOOLS!
YOU ARE NO LONGER IN LOVE WITH MY DAD'S AMAZING DONUTS!
(EVEN THE CINNAMON TOAST DONUT!)
ORDER HERE
STRAWBER
SPRINKLE
DONUT WORRY
YOU ARE NOW IN LOVE WITH--WITH--WITH--

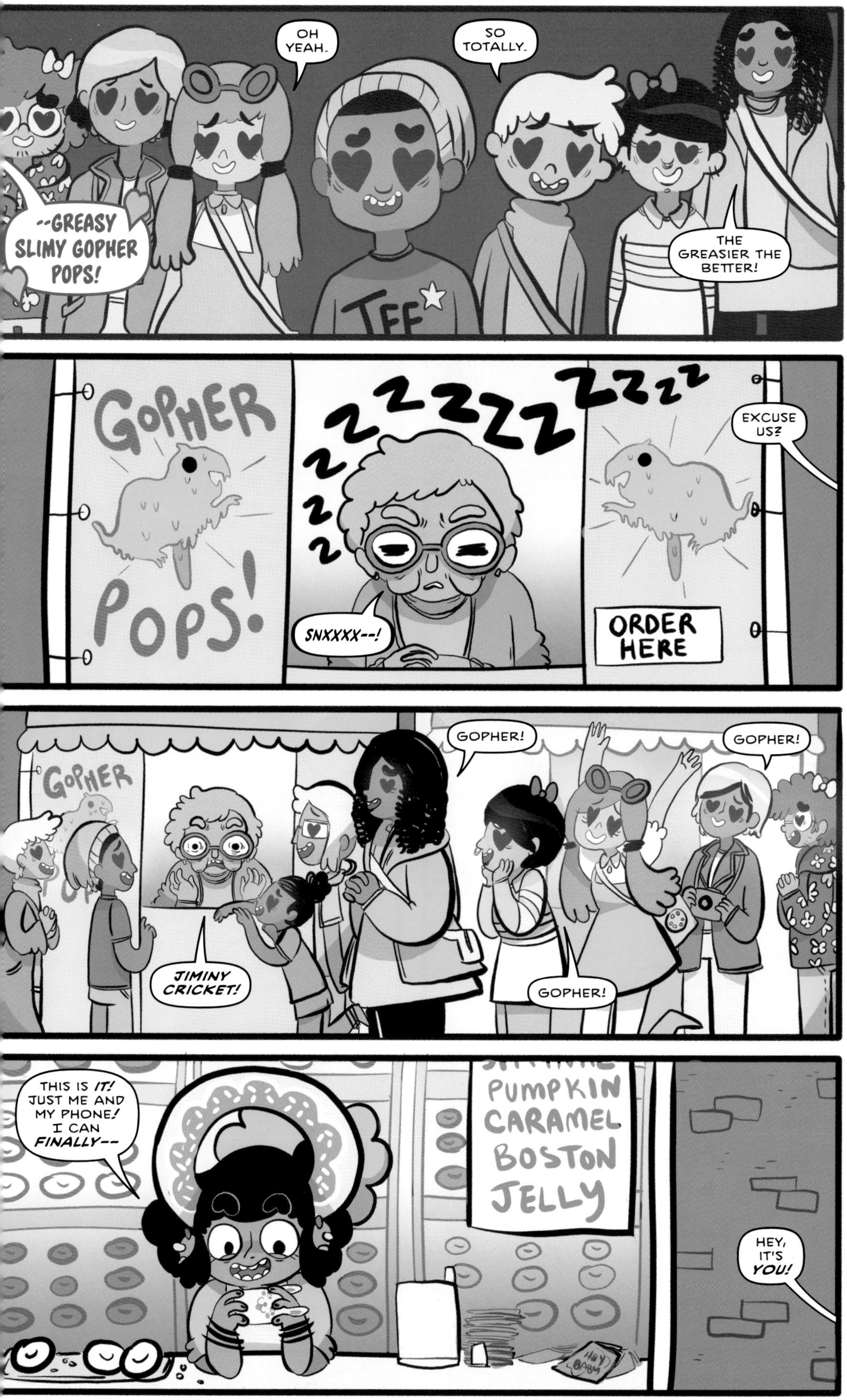
--GREASY SLIMY GOPHER POPS!
OH YEAH.
SO TOTALLY.
THE GREASIER THE BETTER!
TFF
GOPHER POPS!
ZZZZZZZZZZZZZZ
SNXXXX--!
ORDER HERE
EXCUSE US?
GOPHER
JIMINY CRICKET!
GOPHER!
GOPHER!
GOPHER!
THIS IS IT! JUST ME AND MY PHONE! I CAN FINALLY--
PUMPKIN CARAMEL BOSTON JELLY
HEY, IT'S YOU!

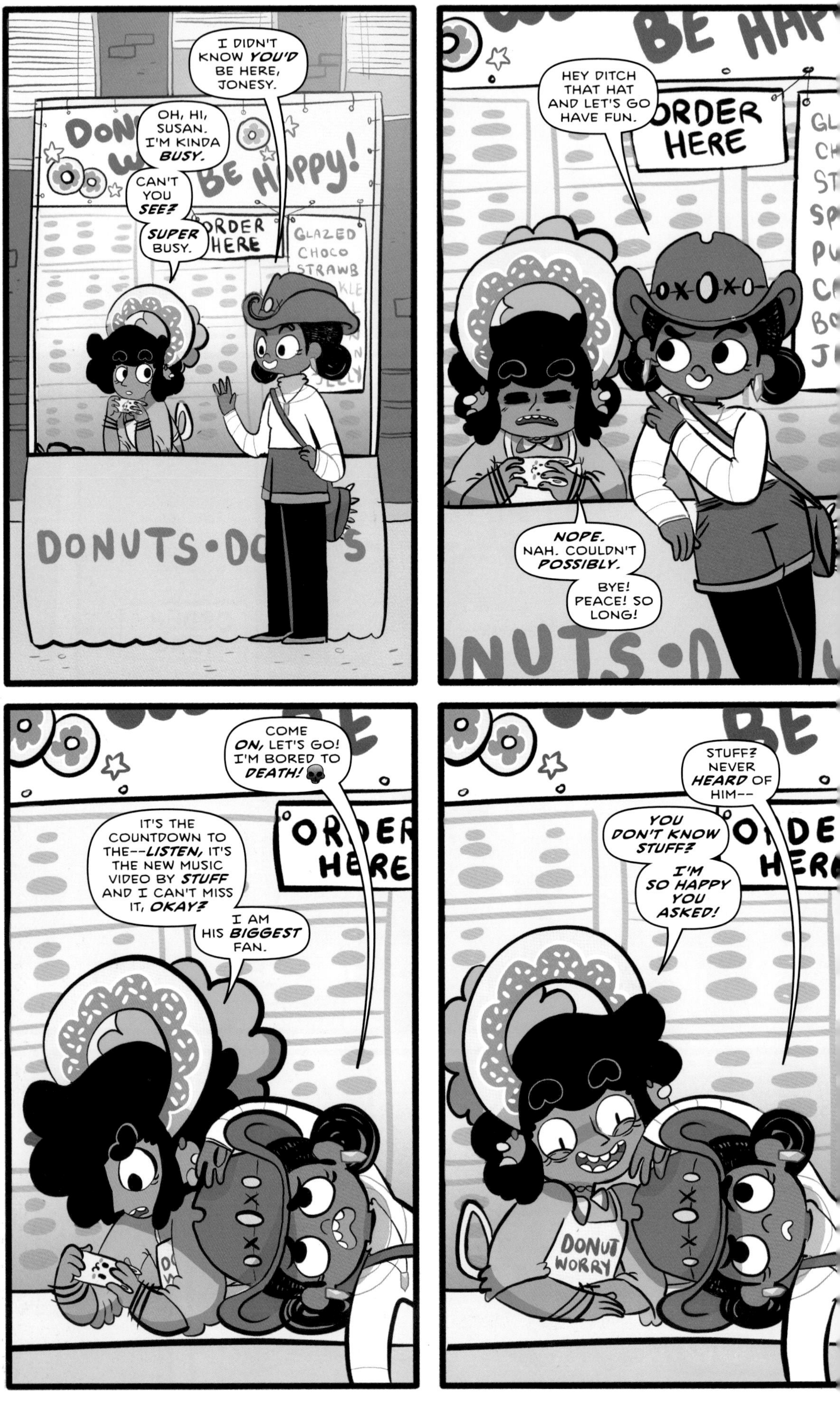

I DIDN'T KNOW YOU'D BE HERE, JONESY.
OH, HI, SUSAN. I'M KINDA BUSY.
CAN'T YOU SEE?
SUPER BUSY.
BE HAPPY!
ORDER HERE
GLAZED
CHOCO
STRAWB
DONUTS • DO S
HEY DITCH THAT HAT AND LET'S GO HAVE FUN.
ORDER HERE
NOPE. NAH. COULDN'T POSSIBLY.
BYE! PEACE! SO LONG!
COME ON, LET'S GO! I'M BORED TO DEATH!
IT'S THE COUNTDOWN TO THE--LISTEN, IT'S THE NEW MUSIC VIDEO BY STUFF AND I CAN'T MISS IT, OKAY?
I AM HIS BIGGEST FAN.
STUFF? NEVER HEARD OF HIM--
YOU DON'T KNOW STUFF?
I'M SO HAPPY YOU ASKED!
DONUT WORRY

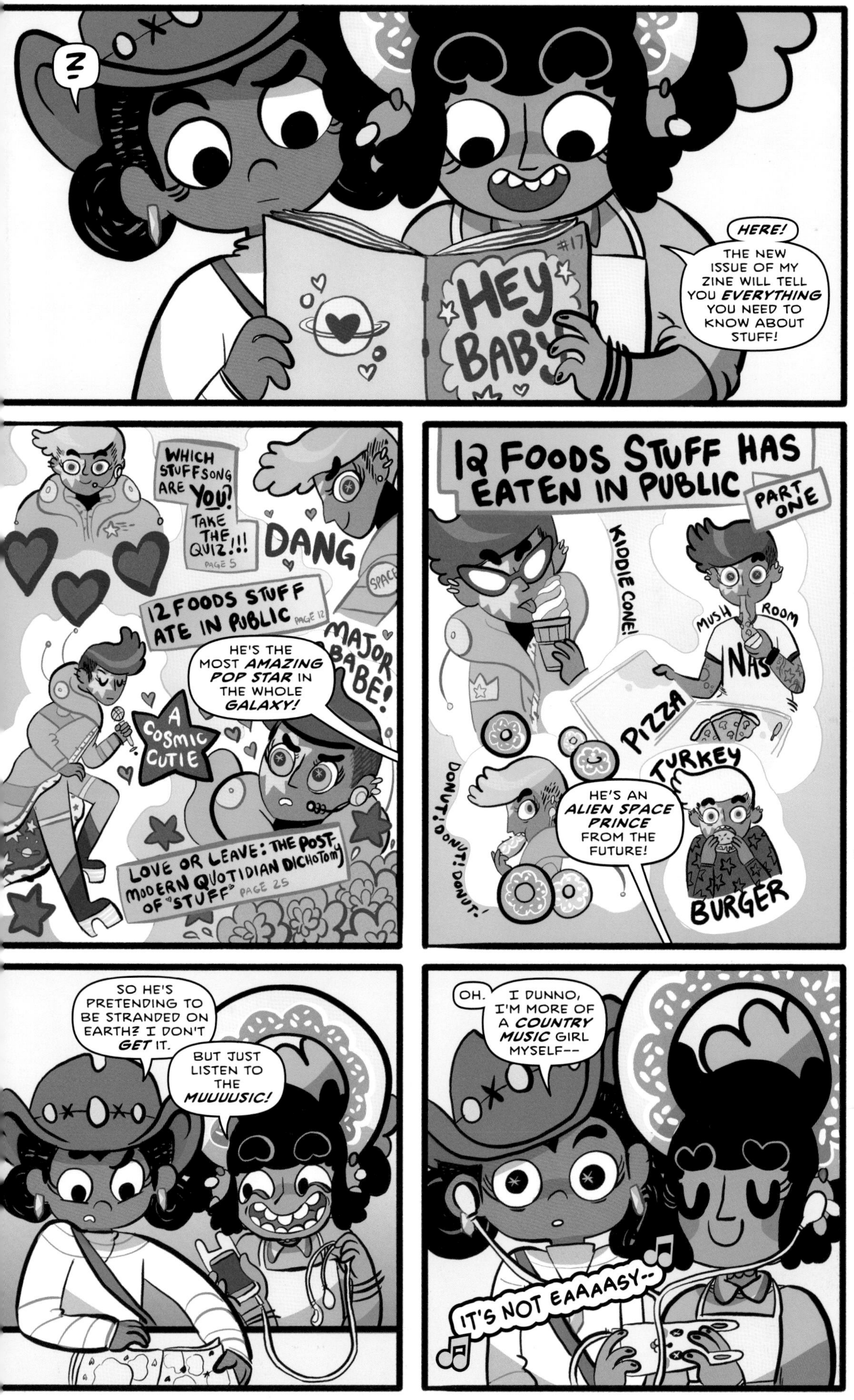
?
HERE!
THE NEW ISSUE OF MY ZINE WILL TELL YOU EVERYTHING YOU NEED TO KNOW ABOUT STUFF!
#17
HEY BABY
WHICH STUFF SONG ARE YOU? TAKE THE QUIZ!!! PAGE 5
DANG
SPACE
12 FOODS STUFF ATE IN PUBLIC PAGE 12
MAJOR BABE!
HE'S THE MOST AMAZING POP STAR IN THE WHOLE GALAXY!
A COSMIC CUTIE
LOVE OR LEAVE: THE POST-MODERN QUOTIDIAN DICHOTOMY OF "STUFF" PAGE 25
12 FOODS STUFF HAS EATEN IN PUBLIC
PART ONE
KIDDIE CONE!
MUSH ROOM
NAS
PIZZA
TURKEY
DONUT! DONUT! DONUT! DONUT!
HE'S AN ALIEN SPACE PRINCE FROM THE FUTURE!
BURGER
SO HE'S PRETENDING TO BE STRANDED ON EARTH? I DON'T GET IT.
BUT JUST LISTEN TO THE MUUUUSIC!
OH.
I DUNNO, I'M MORE OF A COUNTRY MUSIC GIRL MYSELF--
IT'S NOT EAAAASY--

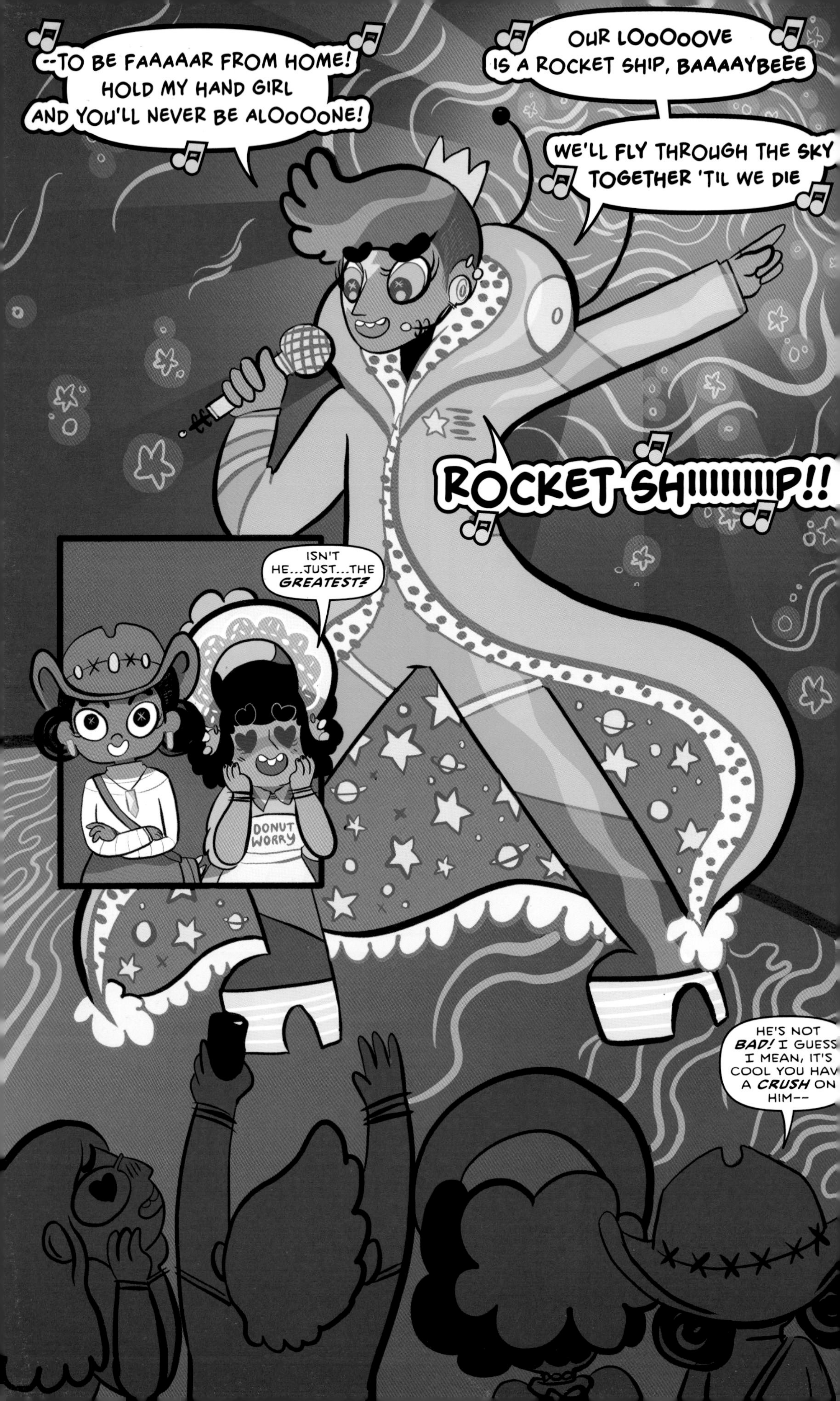
--TO BE FAAAAAR FROM HOME! HOLD MY HAND GIRL AND YOU'LL NEVER BE ALOOOONE!
OUR LOOOOOVE IS A ROCKET SHIP, BAAAAYBEEE
WE'LL FLY THROUGH THE SKY TOGETHER 'TIL WE DIE
ROCKET SHIIIIIIIIP!!
ISN'T HE...JUST...THE GREATEST?
DONUT WORRY
HE'S NOT BAD! I GUESS I MEAN, IT'S COOL YOU HAV A CRUSH ON HIM--

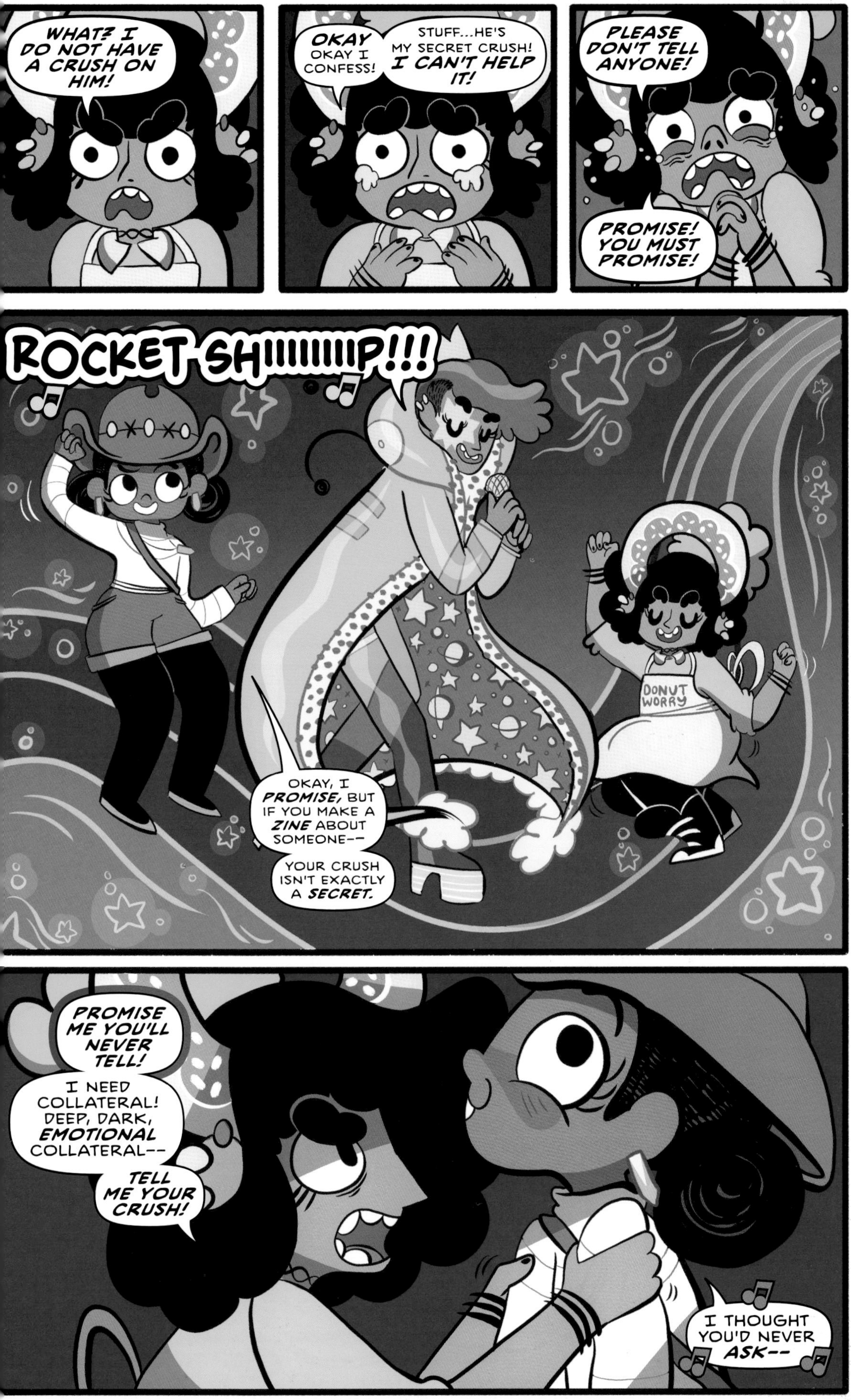
WHAT? I DO NOT HAVE A CRUSH ON HIM!
OKAY OKAY I CONFESS!
STUFF...HE'S MY SECRET CRUSH! I CAN'T HELP IT!
PLEASE DON'T TELL ANYONE!
PROMISE! YOU MUST PROMISE!
ROCKET SHIIIIIIIIIP!!!
OKAY, I PROMISE, BUT IF YOU MAKE A ZINE ABOUT SOMEONE--
YOUR CRUSH ISN'T EXACTLY A SECRET.
DONUT WORRY
PROMISE ME YOU'LL NEVER TELL!
I NEED COLLATERAL! DEEP, DARK, EMOTIONAL COLLATERAL--
TELL ME YOUR CRUSH!
I THOUGHT YOU'D NEVER ASK--

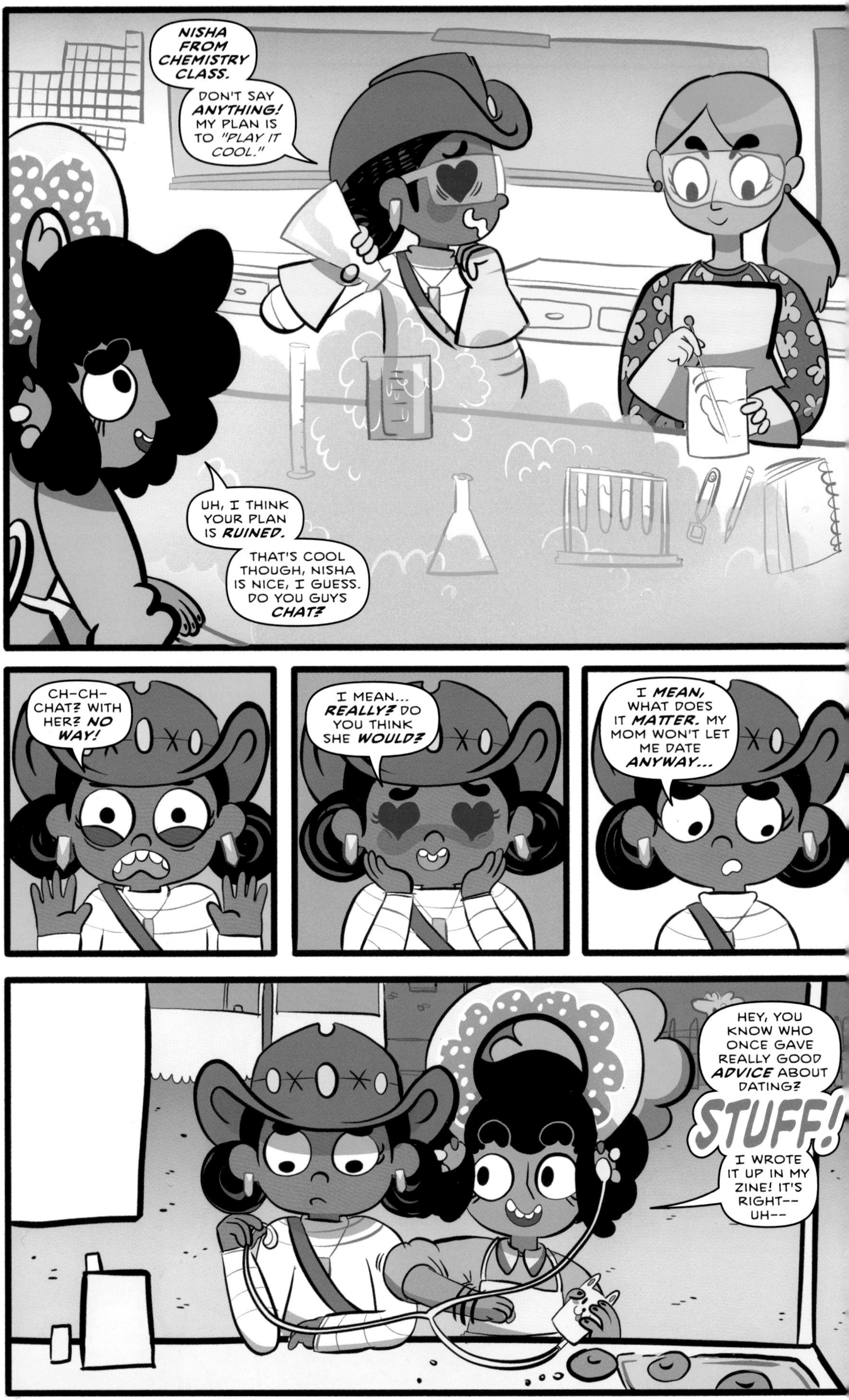
NISHA FROM CHEMISTRY CLASS.
DON'T SAY ANYTHING! MY PLAN IS TO "PLAY IT COOL."
UH, I THINK YOUR PLAN IS RUINED.
THAT'S COOL THOUGH, NISHA IS NICE, I GUESS. DO YOU GUYS CHAT?
CH-CH-CHAT? WITH HER? NO WAY!
I MEAN... REALLY? DO YOU THINK SHE WOULD?
I MEAN, WHAT DOES IT MATTER. MY MOM WON'T LET ME DATE ANYWAY...
HEY, YOU KNOW WHO ONCE GAVE REALLY GOOD ADVICE ABOUT DATING?
STUFF!
I WROTE IT UP IN MY ZINE! IT'S RIGHT-- UH--

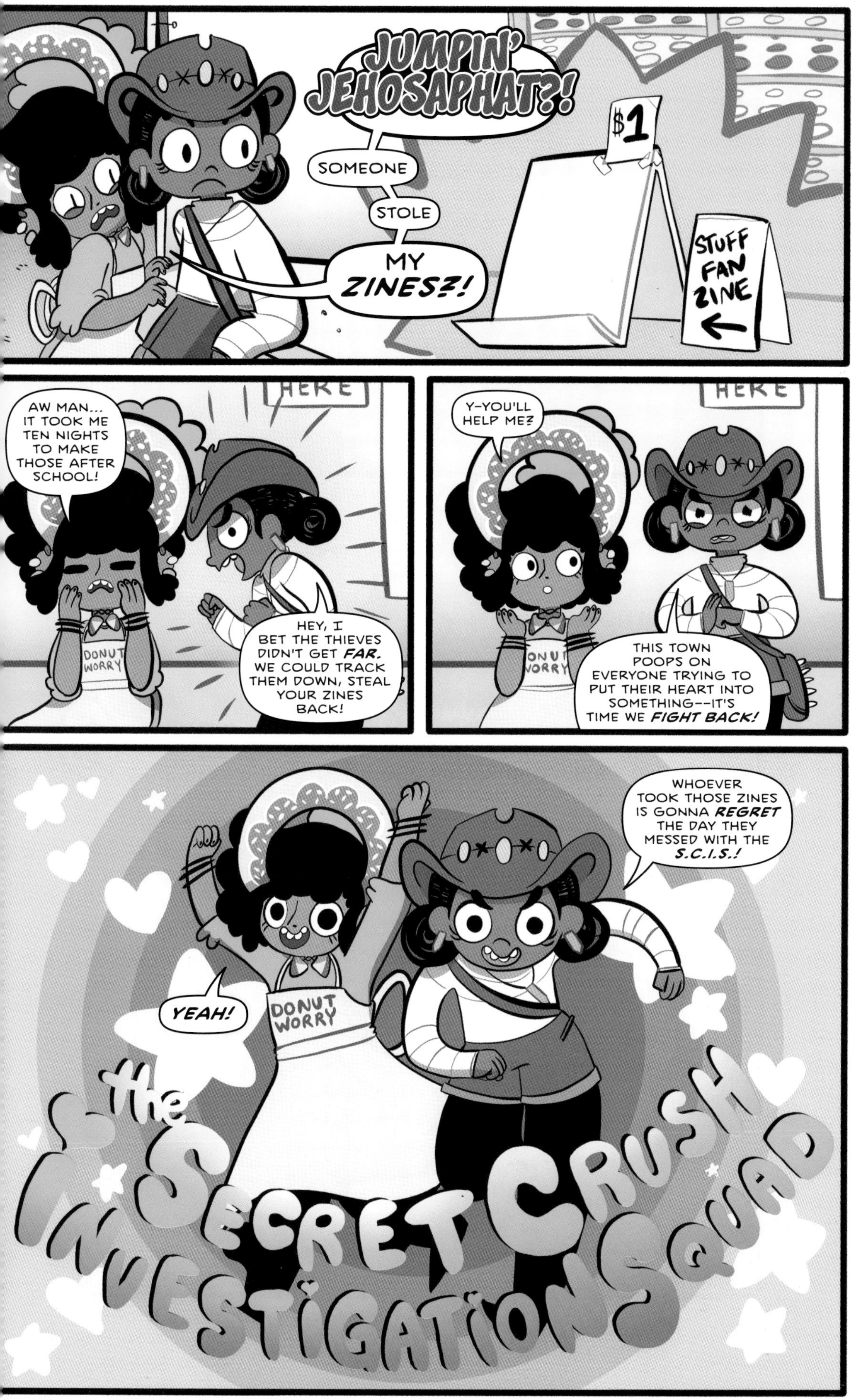

JUMPIN' JEHOSAPHAT?!
SOMEONE
STOLE
MY ZINES?!
$1
STUFF FAN ZINE
AW MAN... IT TOOK ME TEN NIGHTS TO MAKE THOSE AFTER SCHOOL!
HERE
DONUT WORRY
HEY, I BET THE THIEVES DIDN'T GET FAR. WE COULD TRACK THEM DOWN, STEAL YOUR ZINES BACK!
Y-YOU'LL HELP ME?
HERE
THIS TOWN POOPS ON EVERYONE TRYING TO PUT THEIR HEART INTO SOMETHING--IT'S TIME WE FIGHT BACK!
WHOEVER TOOK THOSE ZINES IS GONNA REGRET THE DAY THEY MESSED WITH THE S.C.I.S.!
YEAH!
DONUT WORRY
the SECRET CRUSH INVESTIGATION SQUAD

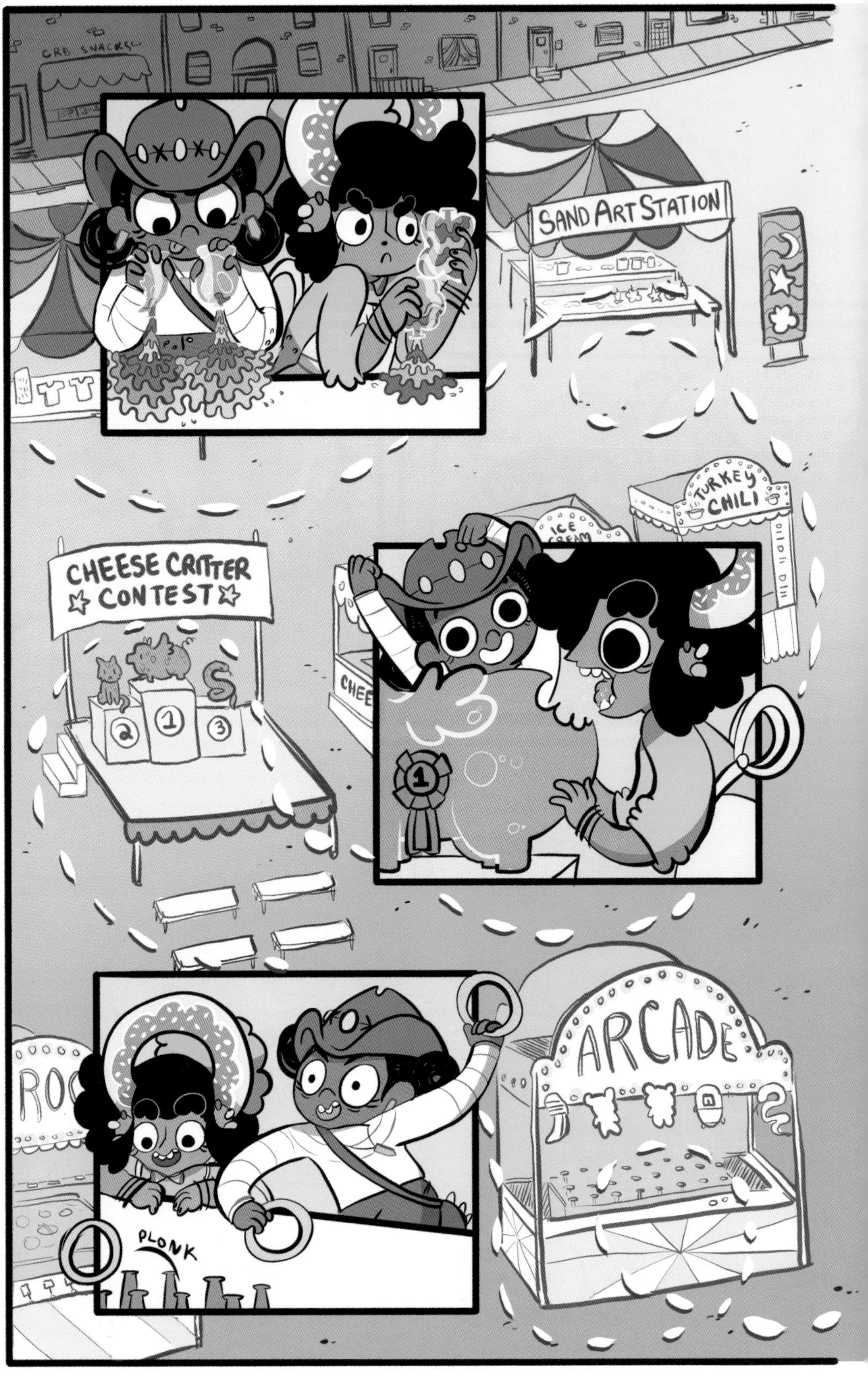

GRB SNACKS
SAND ART STATION
TURKEY CHILI
ICE CREAM
CHEESE CRITTER CONTEST
CHEE
PLONK
ARCADE
ROC

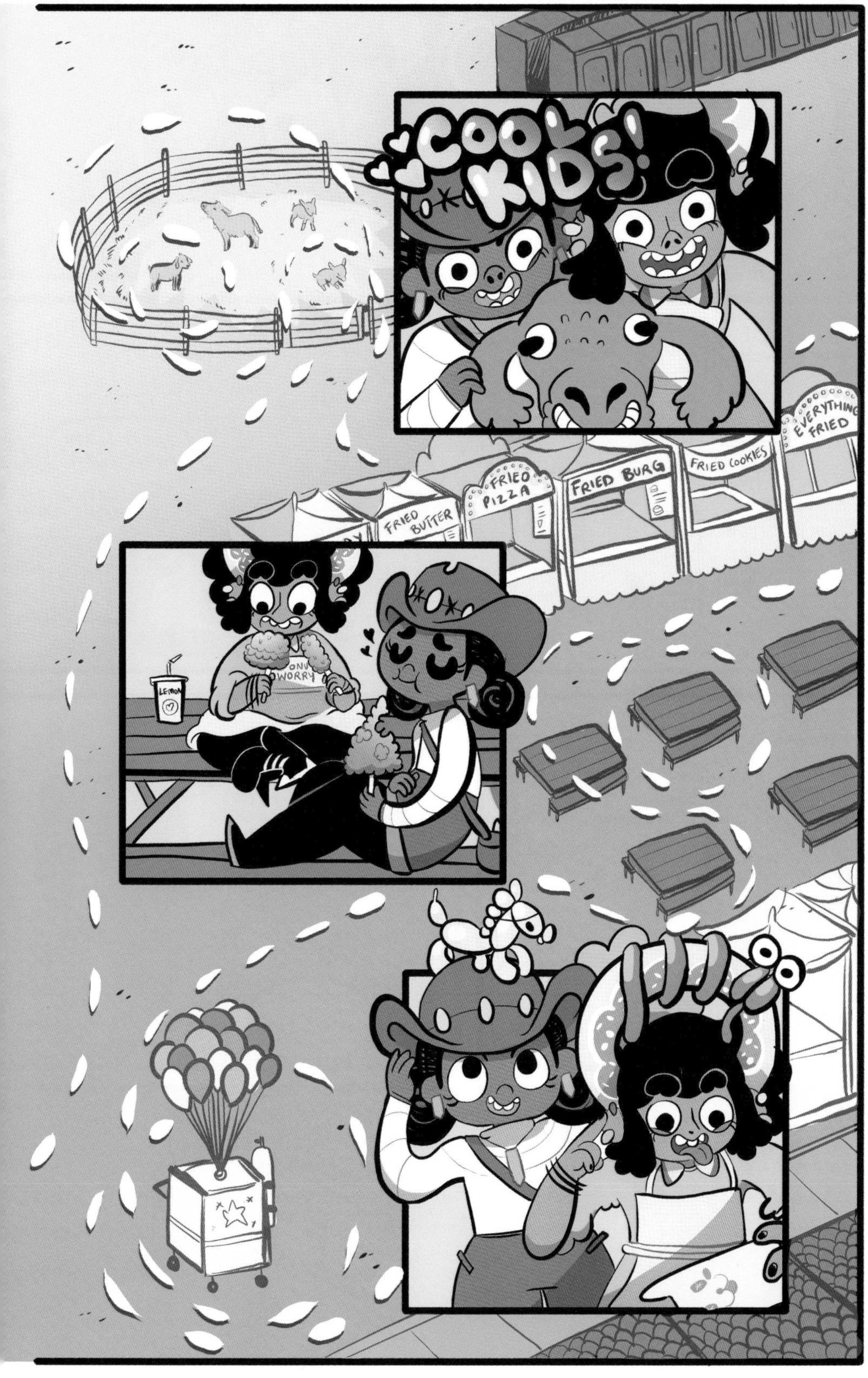

COOL KIDS!
FRIED BUTTER
FRIED PIZZA
FRIED BURG
FRIED COOKIES
EVERYTHING FRIED
LEMON

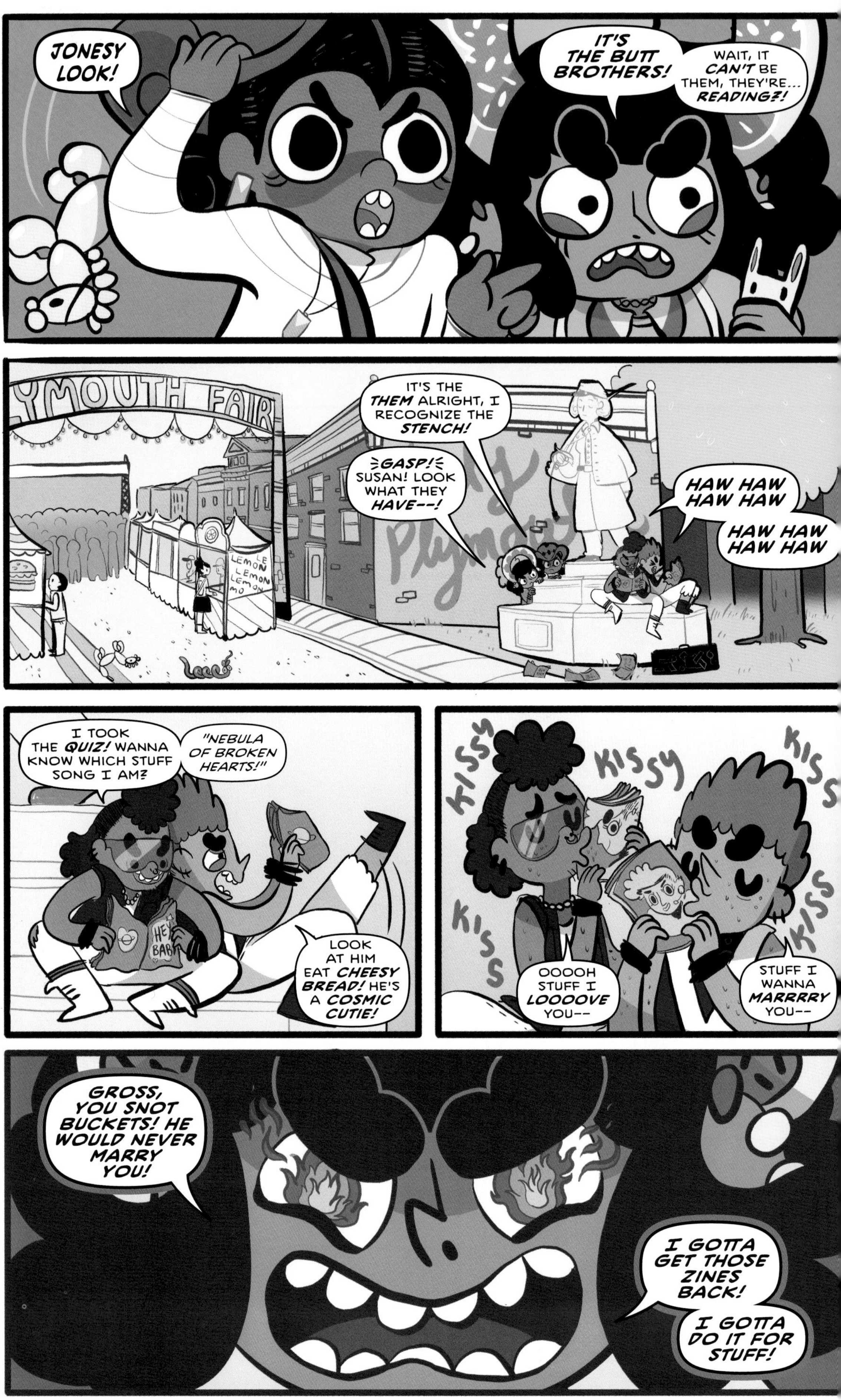
JONESY LOOK!
IT'S THE BUTT BROTHERS!
WAIT, IT CAN'T BE THEM, THEY'RE... READING?!
LYMOUTH FAIR
LEMON LEMON LEMON
IT'S THE THEM ALRIGHT, I RECOGNIZE THE STENCH!
GASP! SUSAN! LOOK WHAT THEY HAVE--!
HAW HAW HAW HAW
HAW HAW HAW HAW
I TOOK THE QUIZ! WANNA KNOW WHICH STUFF SONG I AM?
"NEBULA OF BROKEN HEARTS!"
LOOK AT HIM EAT CHEESY BREAD! HE'S A COSMIC CUTIE!
KISSY KISSY KISS
KISS KISS
OOOOH STUFF I LOOOOVE YOU--
STUFF I WANNA MARRRRY YOU--
GROSS, YOU SNOT BUCKETS! HE WOULD NEVER MARRY YOU!
I GOTTA GET THOSE ZINES BACK!
I GOTTA DO IT FOR STUFF!

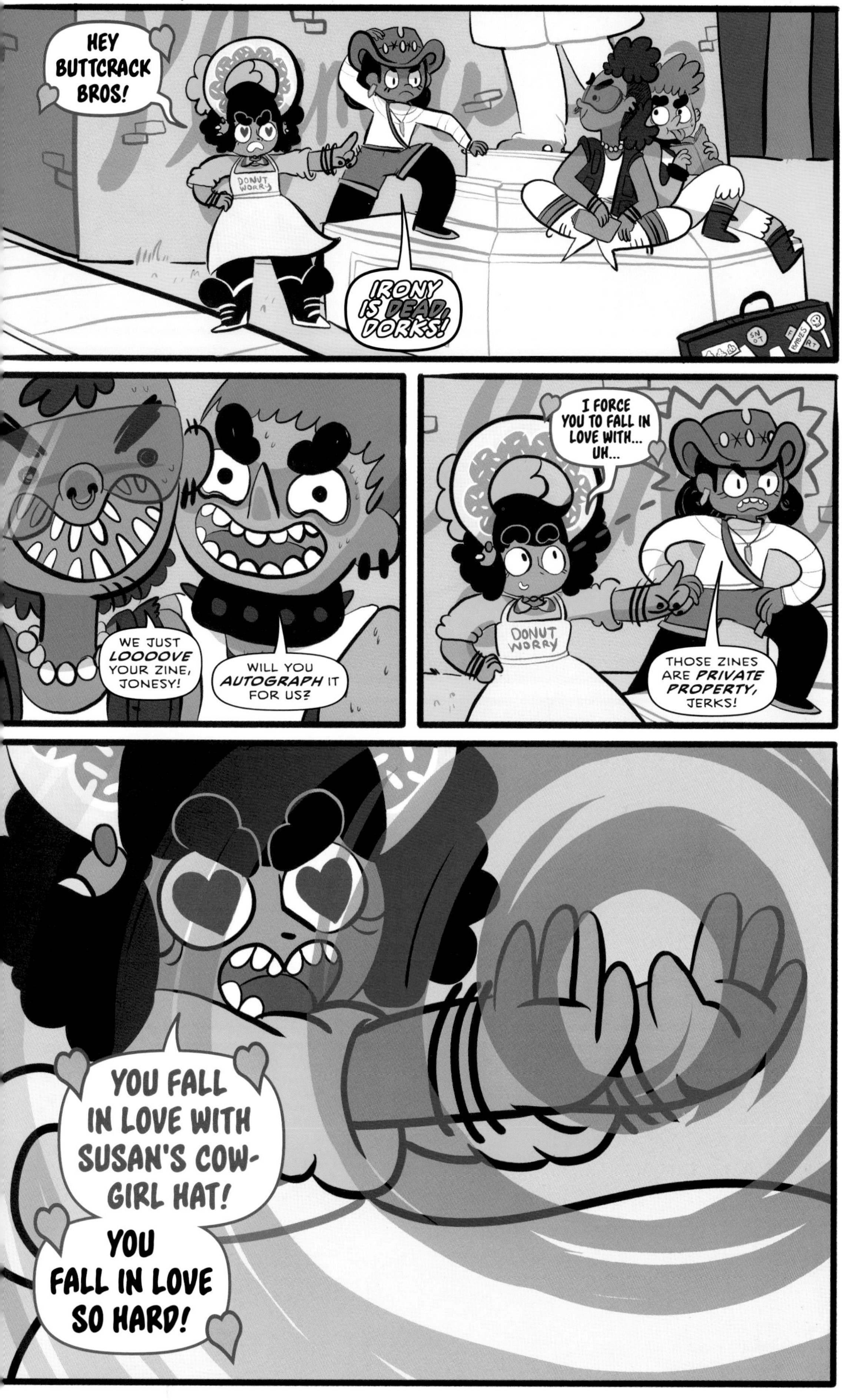
HEY BUTTCRACK BROS!
DONUT WORRY
IRONY IS DEAD, DORKS!
WE JUST LOOOOVE YOUR ZINE, JONESY!
WILL YOU AUTOGRAPH IT FOR US?
I FORCE YOU TO FALL IN LOVE WITH... UH...
DONUT WORRY
THOSE ZINES ARE PRIVATE PROPERTY, JERKS!
YOU FALL IN LOVE WITH SUSAN'S COW-GIRL HAT!
YOU FALL IN LOVE SO HARD!

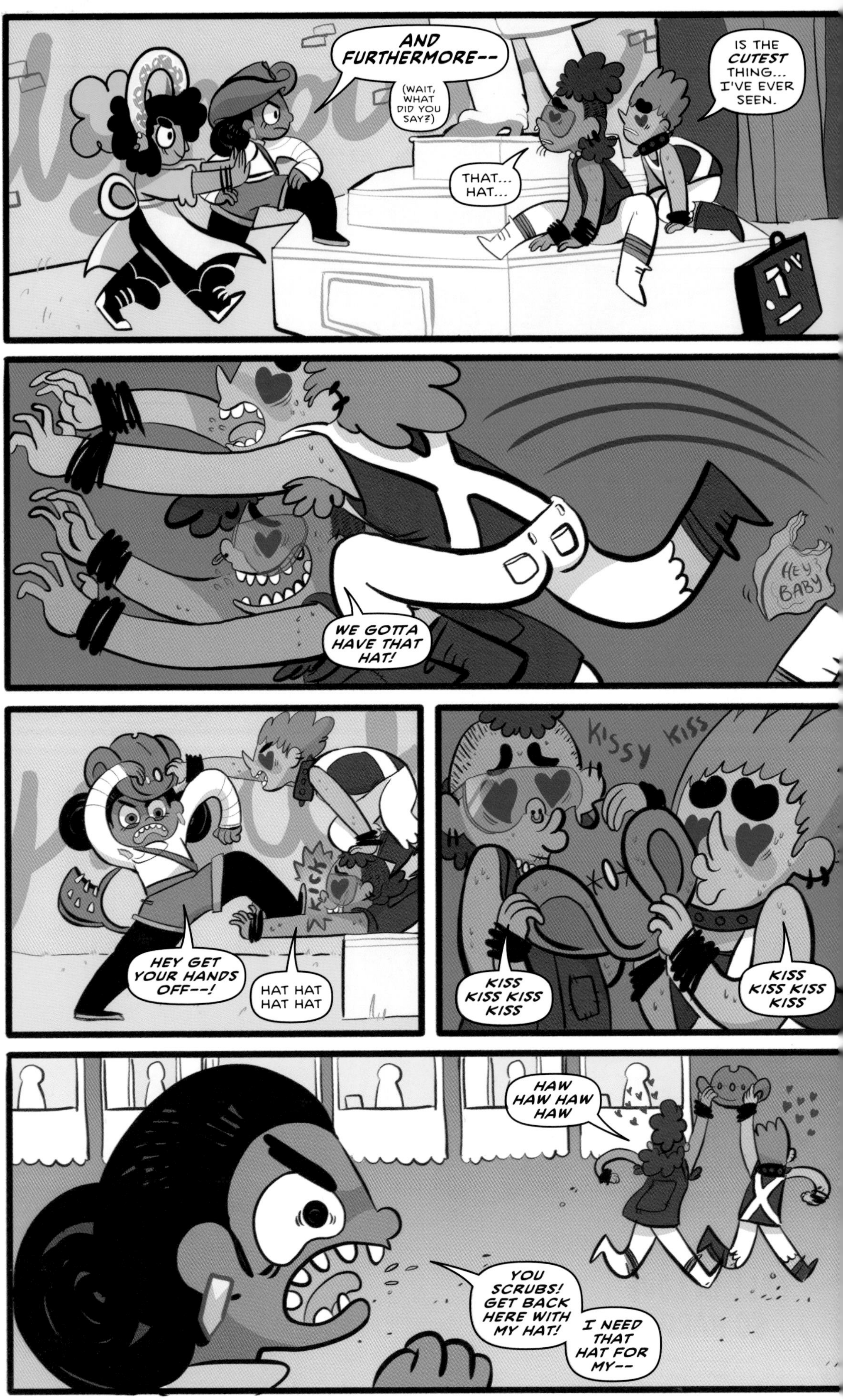
AND FURTHERMORE--
(WAIT, WHAT DID YOU SAY?)
THAT... HAT...
IS THE CUTEST THING... I'VE EVER SEEN.
WE GOTTA HAVE THAT HAT!
HEY BABY
HEY GET YOUR HANDS OFF--!
KICK
HAT HAT HAT HAT
KISSY KISS
KISS KISS KISS KISS
KISS KISS KISS KISS
HAW HAW HAW HAW HAW
YOU SCRUBS! GET BACK HERE WITH MY HAT!
I NEED THAT HAT FOR MY--

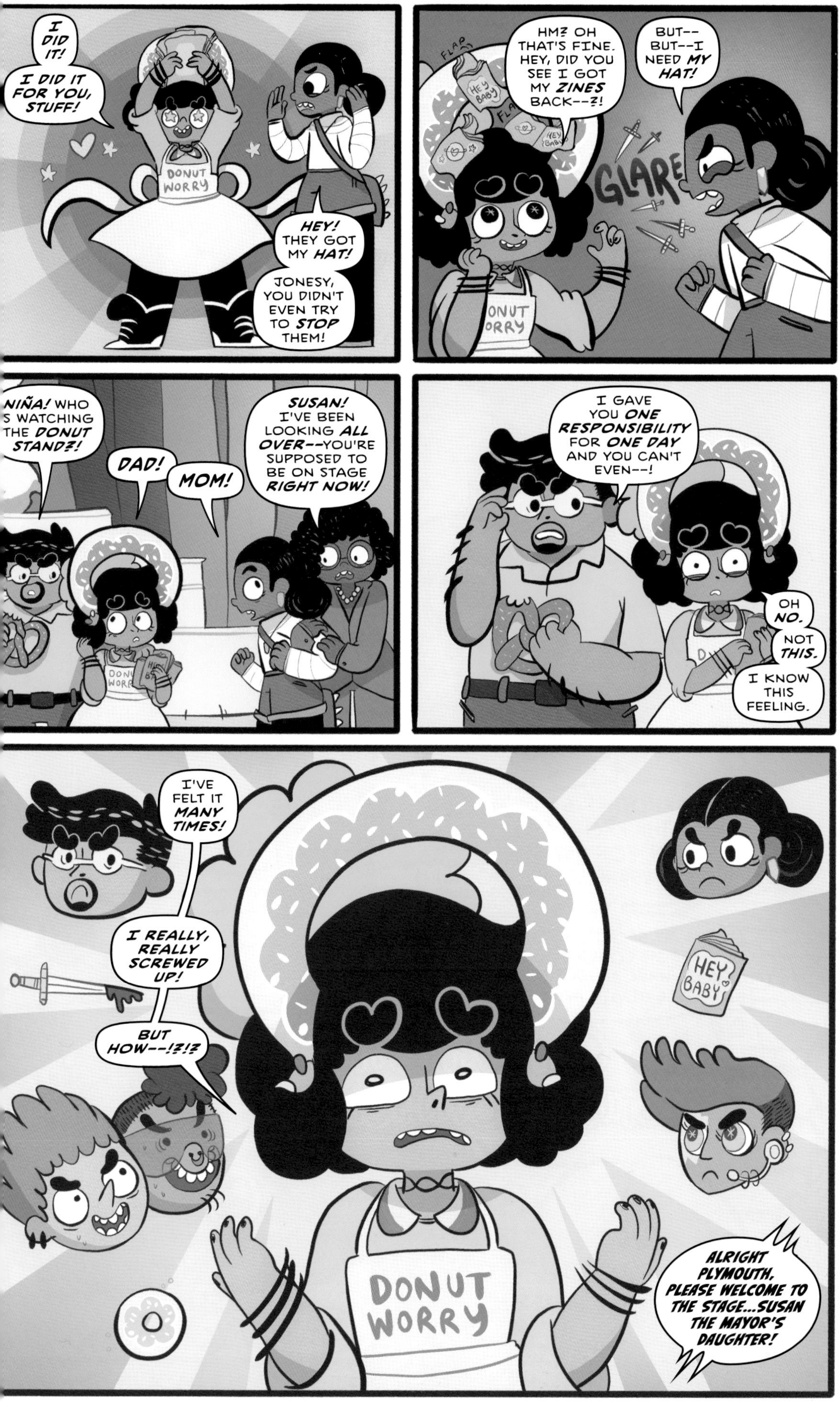
I DID IT!
I DID IT FOR YOU, STUFF!
DONUT WORRY
HEY! THEY GOT MY HAT!
JONESY, YOU DIDN'T EVEN TRY TO STOP THEM!
FLAP
HM? OH THAT'S FINE. HEY, DID YOU SEE I GOT MY ZINES BACK--?!
BUT-- BUT--I NEED MY HAT!
GLARE
NIÑA! WHO S WATCHING THE DONUT STAND?!
DAD!
MOM!
SUSAN! I'VE BEEN LOOKING ALL OVER--YOU'RE SUPPOSED TO BE ON STAGE RIGHT NOW!
I GAVE YOU ONE RESPONSIBILITY FOR ONE DAY AND YOU CAN'T EVEN--!
OH NO.
NOT THIS.
I KNOW THIS FEELING.
I'VE FELT IT MANY TIMES!
I REALLY, REALLY SCREWED UP!
BUT HOW--!?!?
HEY BABY
DONUT WORRY
ALRIGHT PLYMOUTH, PLEASE WELCOME TO THE STAGE...SUSAN THE MAYOR'S DAUGHTER!

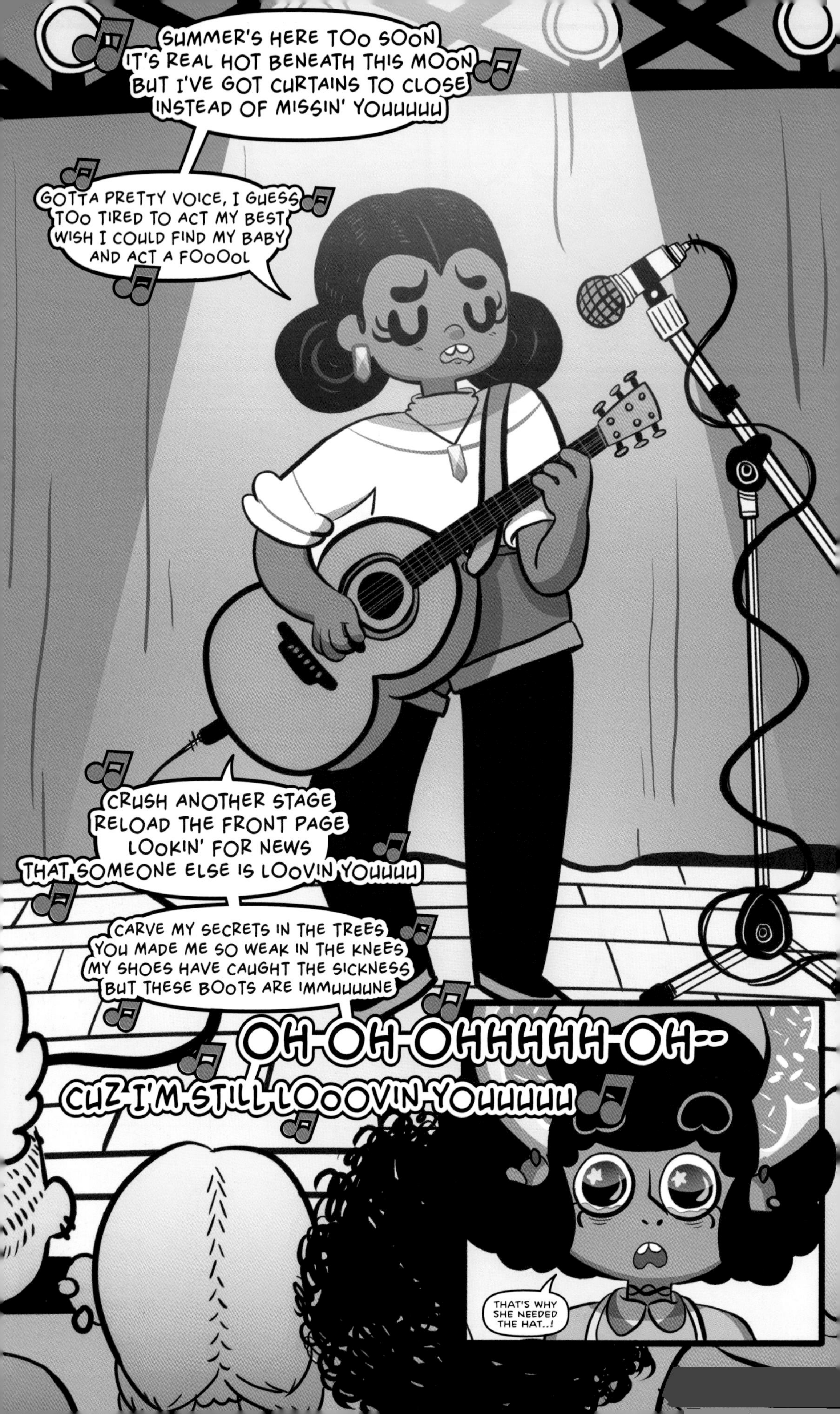
SUMMER'S HERE TOO SOON IT'S REAL HOT BENEATH THIS MOON BUT I'VE GOT CURTAINS TO CLOSE INSTEAD OF MISSIN' YOUUUUU
GOTTA PRETTY VOICE, I GUESS TOO TIRED TO ACT MY BEST WISH I COULD FIND MY BABY AND ACT A FOOOOL
CRUSH ANOTHER STAGE RELOAD THE FRONT PAGE LOOKIN' FOR NEWS THAT SOMEONE ELSE IS LOOVIN YOUUUU
CARVE MY SECRETS IN THE TREES YOU MADE ME SO WEAK IN THE KNEES MY SHOES HAVE CAUGHT THE SICKNESS BUT THESE BOOTS ARE IMMUUUUNE
OH-OH-OHHHHH-OH--
CUZ I'M STILL LOOOVIN YOUUUUU
THAT'S WHY SHE NEEDED THE HAT..!

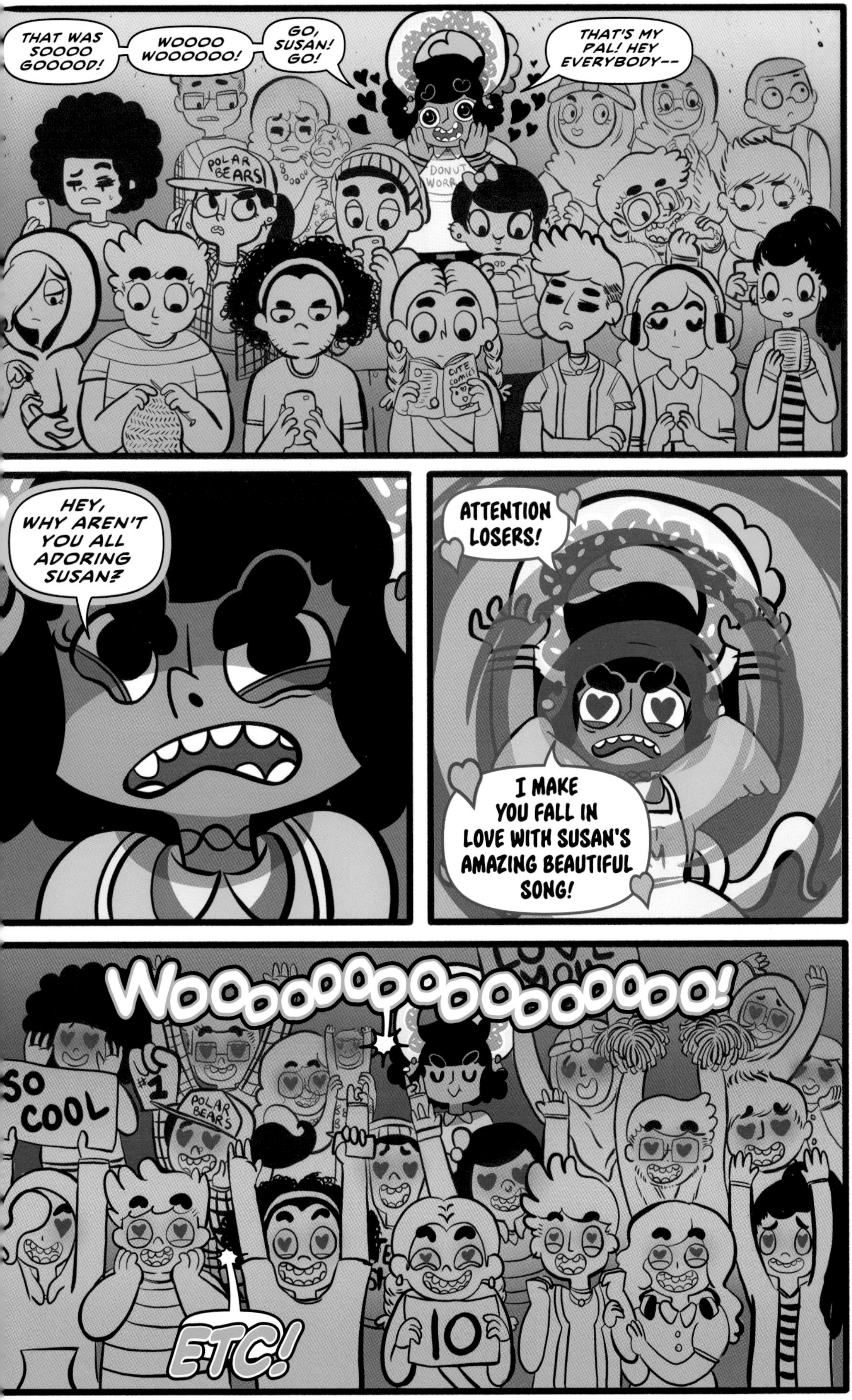
THAT WAS SOOOO GOOOOD!
WOOOO WOOOOOO!
GO, SUSAN! GO!
THAT'S MY PAL! HEY EVERYBODY--
POLAR BEARS
DONUT WORR
CUTE COMICS
HEY, WHY AREN'T YOU ALL ADORING SUSAN?
ATTENTION LOSERS!
I MAKE YOU FALL IN LOVE WITH SUSAN'S AMAZING BEAUTIFUL SONG!
WOOOOOOOOOOOOOOOOO!
SO COOL
#1
POLAR BEARS
10
ETC!

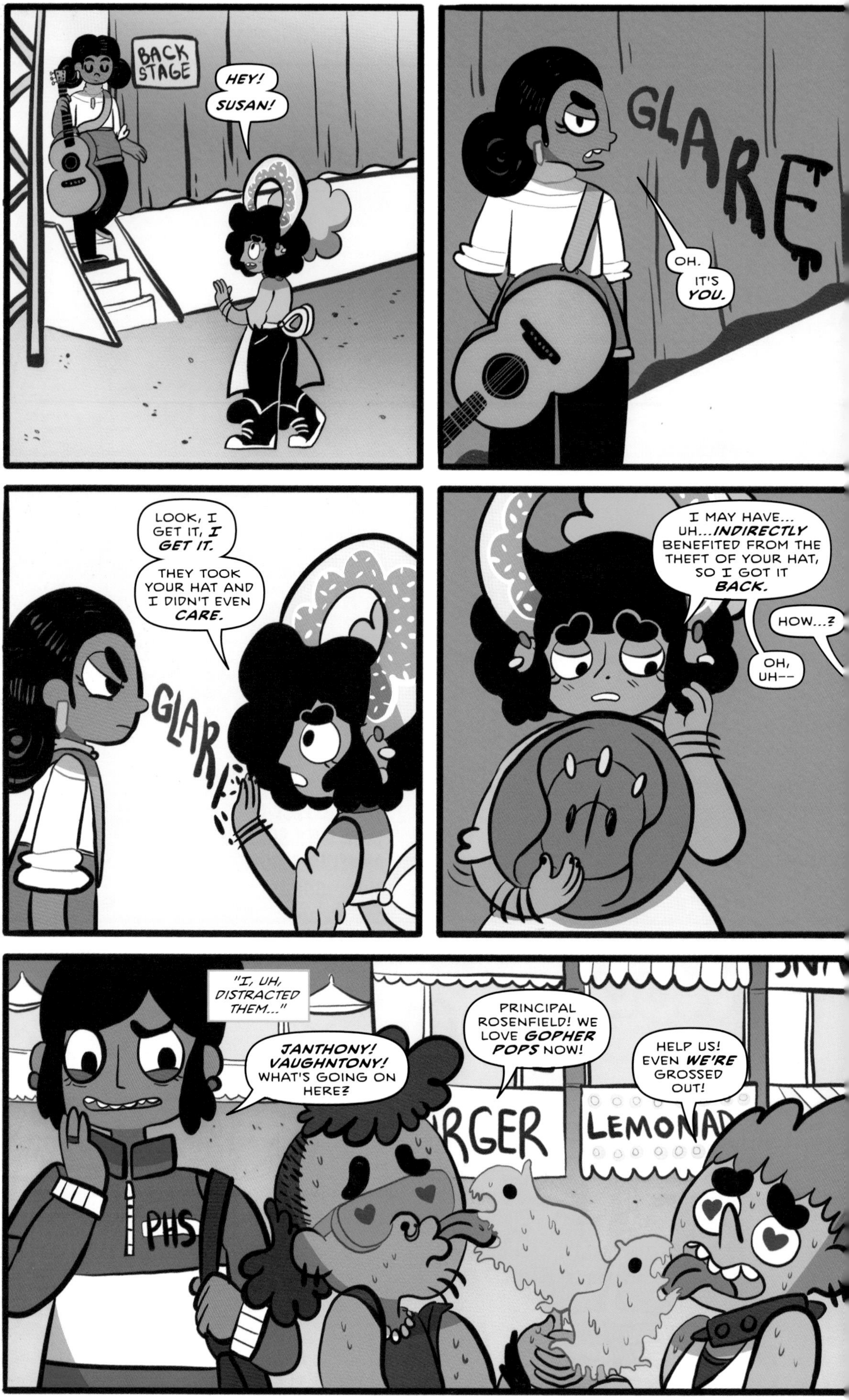
BACK STAGE
HEY!
SUSAN!
GLARE
OH.
IT'S YOU.
LOOK, I GET IT, I GET IT.
THEY TOOK YOUR HAT AND I DIDN'T EVEN CARE.
GLAR
I MAY HAVE... UH...INDIRECTLY BENEFITED FROM THE THEFT OF YOUR HAT, SO I GOT IT BACK.
HOW...?
OH, UH--
"I, UH, DISTRACTED THEM..."
JANTHONY! VAUGHNTONY! WHAT'S GOING ON HERE?
PRINCIPAL ROSENFIELD! WE LOVE GOPHER POPS NOW!
HELP US! EVEN WE'RE GROSSED OUT!
PHS
RGER
LEMONAD

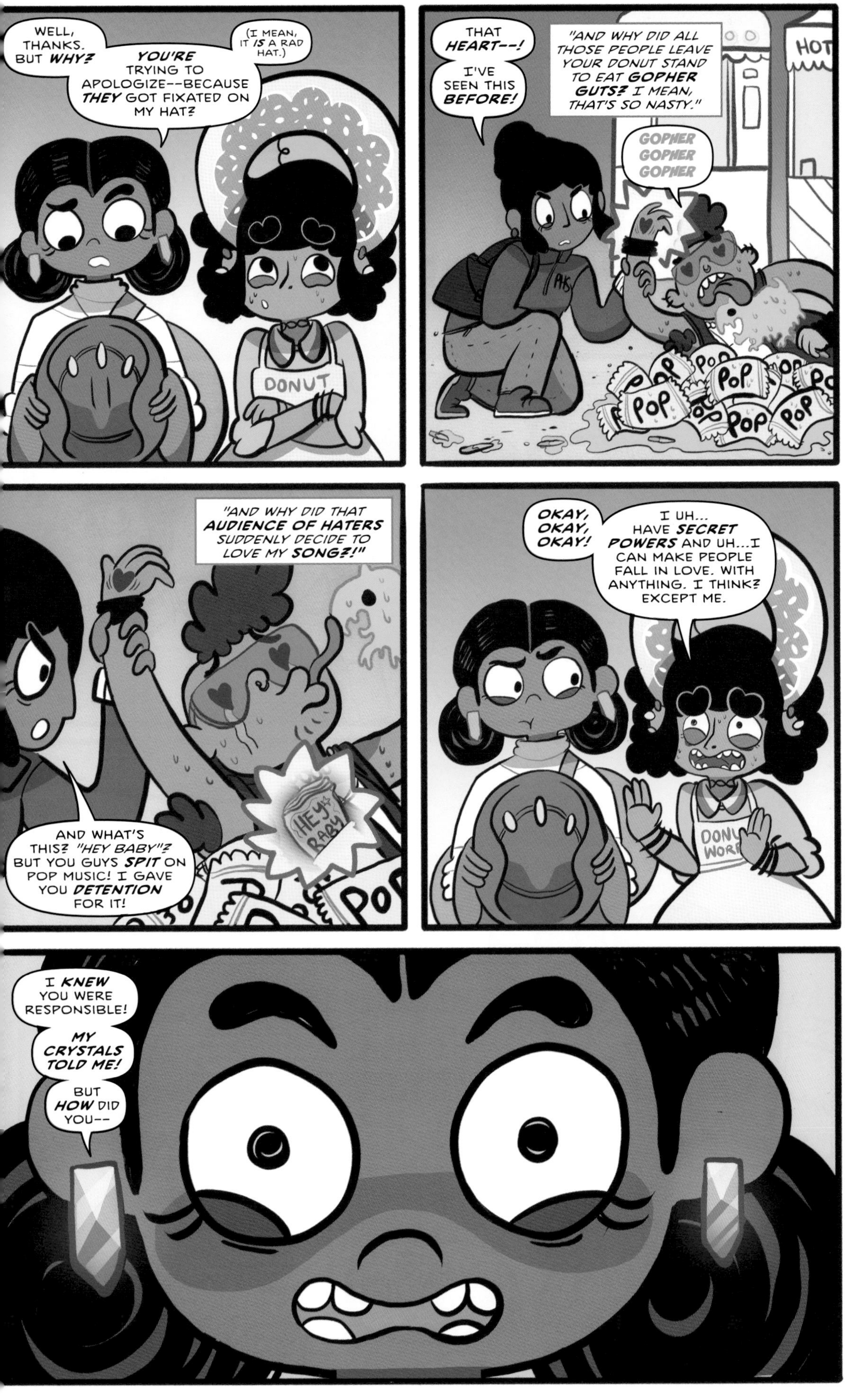
WELL, THANKS. BUT WHY?
YOU'RE TRYING TO APOLOGIZE--BECAUSE THEY GOT FIXATED ON MY HAT?
(I MEAN, IT IS A RAD HAT.)
DONUT
THAT HEART--!
I'VE SEEN THIS BEFORE!
"AND WHY DID ALL THOSE PEOPLE LEAVE YOUR DONUT STAND TO EAT GOPHER GUTS? I MEAN, THAT'S SO NASTY."
HOT
GOPHER GOPHER GOPHER
AHS
POP
"AND WHY DID THAT AUDIENCE OF HATERS SUDDENLY DECIDE TO LOVE MY SONG?!"
AND WHAT'S THIS? "HEY BABY"? BUT YOU GUYS SPIT ON POP MUSIC! I GAVE YOU DETENTION FOR IT!
HEY BABY
POP
OKAY, OKAY, OKAY!
I UH... HAVE SECRET POWERS AND UH...I CAN MAKE PEOPLE FALL IN LOVE. WITH ANYTHING. I THINK? EXCEPT ME.
I KNEW YOU WERE RESPONSIBLE!
MY CRYSTALS TOLD ME!
BUT HOW DID YOU--

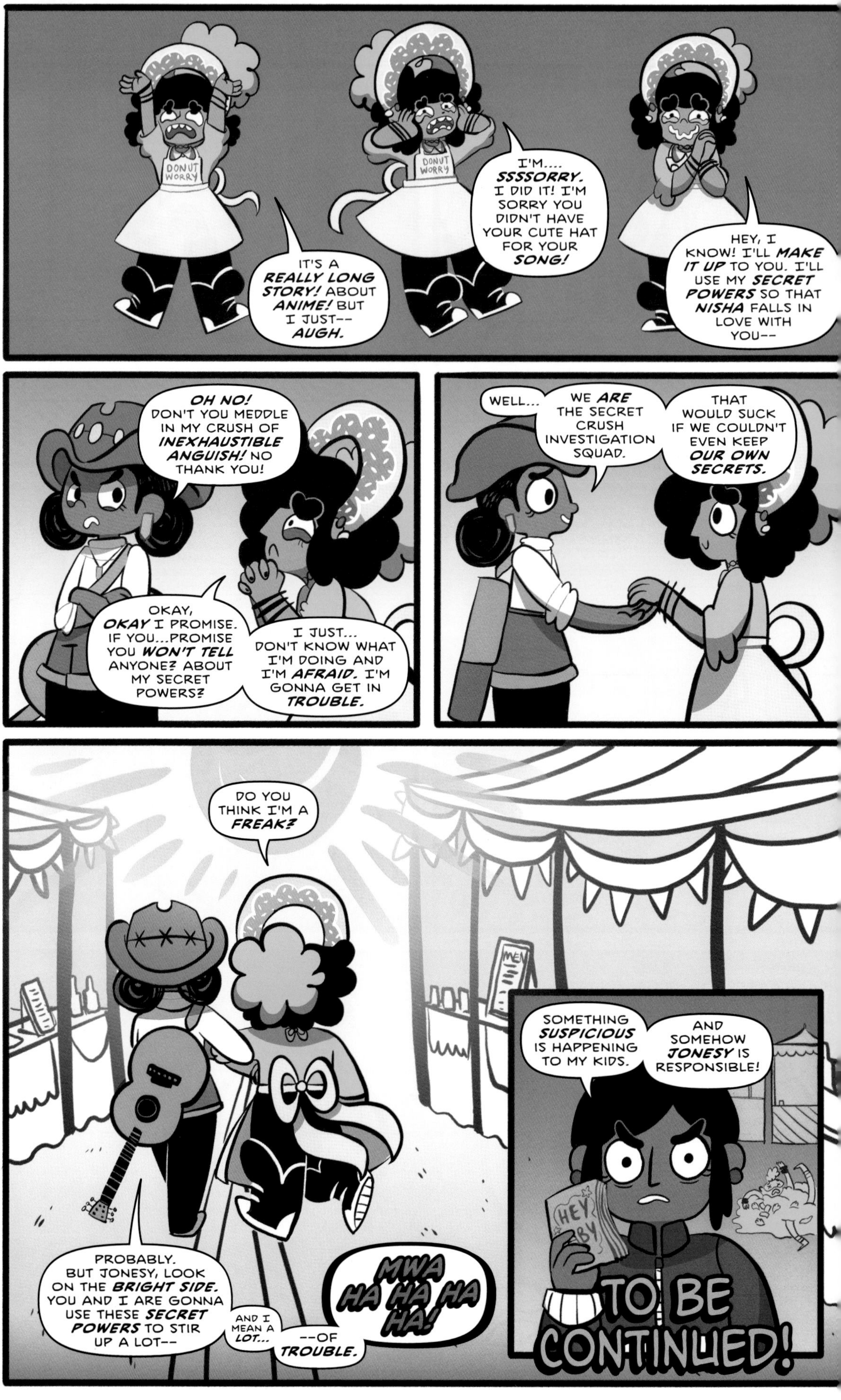

DONUT WORRY
IT'S A REALLY LONG STORY! ABOUT ANIME! BUT I JUST-- AUGH.
DONUT WORRY
I'M.... SSSSORRY. I DID IT! I'M SORRY YOU DIDN'T HAVE YOUR CUTE HAT FOR YOUR SONG!
HEY, I KNOW! I'LL MAKE IT UP TO YOU. I'LL USE MY SECRET POWERS SO THAT NISHA FALLS IN LOVE WITH YOU--
OH NO! DON'T YOU MEDDLE IN MY CRUSH OF INEXHAUSTIBLE ANGUISH! NO THANK YOU!
OKAY, OKAY I PROMISE. IF YOU...PROMISE YOU WON'T TELL ANYONE? ABOUT MY SECRET POWERS?
I JUST... DON'T KNOW WHAT I'M DOING AND I'M AFRAID. I'M GONNA GET IN TROUBLE.
WELL...
WE ARE THE SECRET CRUSH INVESTIGATION SQUAD.
THAT WOULD SUCK IF WE COULDN'T EVEN KEEP OUR OWN SECRETS.
DO YOU THINK I'M A FREAK?
PROBABLY. BUT JONESY, LOOK ON THE BRIGHT SIDE. YOU AND I ARE GONNA USE THESE SECRET POWERS TO STIR UP A LOT--
AND I MEAN A LOT...
--OF TROUBLE.
MWA HA HA HA HA!
SOMETHING SUSPICIOUS IS HAPPENING TO MY KIDS.
AND SOMEHOW JONESY IS RESPONSIBLE!
TO BE CONTINUED!

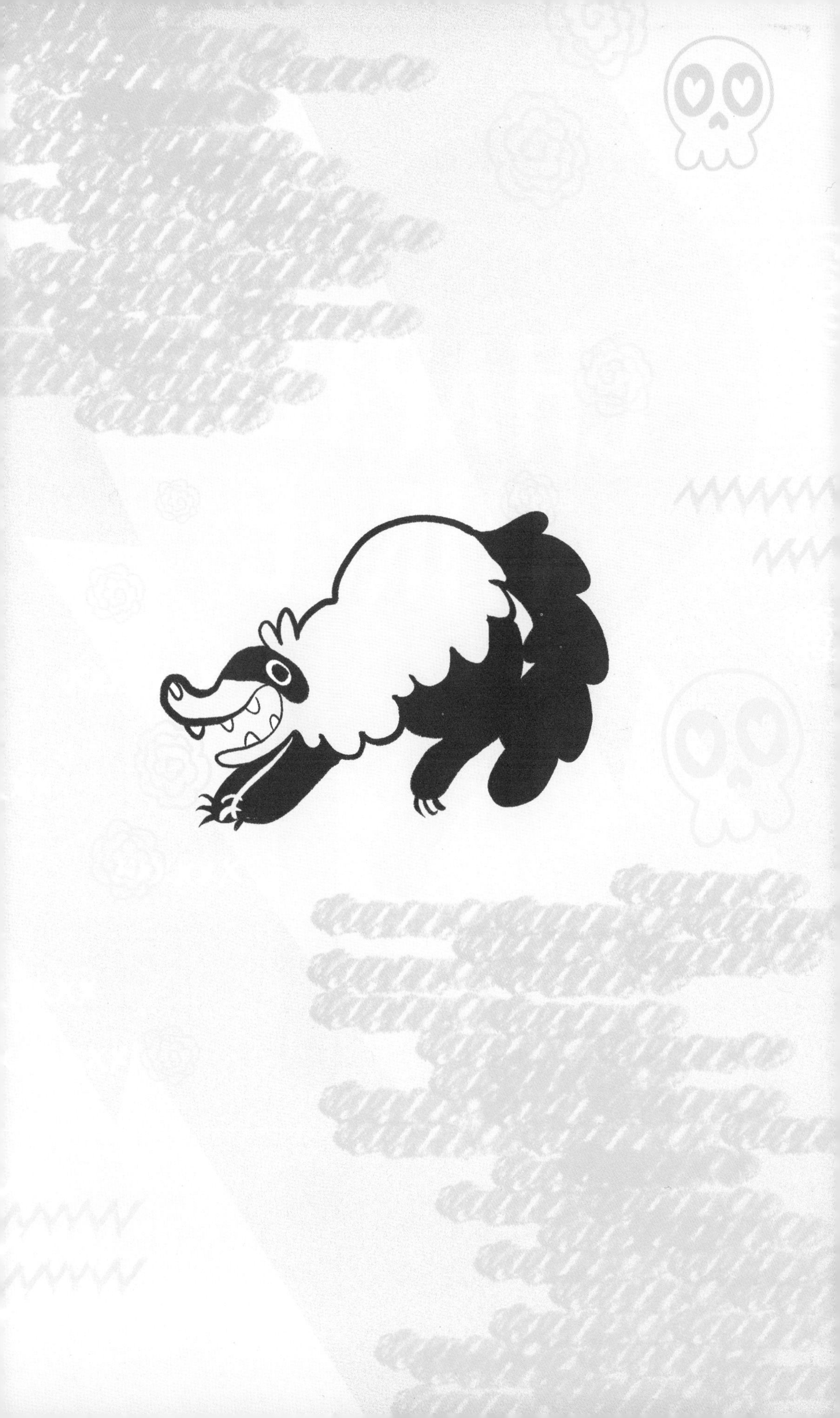

# CHAPTER THREE

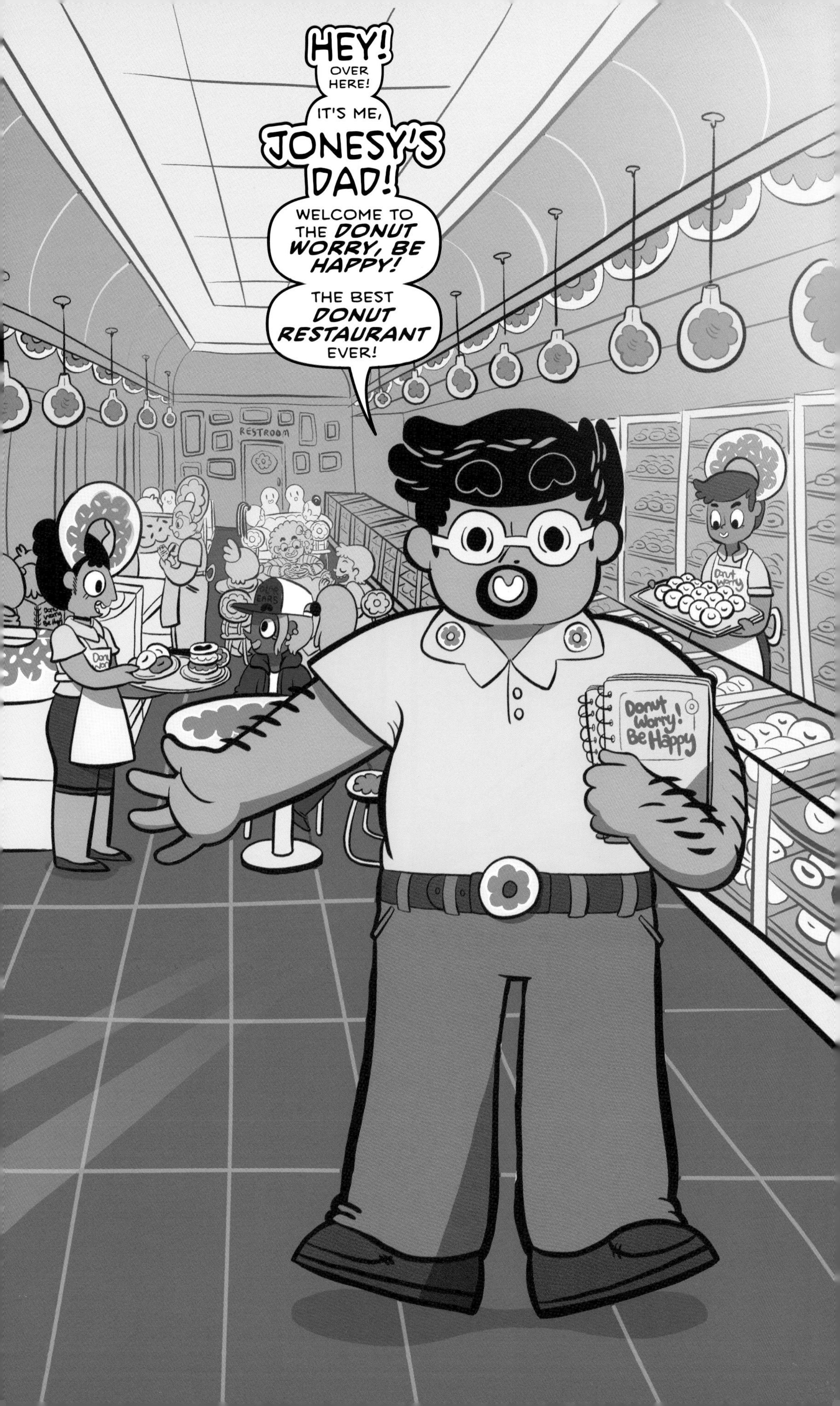
HEY! OVER HERE!
IT'S ME, JONESY'S DAD!
WELCOME TO THE DONUT WORRY, BE HAPPY!
THE BEST DONUT RESTAURANT EVER!
RESTROOM
Donut Worry! Be Happy

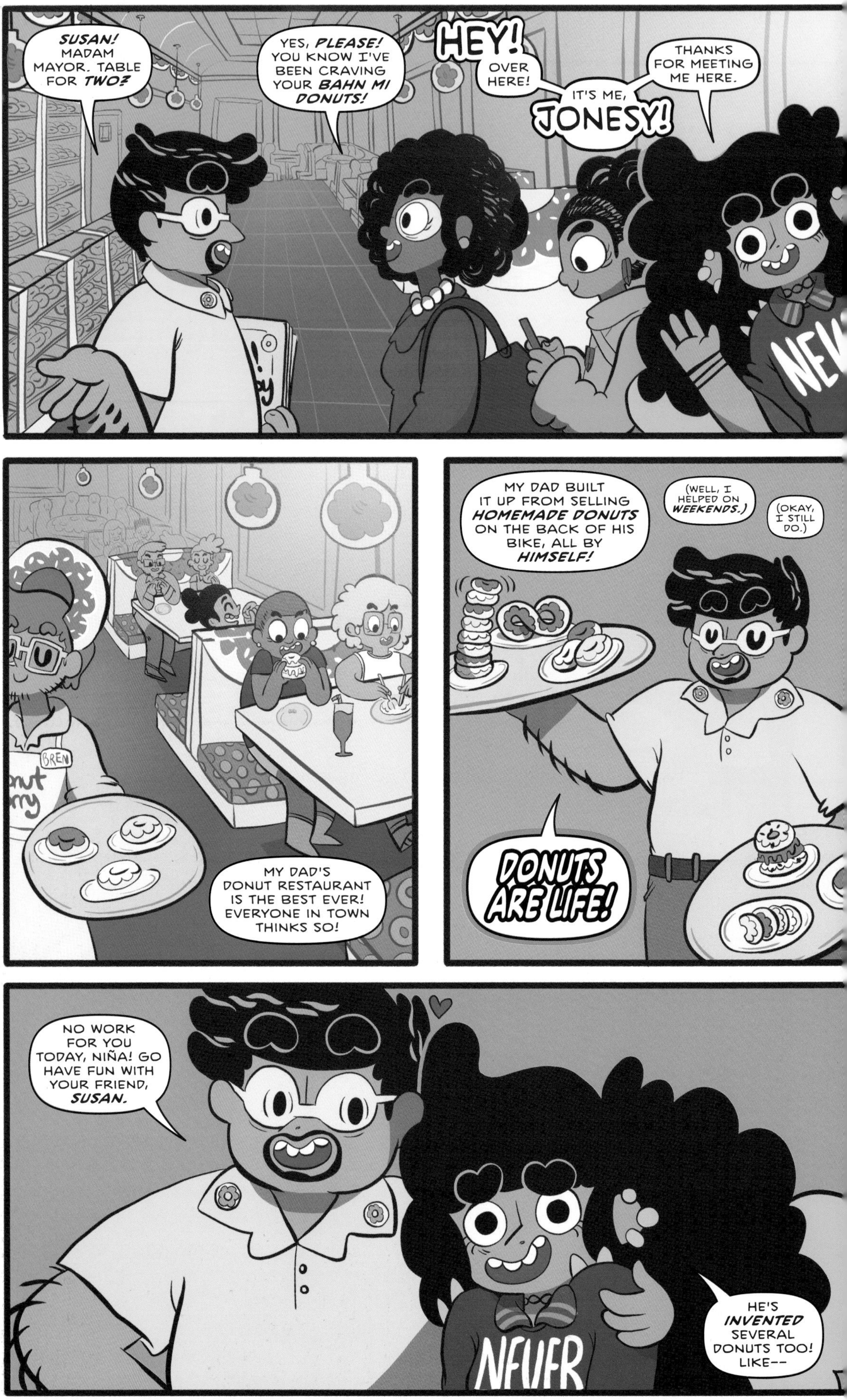
SUSAN! MADAM MAYOR. TABLE FOR TWO?
YES, PLEASE! YOU KNOW I'VE BEEN CRAVING YOUR BAHN MI DONUTS!
HEY!
OVER HERE!
IT'S ME, JONESY!
THANKS FOR MEETING ME HERE.
MY DAD'S DONUT RESTAURANT IS THE BEST EVER! EVERYONE IN TOWN THINKS SO!
MY DAD BUILT IT UP FROM SELLING HOMEMADE DONUTS ON THE BACK OF HIS BIKE, ALL BY HIMSELF!
(WELL, I HELPED ON WEEKENDS.)
(OKAY, I STILL DO.)
DONUTS ARE LIFE!
NO WORK FOR YOU TODAY, NIÑA! GO HAVE FUN WITH YOUR FRIEND, SUSAN.
HE'S INVENTED SEVERAL DONUTS TOO! LIKE--
NEVER

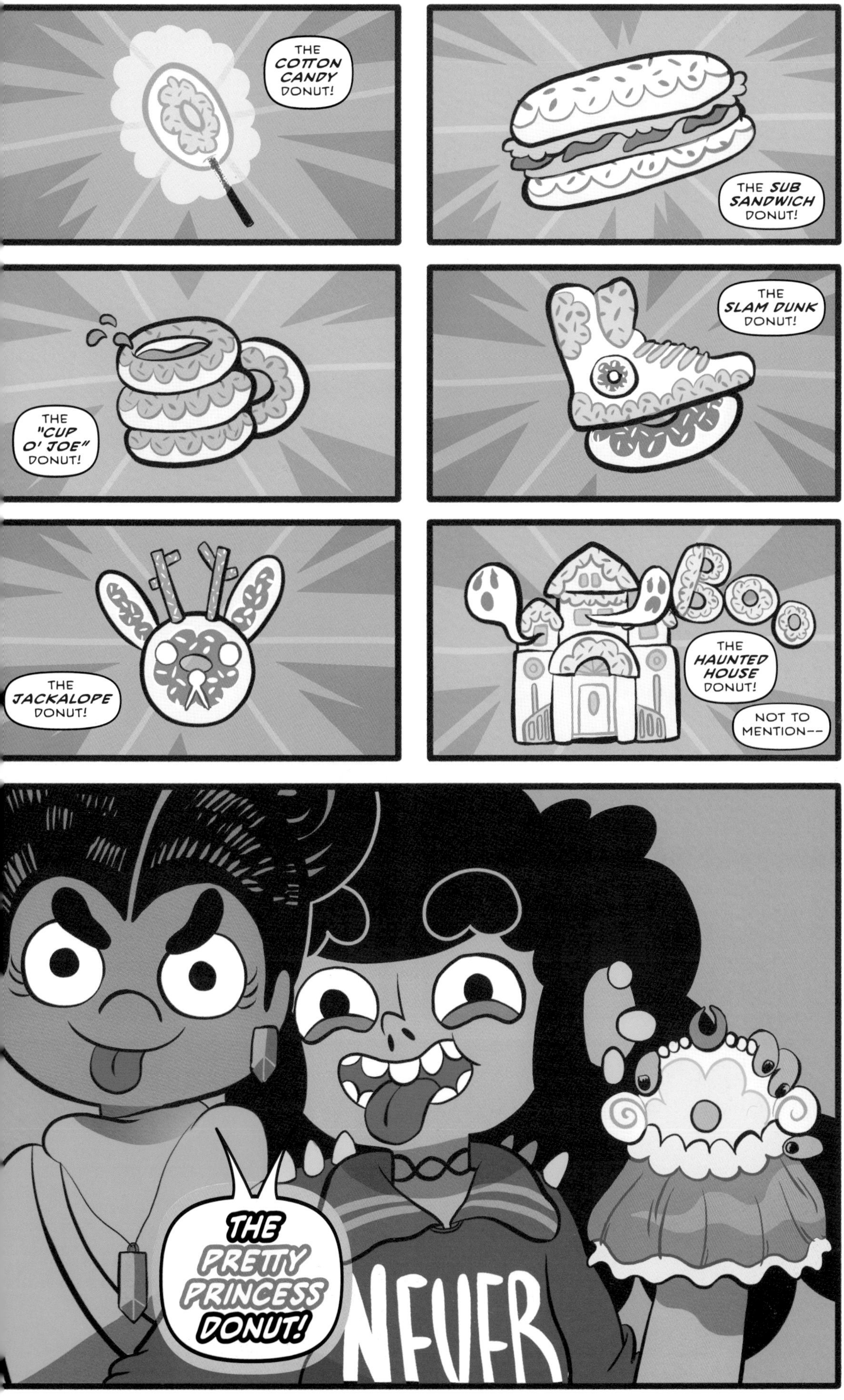
THE COTTON CANDY DONUT!
THE SUB SANDWICH DONUT!
THE "CUP O' JOE" DONUT!
THE SLAM DUNK DONUT!
THE JACKALOPE DONUT!
BOO
THE HAUNTED HOUSE DONUT!
NOT TO MENTION--
THE PRETTY PRINCESS DONUT!
NEVER

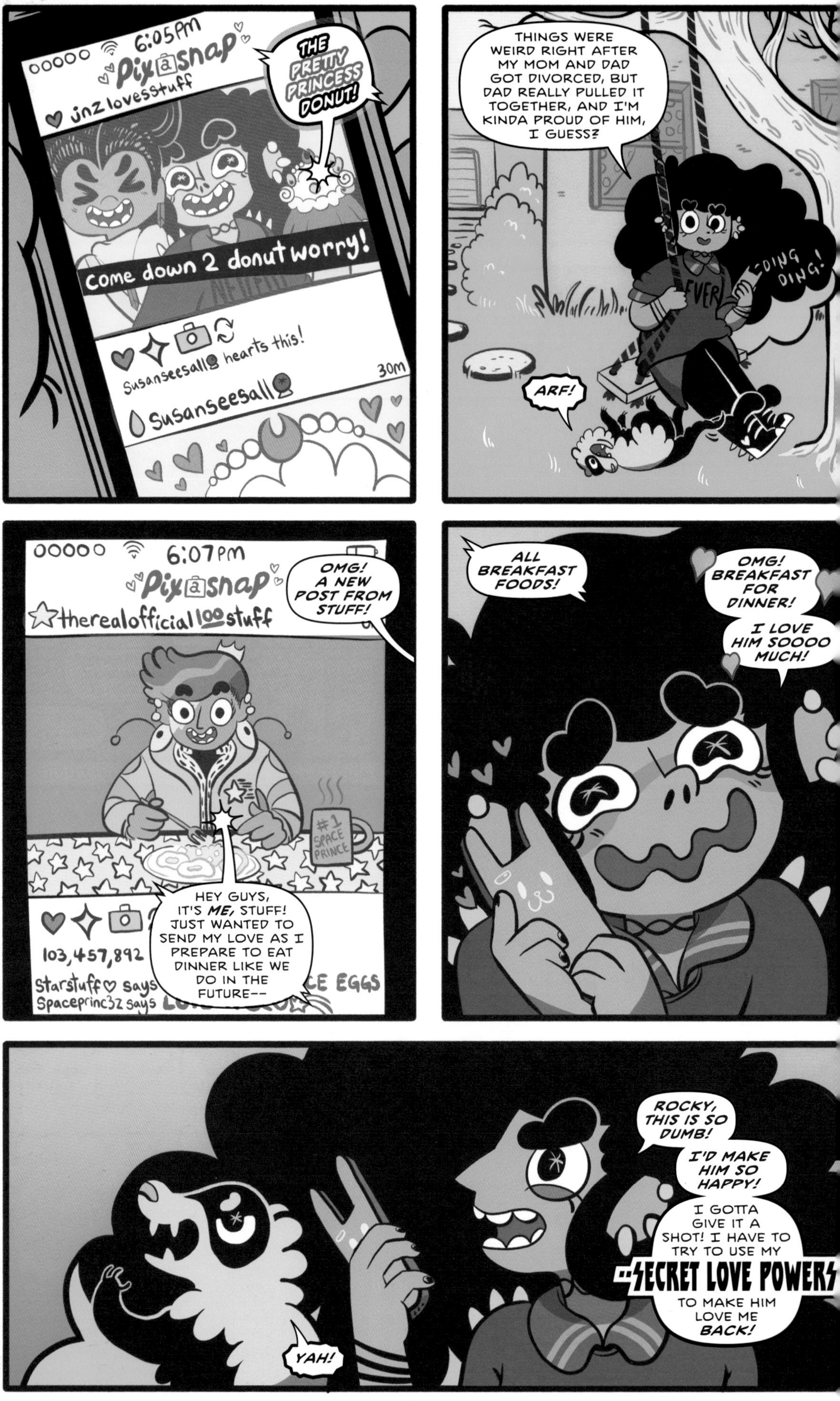

6:05PM
Pixasnap
unzlovesstuff
THE PRETTY PRINCESS DONUT!
come down 2 donut worry!
hearts this!
Susanseesall
30m
susanseesall
THINGS WERE WEIRD RIGHT AFTER MY MOM AND DAD GOT DIVORCED, BUT DAD REALLY PULLED IT TOGETHER, AND I'M KINDA PROUD OF HIM, I GUESS?
DING DING!
ARF!
6:07PM
Pixasnap
therealofficial100stuff
OMG! A NEW POST FROM STUFF!
#1 SPACE PRINCE
HEY GUYS, IT'S ME, STUFF! JUST WANTED TO SEND MY LOVE AS I PREPARE TO EAT DINNER LIKE WE DO IN THE FUTURE--
103,457,892
starstuff says
Spaceprinc3z says
CE EGGS
ALL BREAKFAST FOODS!
OMG! BREAKFAST FOR DINNER!
I LOVE HIM SOOOO MUCH!
ROCKY, THIS IS SO DUMB!
I'D MAKE HIM SO HAPPY!
I GOTTA GIVE IT A SHOT! I HAVE TO TRY TO USE MY ...SECRET LOVE POWERS TO MAKE HIM LOVE ME BACK!
YAH!

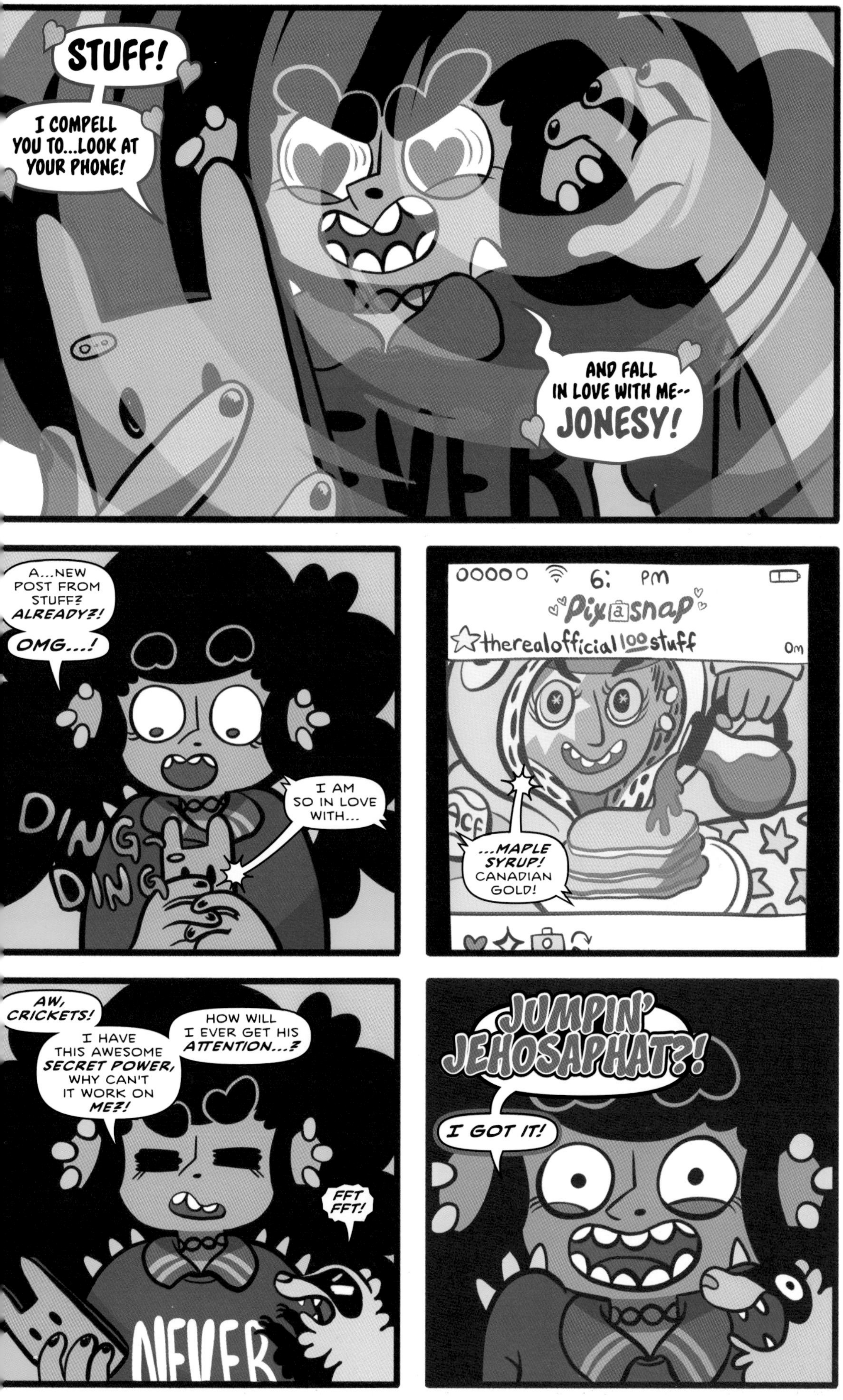
STUFF!
I COMPELL YOU TO...LOOK AT YOUR PHONE!
AND FALL IN LOVE WITH ME-- JONESY!
A...NEW POST FROM STUFF? ALREADY?!
OMG...!
DING DING
I AM SO IN LOVE WITH...
6: PM
Pix a snap
therealofficial100stuff
0m
...MAPLE SYRUP! CANADIAN GOLD!
AW, CRICKETS!
I HAVE THIS AWESOME SECRET POWER, WHY CAN'T IT WORK ON ME?!
HOW WILL I EVER GET HIS ATTENTION...?
FFT FFT!
JUMPIN' JEHOSAPHAT?!
I GOT IT!

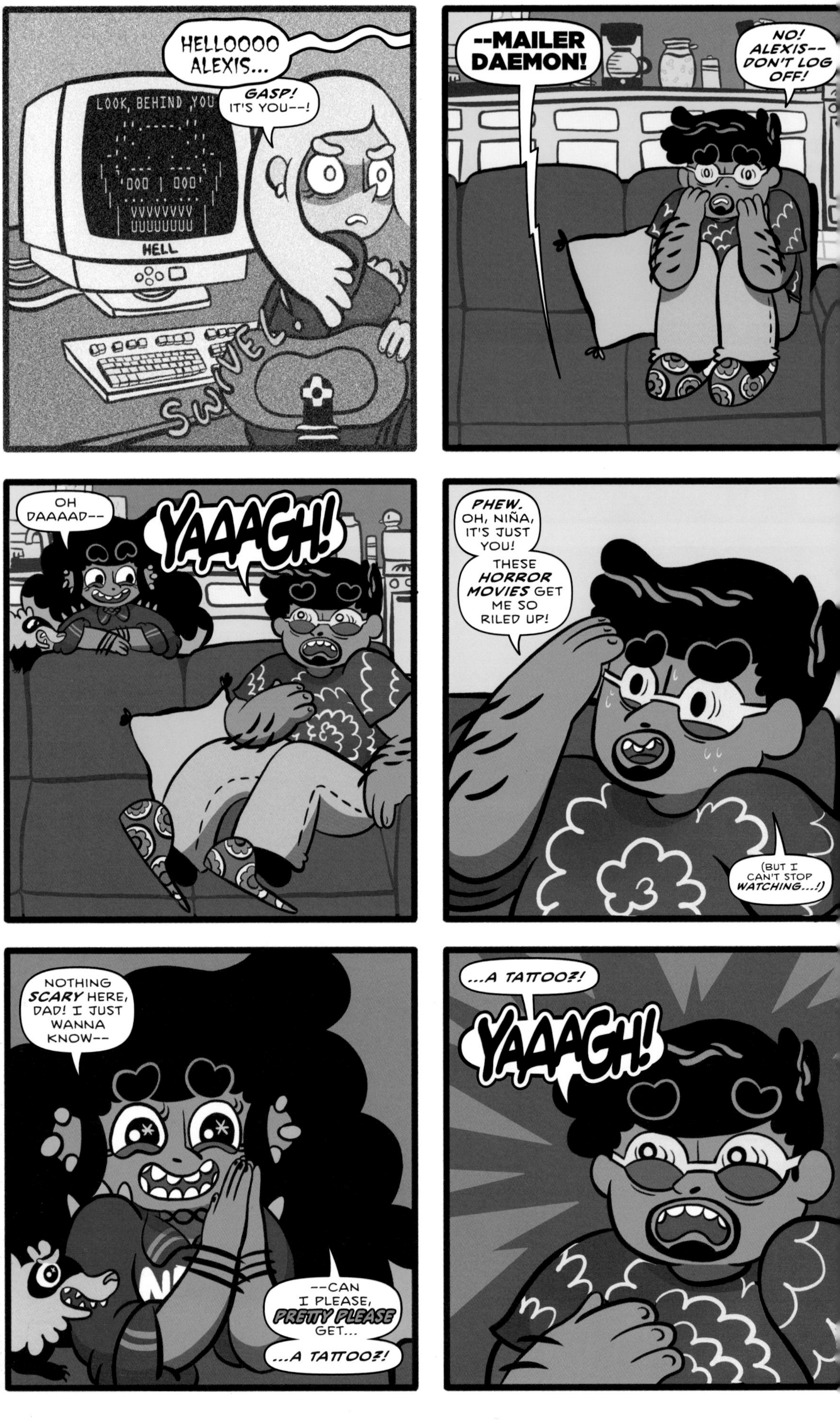
HELLOOOO ALEXIS...
LOOK, BEHIND YOU
HELL
GASP! IT'S YOU--!
SWIVEL
--MAILER DAEMON!
NO! ALEXIS-- DON'T LOG OFF!
OH DAAAAD--
YAAAGH!
PHEW. OH, NIÑA, IT'S JUST YOU!
THESE HORROR MOVIES GET ME SO RILED UP!
(BUT I CAN'T STOP WATCHING...!)
NOTHING SCARY HERE, DAD! I JUST WANNA KNOW--
--CAN I PLEASE, PRETTY PLEASE GET...
...A TATTOO?!
...A TATTOO?!
YAAAGH!

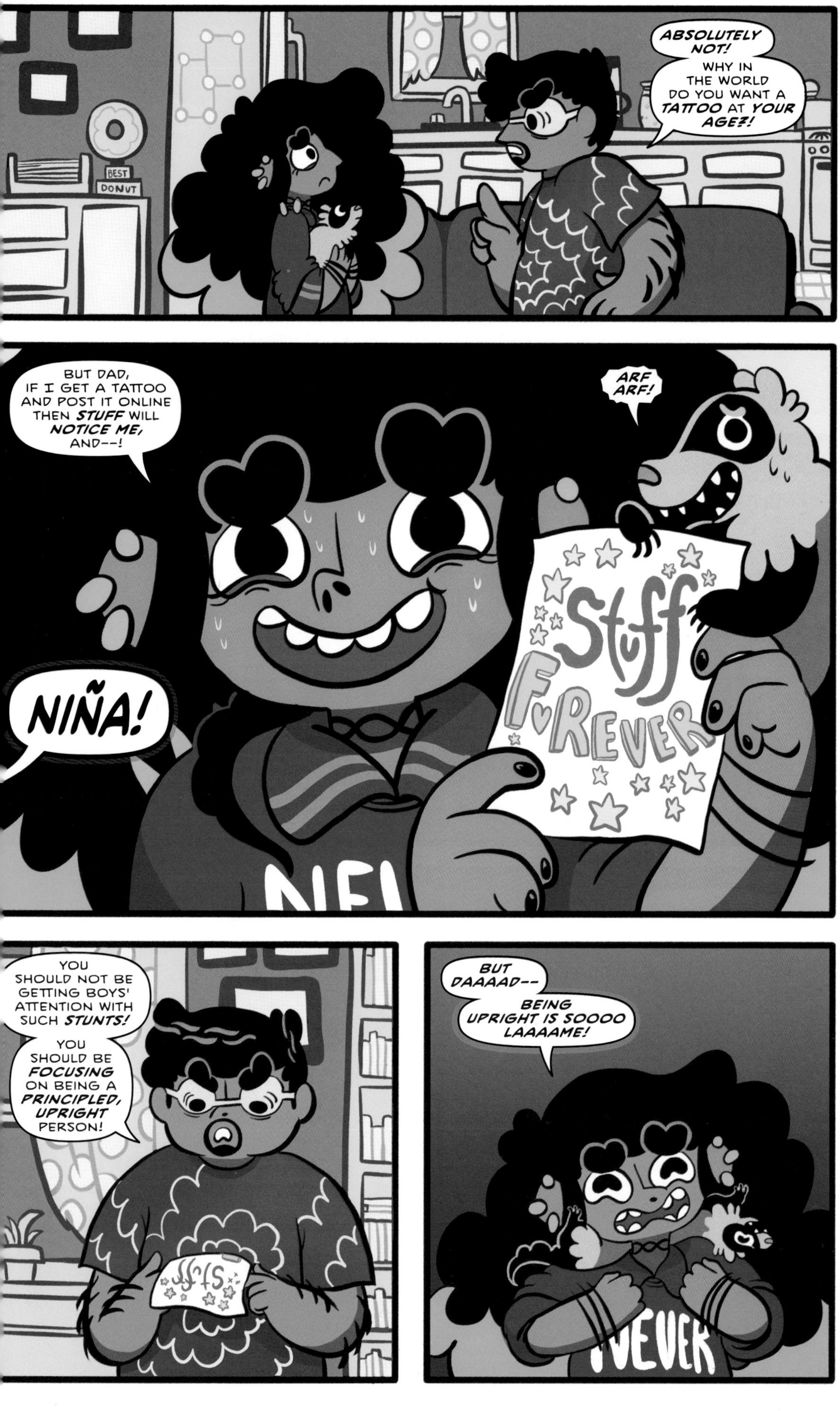
ABSOLUTELY NOT! WHY IN THE WORLD DO YOU WANT A TATTOO AT YOUR AGE?!
BEST DONUT
BUT DAD, IF I GET A TATTOO AND POST IT ONLINE THEN STUFF WILL NOTICE ME, AND--!
ARF ARF!
NIÑA!
Stuff FOREVER
YOU SHOULD NOT BE GETTING BOYS' ATTENTION WITH SUCH STUNTS!
YOU SHOULD BE FOCUSING ON BEING A PRINCIPLED, UPRIGHT PERSON!
BUT DAAAAD--
BEING UPRIGHT IS SOOOO LAAAAME!

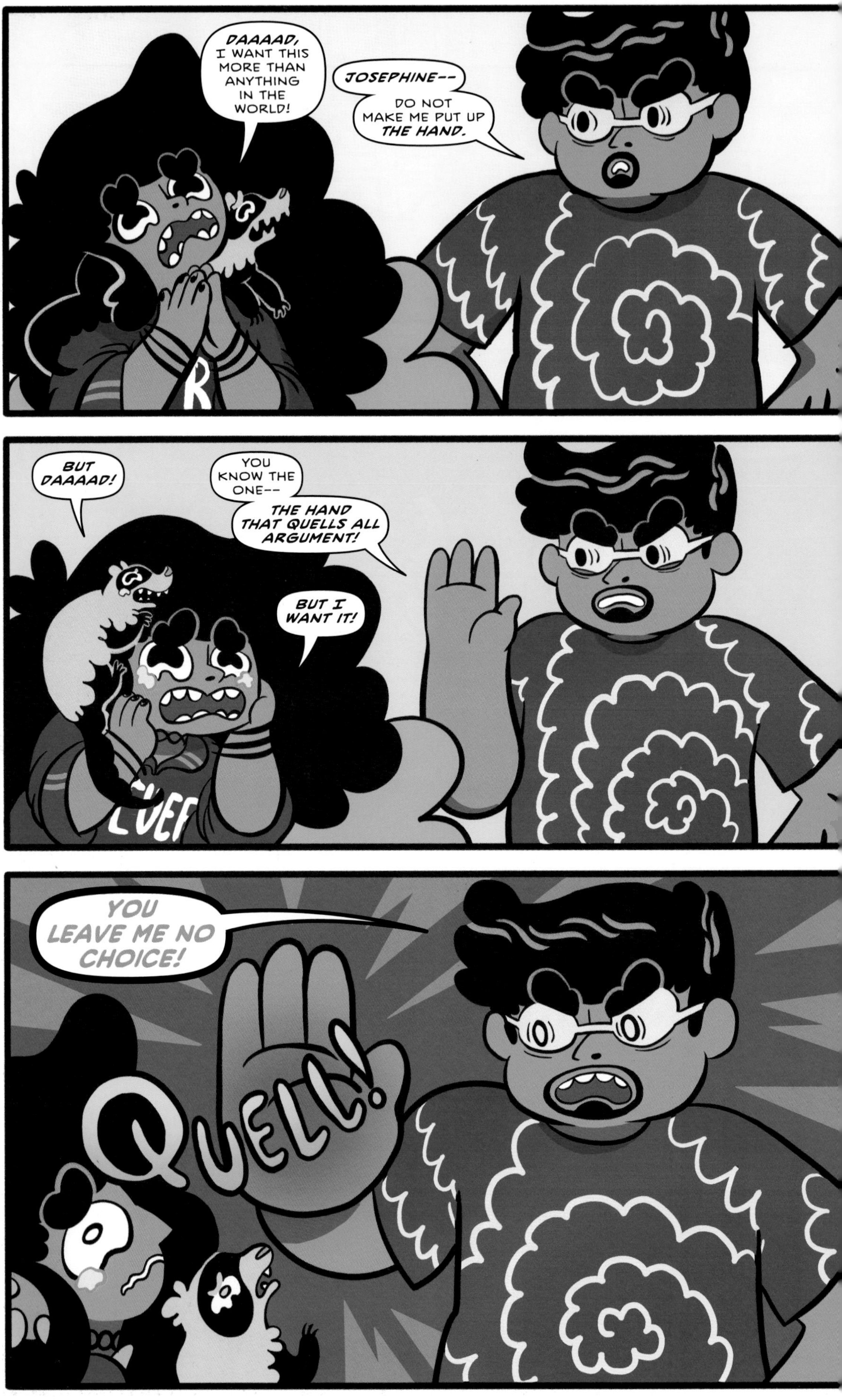
DAAAAD, I WANT THIS MORE THAN ANYTHING IN THE WORLD!
JOSEPHINE--
DO NOT MAKE ME PUT UP THE HAND.
BUT DAAAAD!
YOU KNOW THE ONE--
THE HAND THAT QUELLS ALL ARGUMENT!
BUT I WANT IT!
YOU LEAVE ME NO CHOICE!
QUELL!

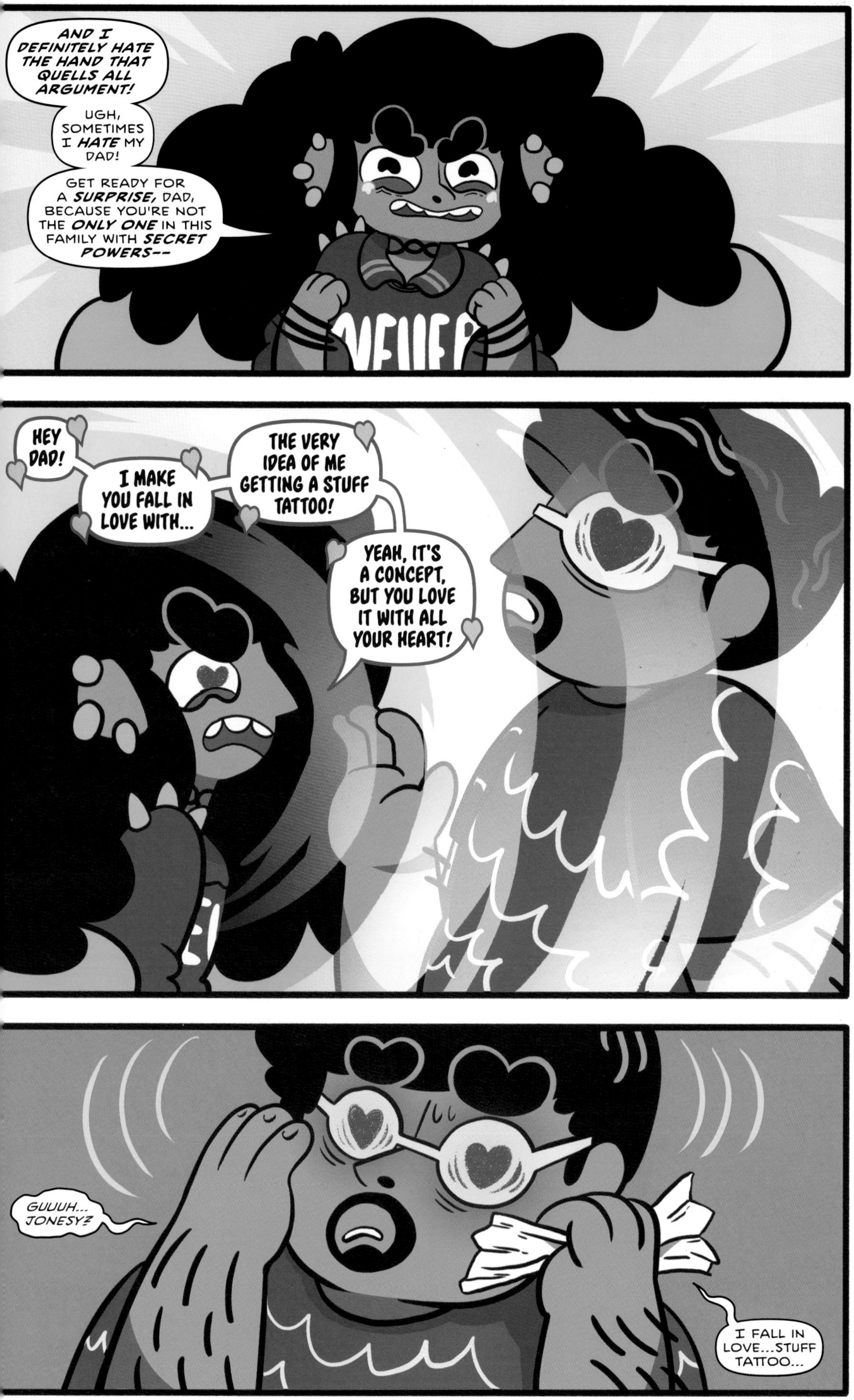

AND I DEFINITELY HATE THE HAND THAT QUELLS ALL ARGUMENT!
UGH, SOMETIMES I HATE MY DAD!
GET READY FOR A SURPRISE, DAD, BECAUSE YOU'RE NOT THE ONLY ONE IN THIS FAMILY WITH SECRET POWERS--
HEY DAD!
I MAKE YOU FALL IN LOVE WITH...
THE VERY IDEA OF ME GETTING A STUFF TATTOO!
YEAH, IT'S A CONCEPT, BUT YOU LOVE IT WITH ALL YOUR HEART!
GUUUH... JONESY?
I FALL IN LOVE...STUFF TATTOO...

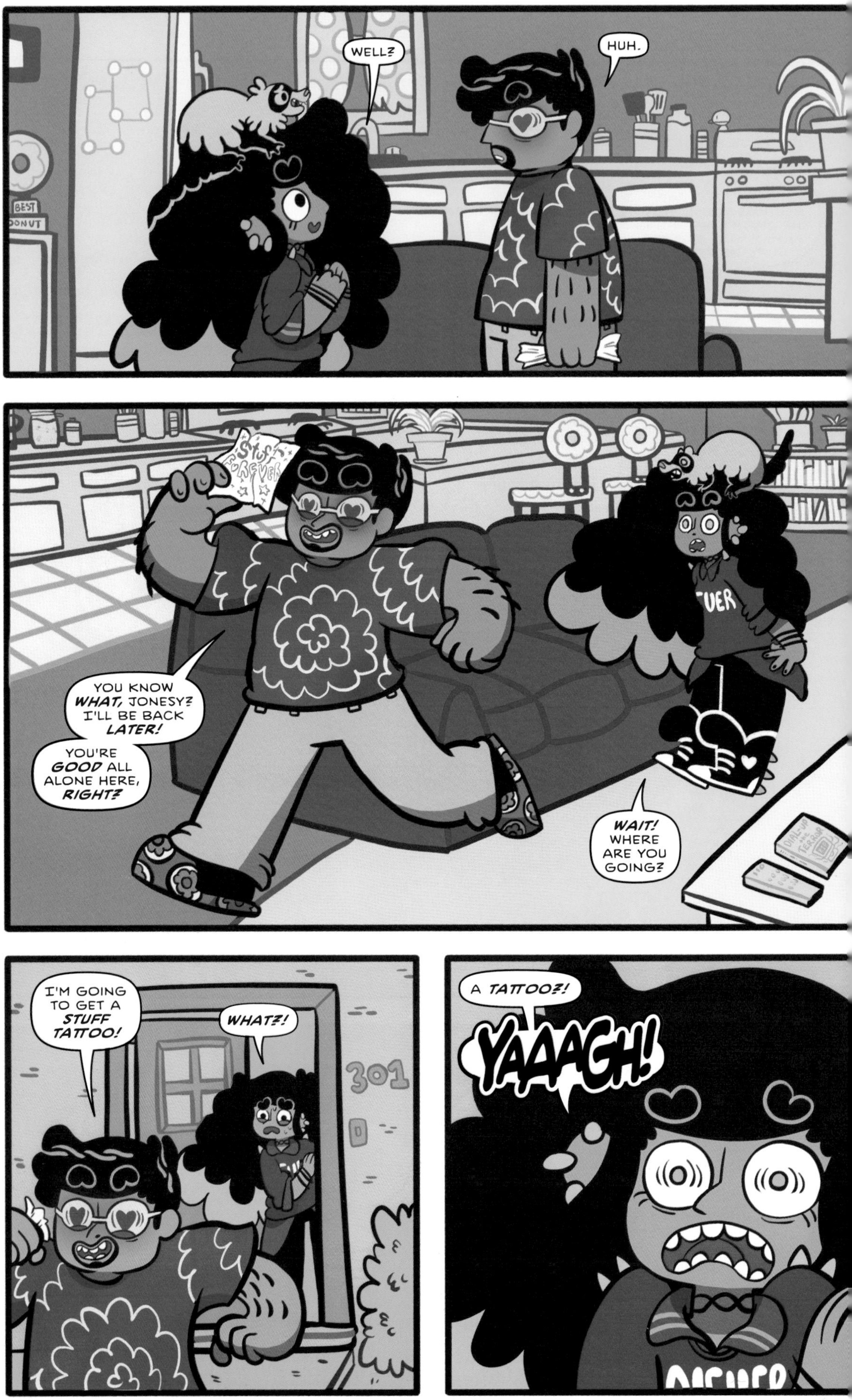

BEST
DONUT
WELL?
HUH.
STUFF FOREVER
YOU KNOW WHAT, JONESY? I'LL BE BACK LATER!
YOU'RE GOOD ALL ALONE HERE, RIGHT?
WAIT! WHERE ARE YOU GOING?
DIAL-UP THE TERROR
I'M GOING TO GET A STUFF TATTOO!
WHAT?!
301
A TATTOO?!
YAAAGH!

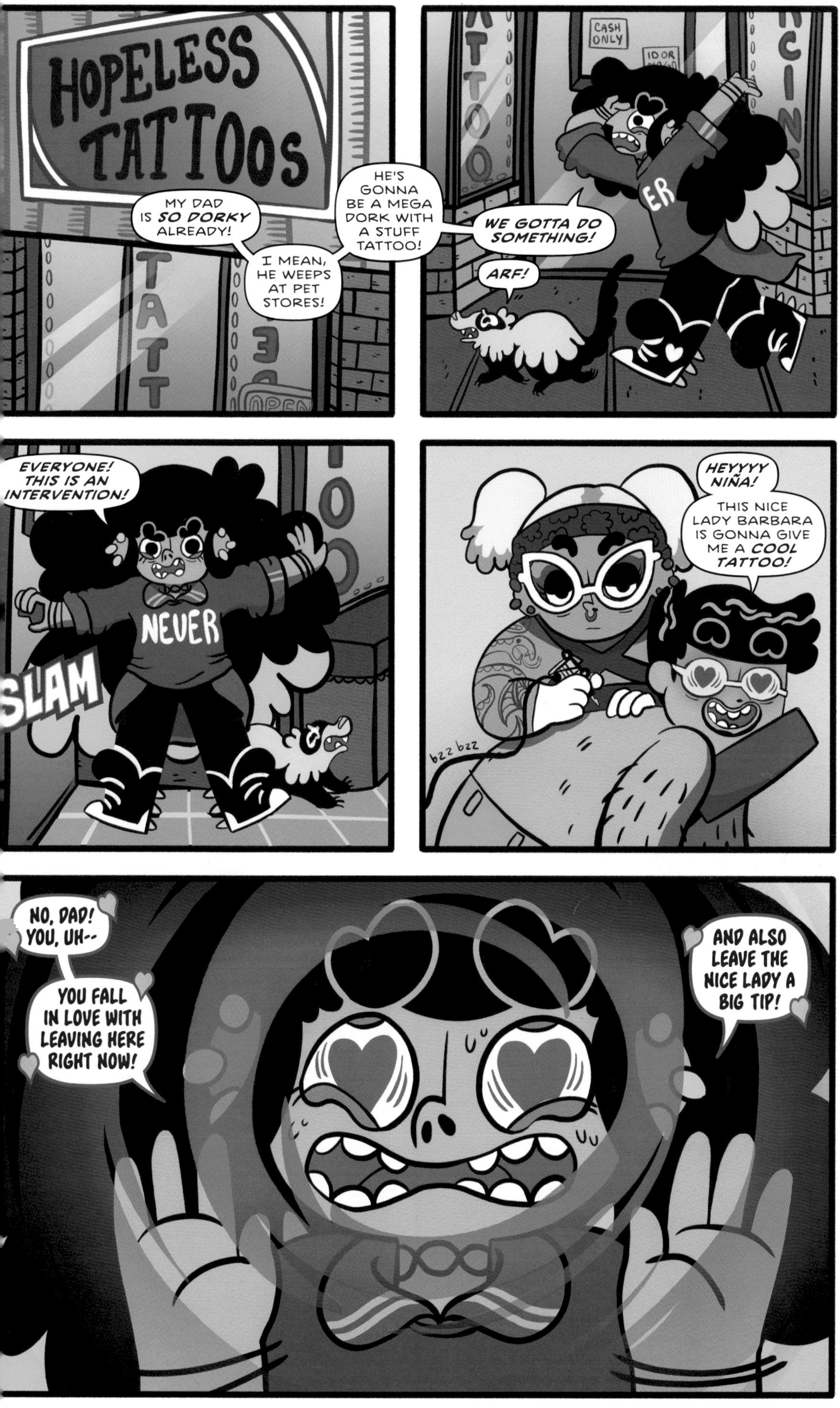
HOPELESS TATTOOS
MY DAD IS SO DORKY ALREADY!
I MEAN, HE WEEPS AT PET STORES!
HE'S GONNA BE A MEGA DORK WITH A STUFF TATTOO!
CASH ONLY
WE GOTTA DO SOMETHING!
ARF!
EVERYONE! THIS IS AN INTERVENTION!
NEVER
SLAM
HEYYYY NIÑA!
THIS NICE LADY BARBARA IS GONNA GIVE ME A COOL TATTOO!
bzz bzz
NO, DAD! YOU, UH--
YOU FALL IN LOVE WITH LEAVING HERE RIGHT NOW!
AND ALSO LEAVE THE NICE LADY A BIG TIP!

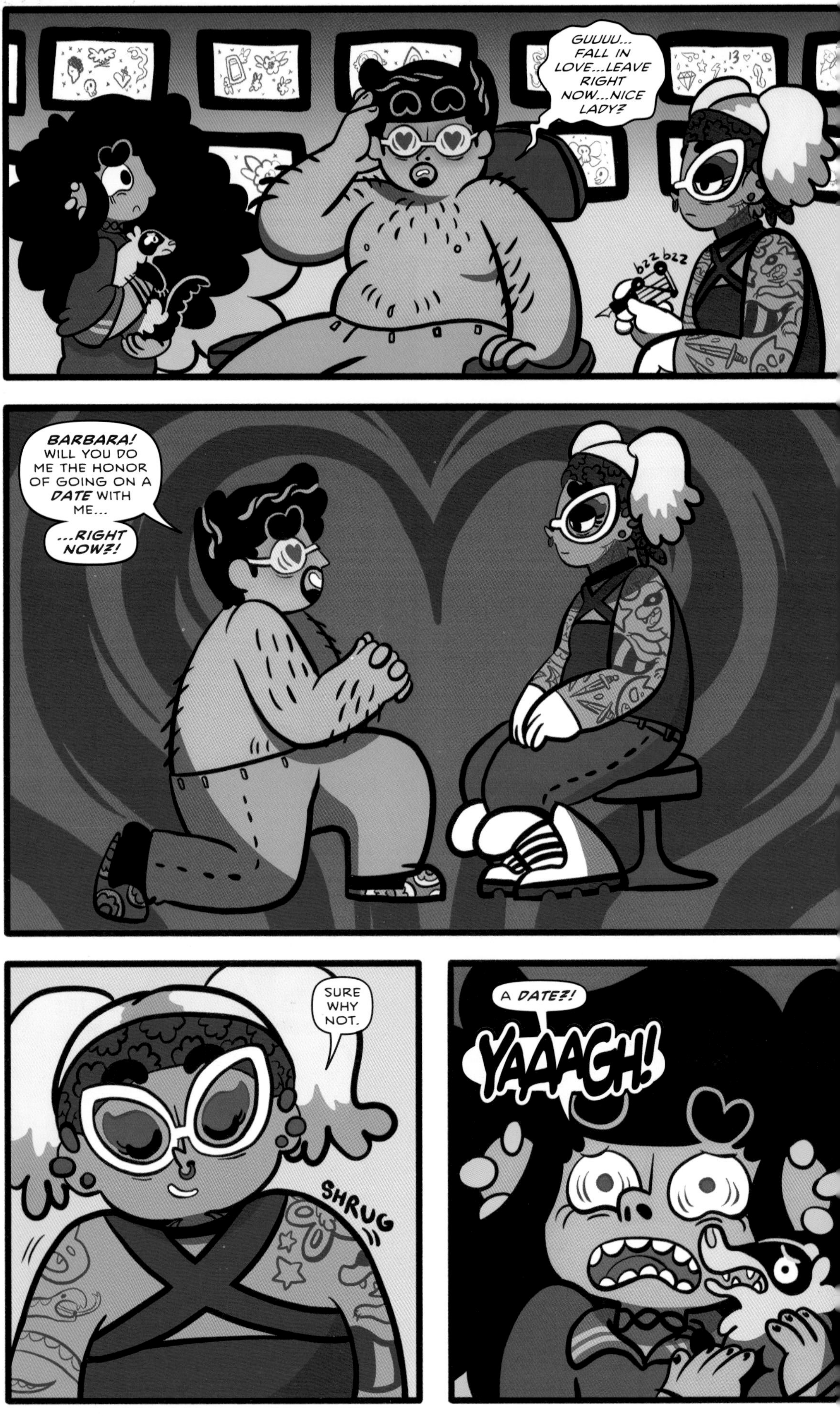
GUUUU... FALL IN LOVE...LEAVE RIGHT NOW...NICE LADY?
bzz bzz
BARBARA! WILL YOU DO ME THE HONOR OF GOING ON A DATE WITH ME...
...RIGHT NOW?!
SURE WHY NOT.
SHRUG
A DATE?!
YAAAGH!

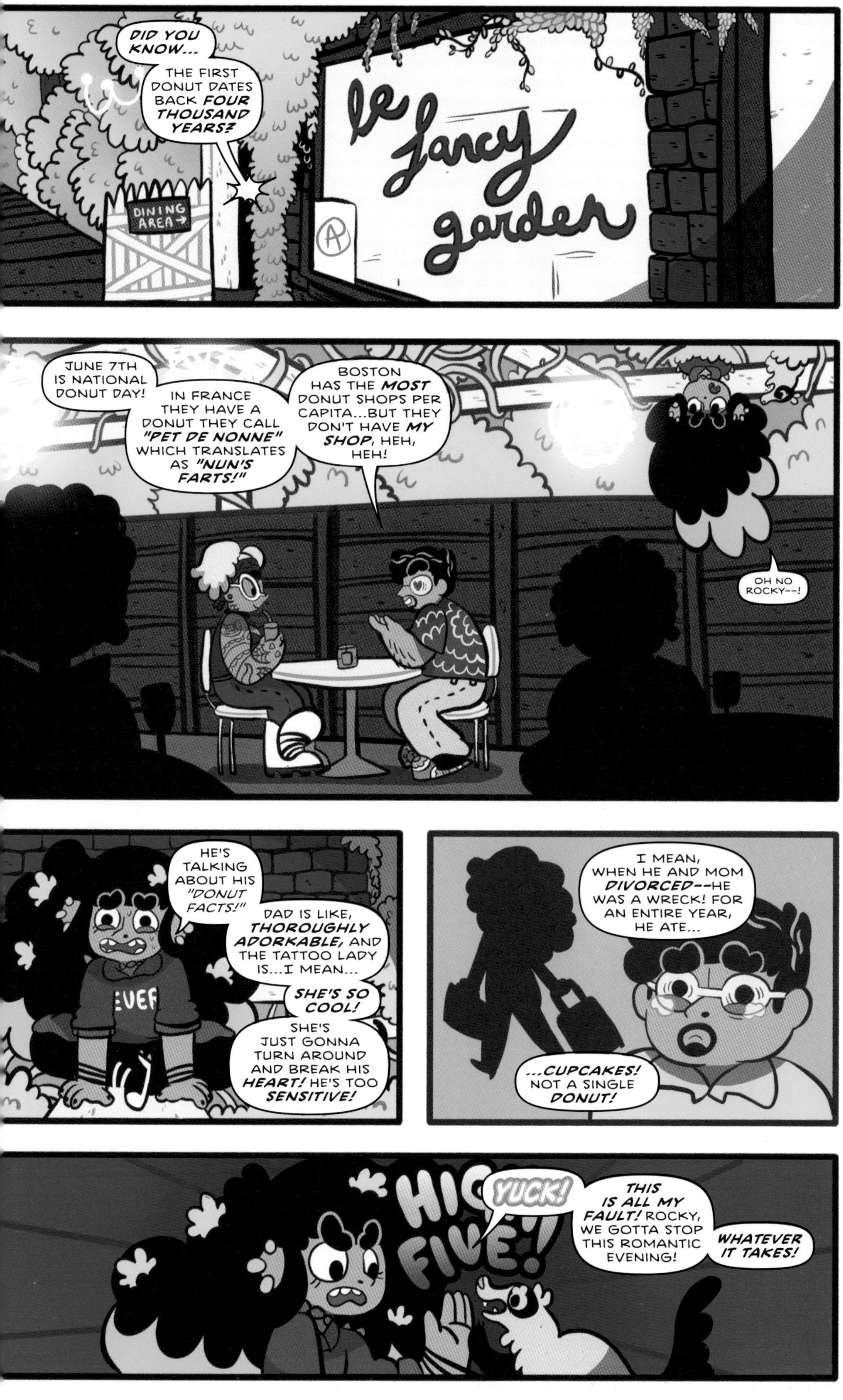
DID YOU KNOW...
THE FIRST DONUT DATES BACK FOUR THOUSAND YEARS?
DINING AREA →
le fancy garden
JUNE 7TH IS NATIONAL DONUT DAY!
IN FRANCE THEY HAVE A DONUT THEY CALL "PET DE NONNE" WHICH TRANSLATES AS "NUN'S FARTS!"
BOSTON HAS THE MOST DONUT SHOPS PER CAPITA...BUT THEY DON'T HAVE MY SHOP, HEH, HEH!
OH NO ROCKY--!
HE'S TALKING ABOUT HIS "DONUT FACTS!"
DAD IS LIKE, THOROUGHLY ADORKABLE, AND THE TATTOO LADY IS...I MEAN...
SHE'S SO COOL!
SHE'S JUST GONNA TURN AROUND AND BREAK HIS HEART! HE'S TOO SENSITIVE!
I MEAN, WHEN HE AND MOM DIVORCED--HE WAS A WRECK! FOR AN ENTIRE YEAR, HE ATE...
...CUPCAKES! NOT A SINGLE DONUT!
HIGH FIVE!
YUCK!
THIS IS ALL MY FAULT! ROCKY, WE GOTTA STOP THIS ROMANTIC EVENING!
WHATEVER IT TAKES!

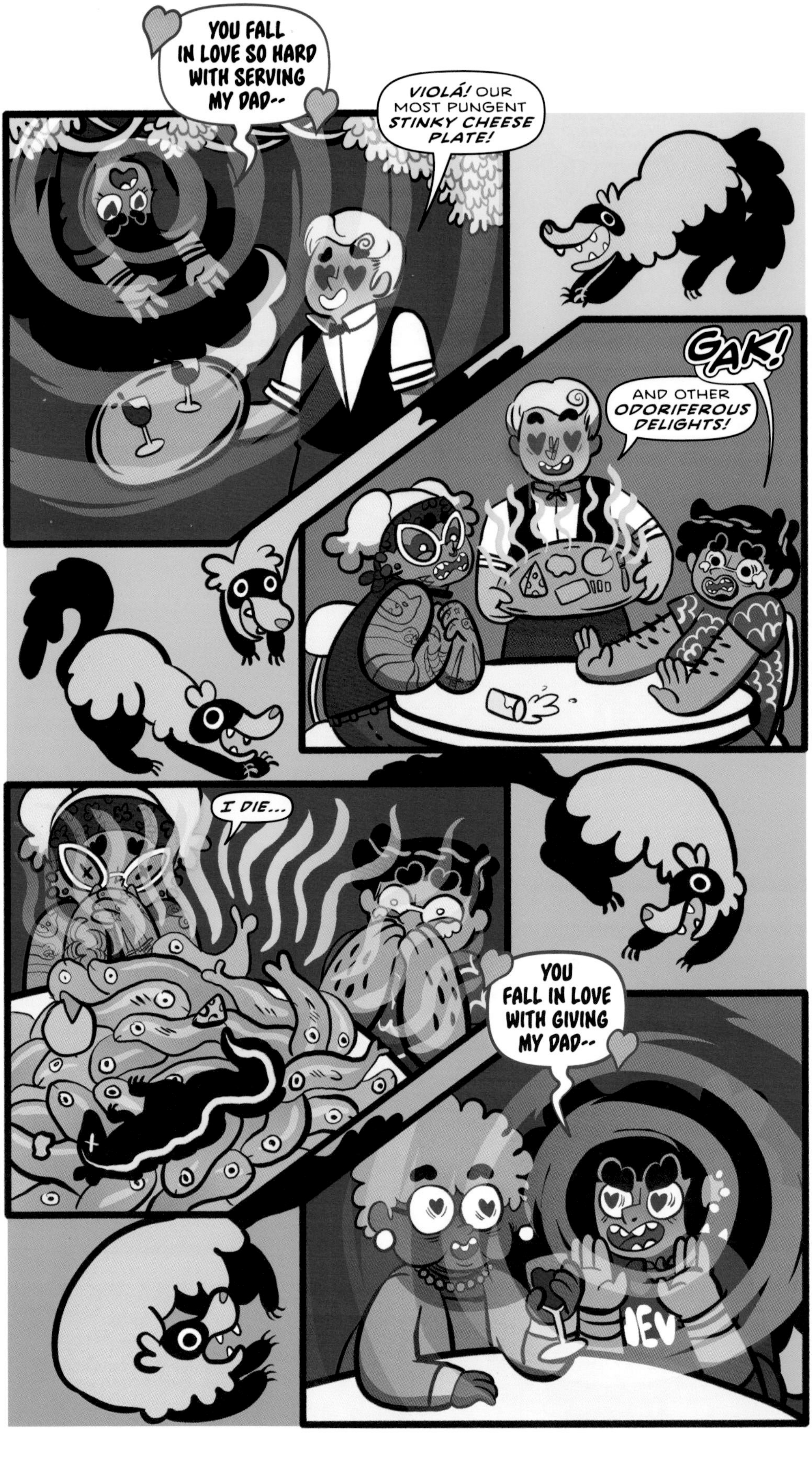

YOU FALL IN LOVE SO HARD WITH SERVING MY DAD--
VIOLÁ! OUR MOST PUNGENT STINKY CHEESE PLATE!
GAK!
AND OTHER ODORIFEROUS DELIGHTS!
I DIE...
YOU FALL IN LOVE WITH GIVING MY DAD--

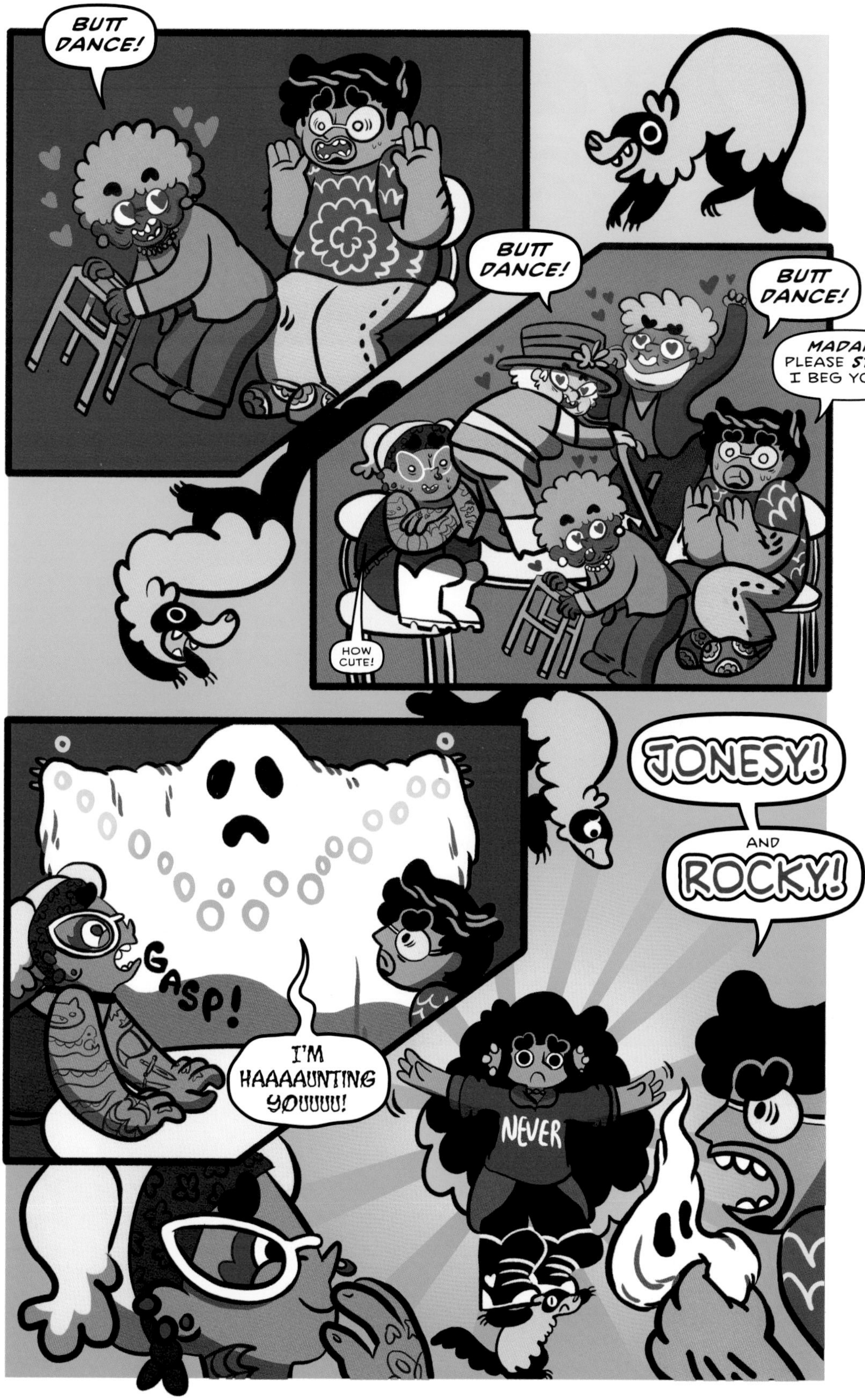
BUTT DANCE!
BUTT DANCE!
BUTT DANCE!
MADAM! PLEASE STOP! I BEG YOU--
HOW CUTE!
GASP!
I'M HAAAAUNTING YOUUUU!
JONESY!
AND
ROCKY!
NEVER

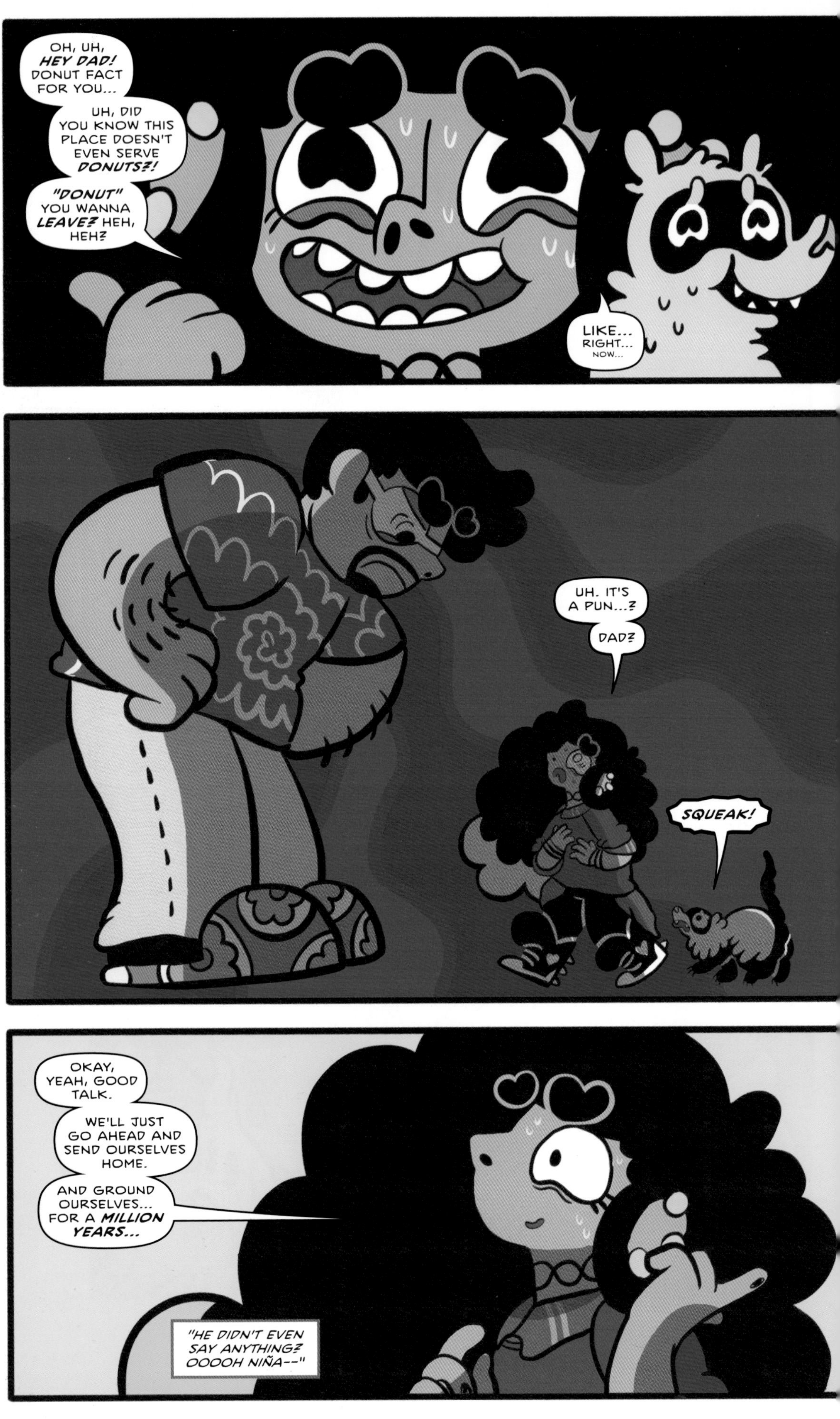

OH, UH, **HEY DAD!** DONUT FACT FOR YOU...
UH, DID YOU KNOW THIS PLACE DOESN'T EVEN SERVE ***DONUTS?!***
***"DONUT"*** YOU WANNA ***LEAVE?*** HEH, HEH?
LIKE... RIGHT... NOW...
UH. IT'S A PUN...?
DAD?
***SQUEAK!***
OKAY, YEAH, GOOD TALK.
WE'LL JUST GO AHEAD AND SEND OURSELVES HOME.
AND GROUND OURSELVES... FOR A ***MILLION YEARS...***
*"HE DIDN'T EVEN SAY ANYTHING? OOOOH NIÑA--"*

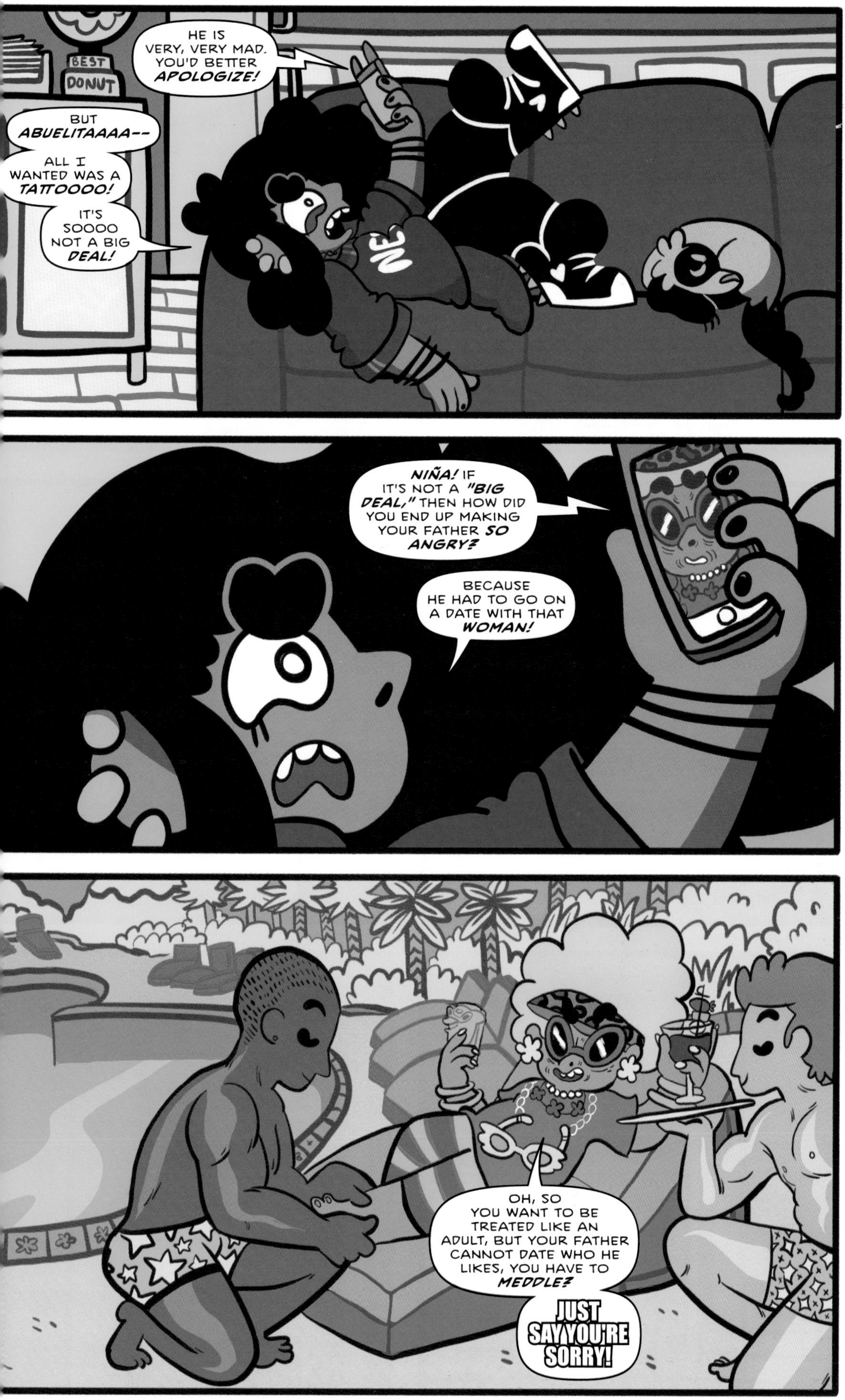

HE IS VERY, VERY MAD. YOU'D BETTER *APOLOGIZE!*
BUT *ABUELITAAAA--*
ALL I WANTED WAS A *TATTOOOO!*
IT'S SOOOO NOT A BIG *DEAL!*
*NIÑA!* IF IT'S NOT A *"BIG DEAL,"* THEN HOW DID YOU END UP MAKING YOUR FATHER *SO ANGRY?*
BECAUSE HE HAD TO GO ON A DATE WITH THAT *WOMAN!*
OH, SO YOU WANT TO BE TREATED LIKE AN ADULT, BUT YOUR FATHER CANNOT DATE WHO HE LIKES, YOU HAVE TO *MEDDLE?*
JUST SAY YOU'RE SORRY!
BEST DONUT

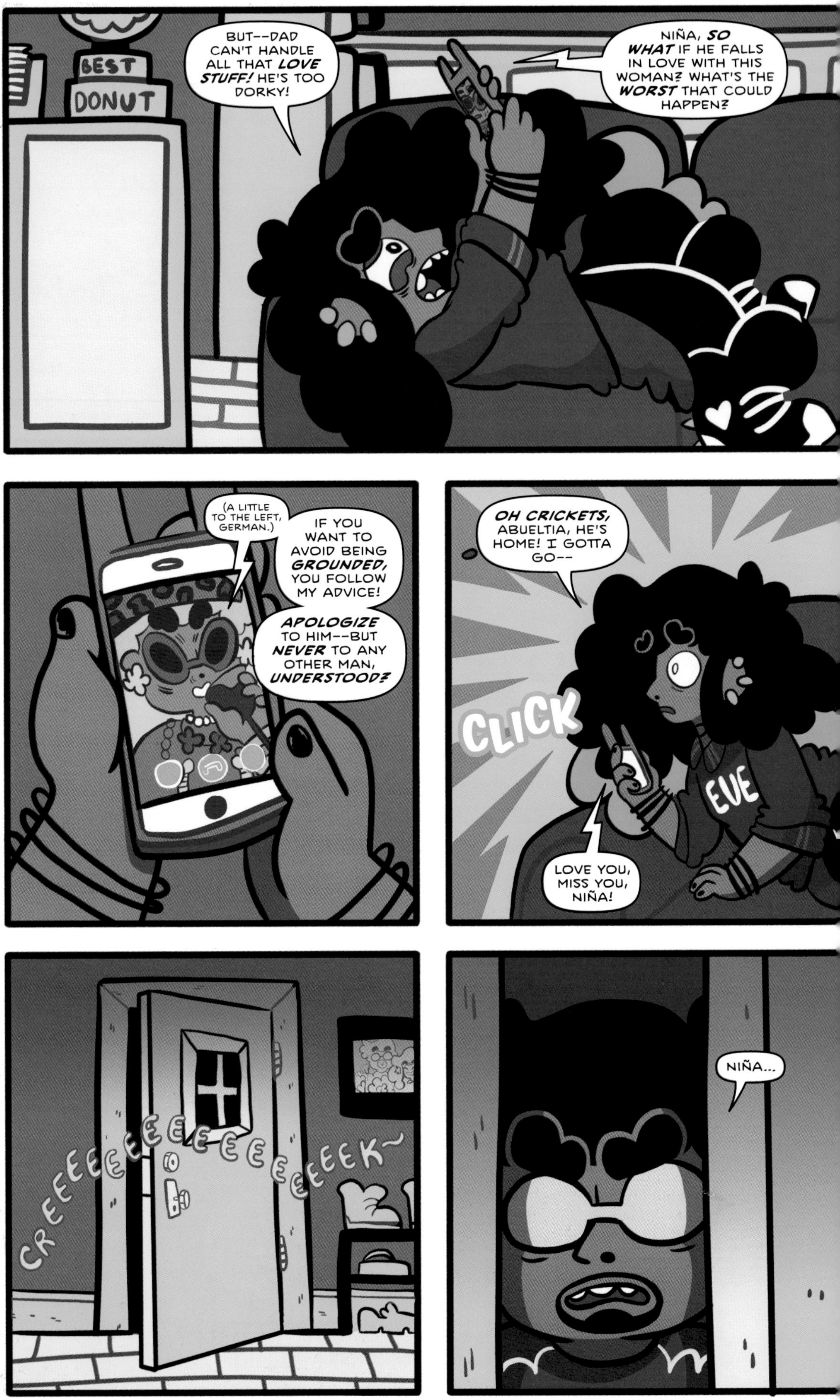
BEST
DONUT
BUT--DAD CAN'T HANDLE ALL THAT *LOVE STUFF!* HE'S TOO DORKY!
NIÑA, ***SO WHAT*** IF HE FALLS IN LOVE WITH THIS WOMAN? WHAT'S THE ***WORST*** THAT COULD HAPPEN?
(A LITTLE TO THE LEFT, GERMAN.)
IF YOU WANT TO AVOID BEING ***GROUNDED,*** YOU FOLLOW MY ADVICE!
***APOLOGIZE*** TO HIM--BUT ***NEVER*** TO ANY OTHER MAN, ***UNDERSTOOD?***
***OH CRICKETS,*** ABUELTIA, HE'S HOME! I GOTTA GO--
CLICK
EVE
LOVE YOU, MISS YOU, NIÑA!
CREEEEEEEEEEEEEEEEEK~
NIÑA...

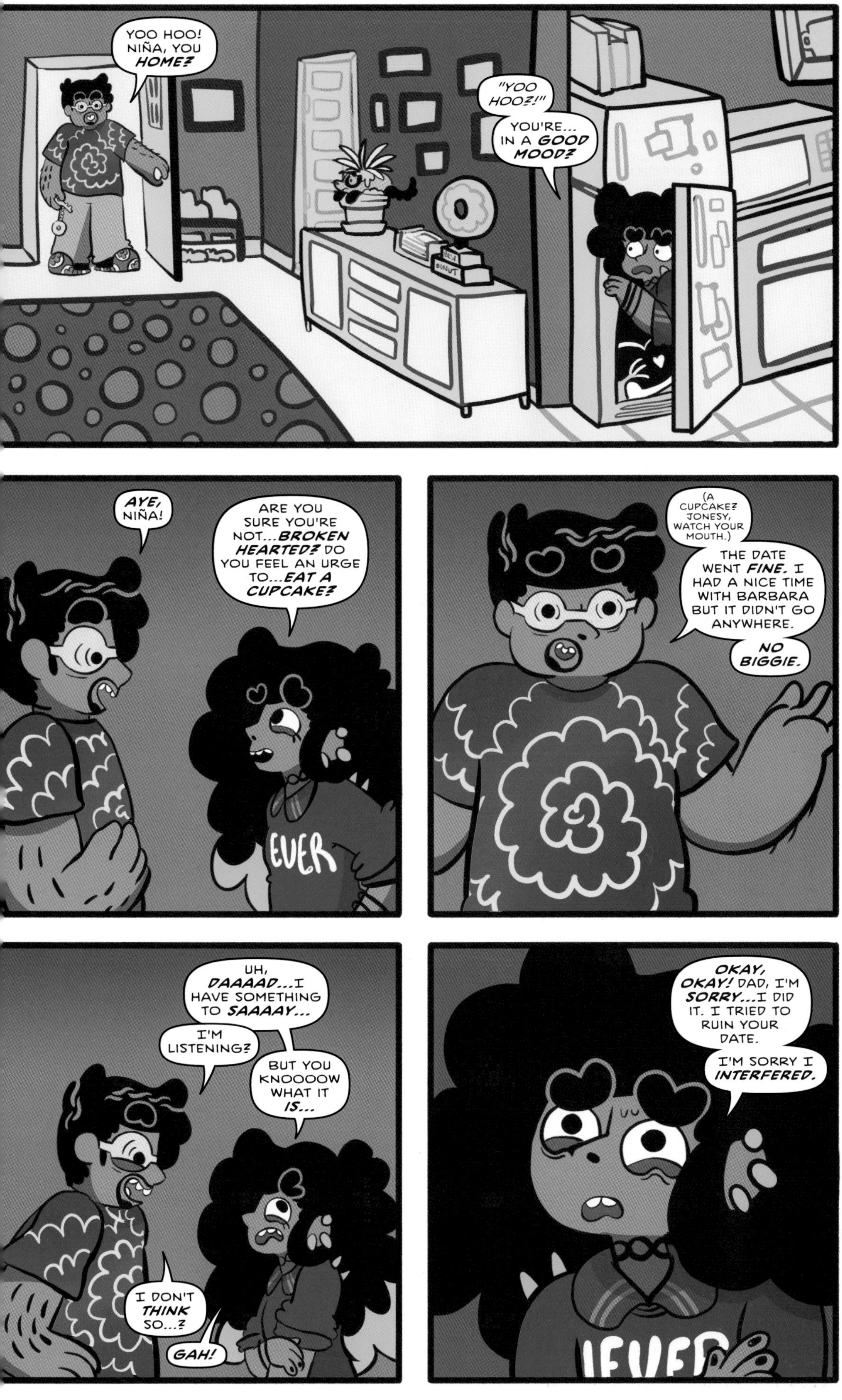
YOO HOO! NIÑA, YOU HOME?
"YOO HOO?!"
YOU'RE... IN A GOOD MOOD?
DESI DONUT
AYE, NIÑA!
ARE YOU SURE YOU'RE NOT...BROKEN HEARTED? DO YOU FEEL AN URGE TO...EAT A CUPCAKE?
EVER
(A CUPCAKE? JONESY, WATCH YOUR MOUTH.)
THE DATE WENT FINE. I HAD A NICE TIME WITH BARBARA BUT IT DIDN'T GO ANYWHERE.
NO BIGGIE.
UH, DAAAAAD...I HAVE SOMETHING TO SAAAAY...
I'M LISTENING?
BUT YOU KNOOOOW WHAT IT IS...
I DON'T THINK SO...?
GAH!
OKAY, OKAY! DAD, I'M SORRY...I DID IT. I TRIED TO RUIN YOUR DATE.
I'M SORRY I INTERFERED.

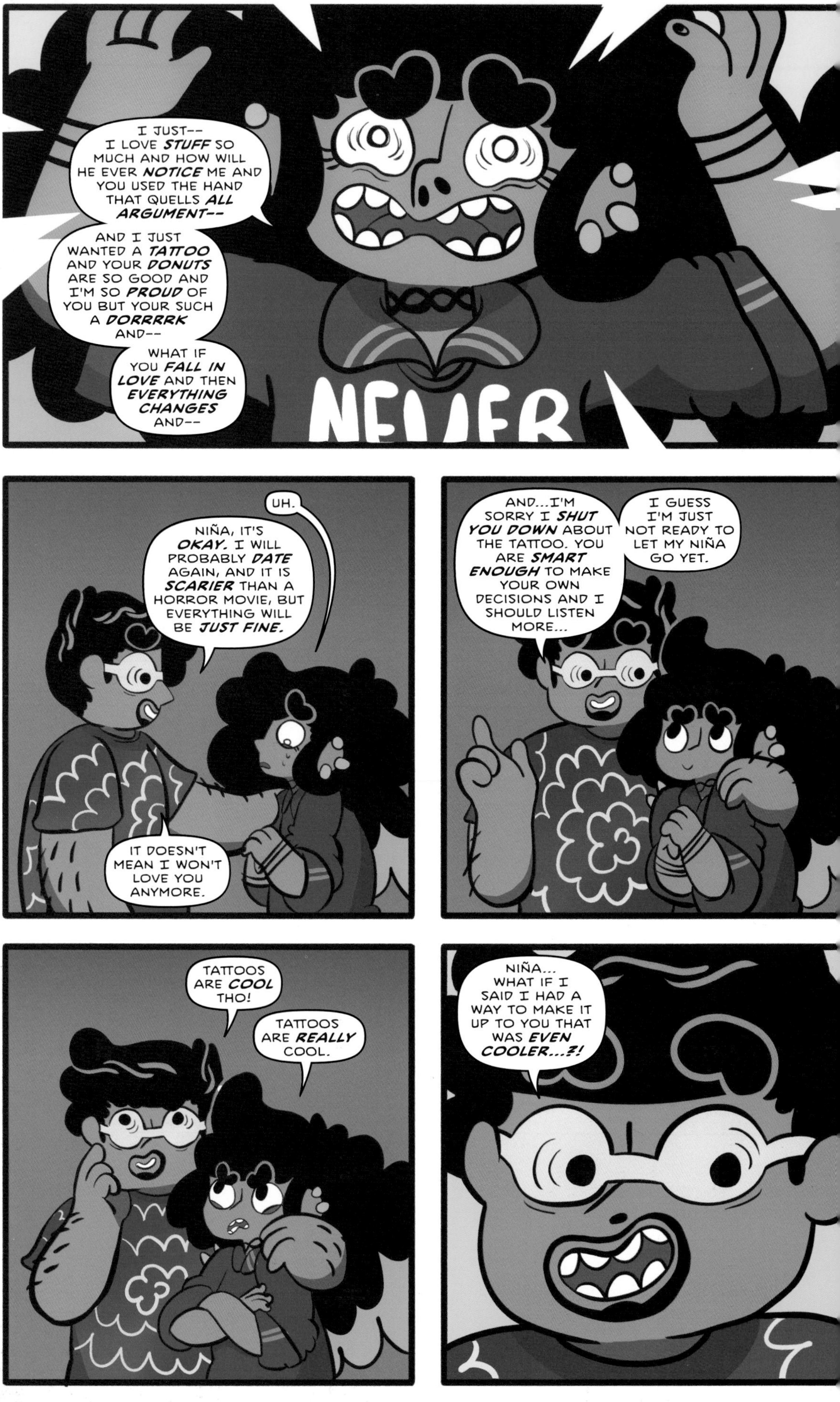

I JUST-- I LOVE STUFF SO MUCH AND HOW WILL HE EVER NOTICE ME AND YOU USED THE HAND THAT QUELLS ALL ARGUMENT--
AND I JUST WANTED A TATTOO AND YOUR DONUTS ARE SO GOOD AND I'M SO PROUD OF YOU BUT YOUR SUCH A DORRRRK AND--
WHAT IF YOU FALL IN LOVE AND THEN EVERYTHING CHANGES AND--
NEVER
UH.
NIÑA, IT'S OKAY. I WILL PROBABLY DATE AGAIN, AND IT IS SCARIER THAN A HORROR MOVIE, BUT EVERYTHING WILL BE JUST FINE.
IT DOESN'T MEAN I WON'T LOVE YOU ANYMORE.
AND...I'M SORRY I SHUT YOU DOWN ABOUT THE TATTOO. YOU ARE SMART ENOUGH TO MAKE YOUR OWN DECISIONS AND I SHOULD LISTEN MORE...
I GUESS I'M JUST NOT READY TO LET MY NIÑA GO YET.
TATTOOS ARE COOL THO!
TATTOOS ARE REALLY COOL.
NIÑA... WHAT IF I SAID I HAD A WAY TO MAKE IT UP TO YOU THAT WAS EVEN COOLER...?!

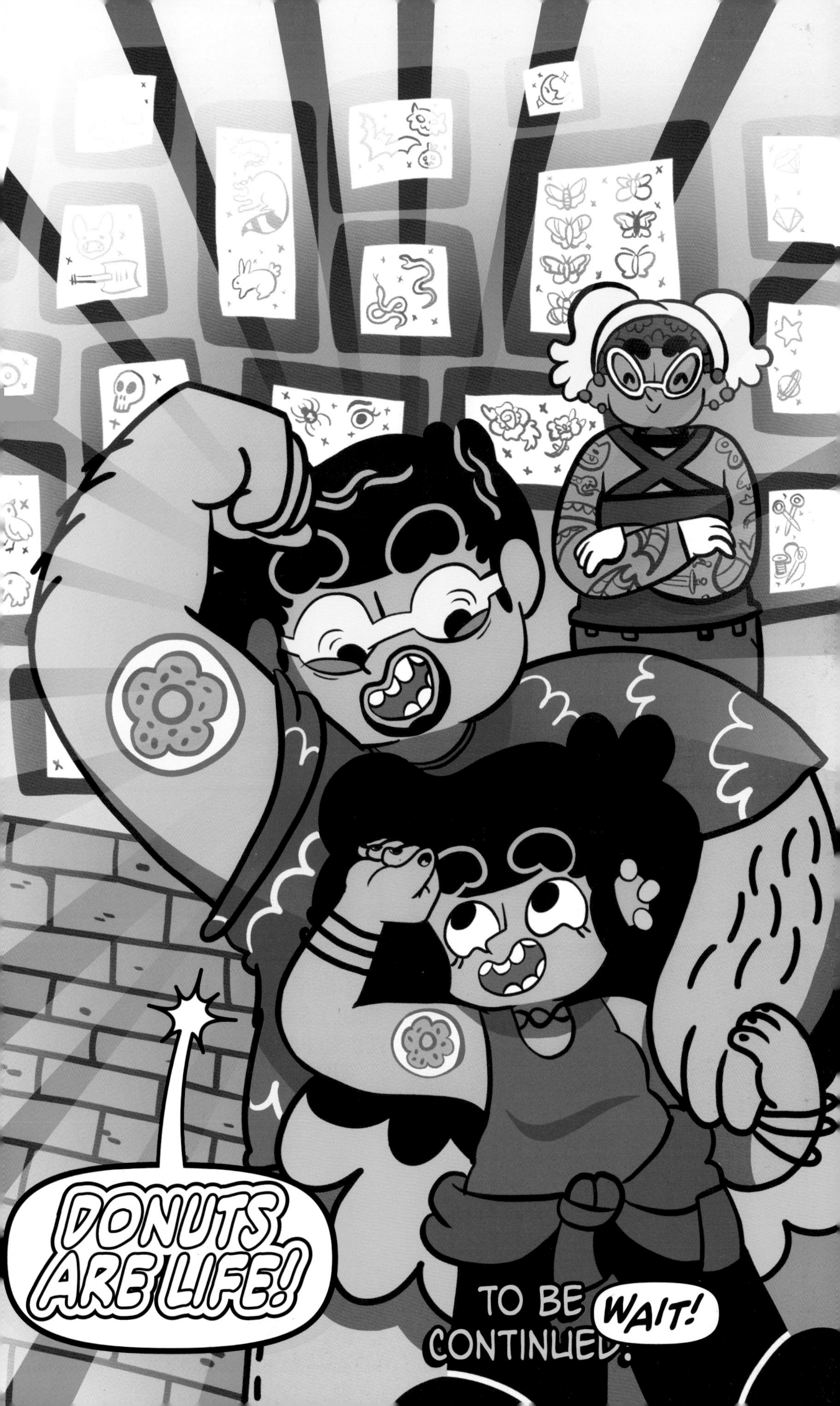
DONUTS ARE LIFE!
TO BE CONTINUED.
WAIT!

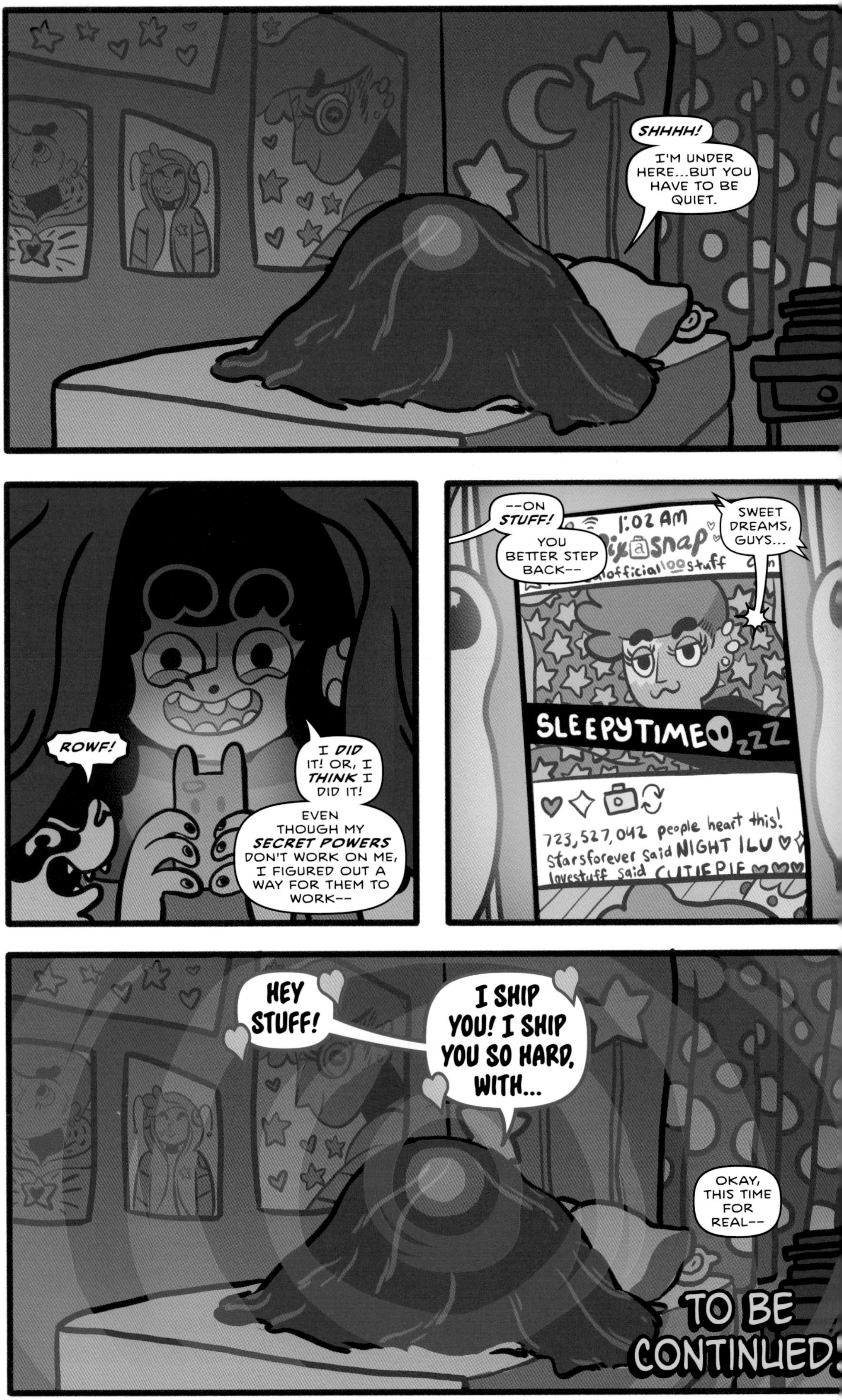
SHHHH!
I'M UNDER HERE...BUT YOU HAVE TO BE QUIET.
ROWF!
I DID IT! OR, I THINK I DID IT!
EVEN THOUGH MY SECRET POWERS DON'T WORK ON ME, I FIGURED OUT A WAY FOR THEM TO WORK--
--ON STUFF!
YOU BETTER STEP BACK--
SWEET DREAMS, GUYS...
1:02 AM
officialstuff
SLEEPYTIME zzz
723,527,042 people heart this!
Starsforever said NIGHT ILU
lovestuff said CUTIEPIE
HEY STUFF!
I SHIP YOU! I SHIP YOU SO HARD, WITH...
OKAY, THIS TIME FOR REAL--
TO BE CONTINUED!

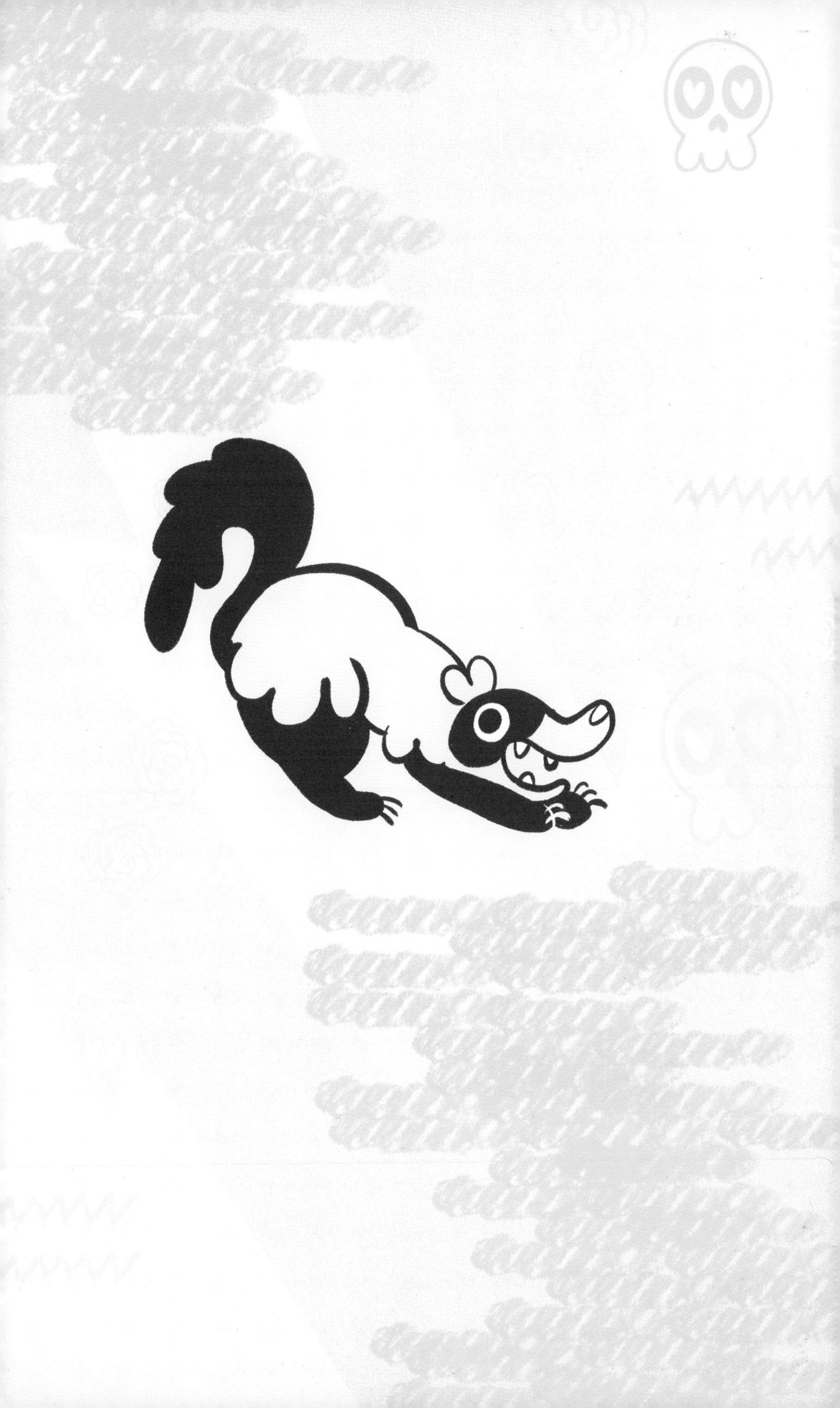

# CHAPTER FOUR

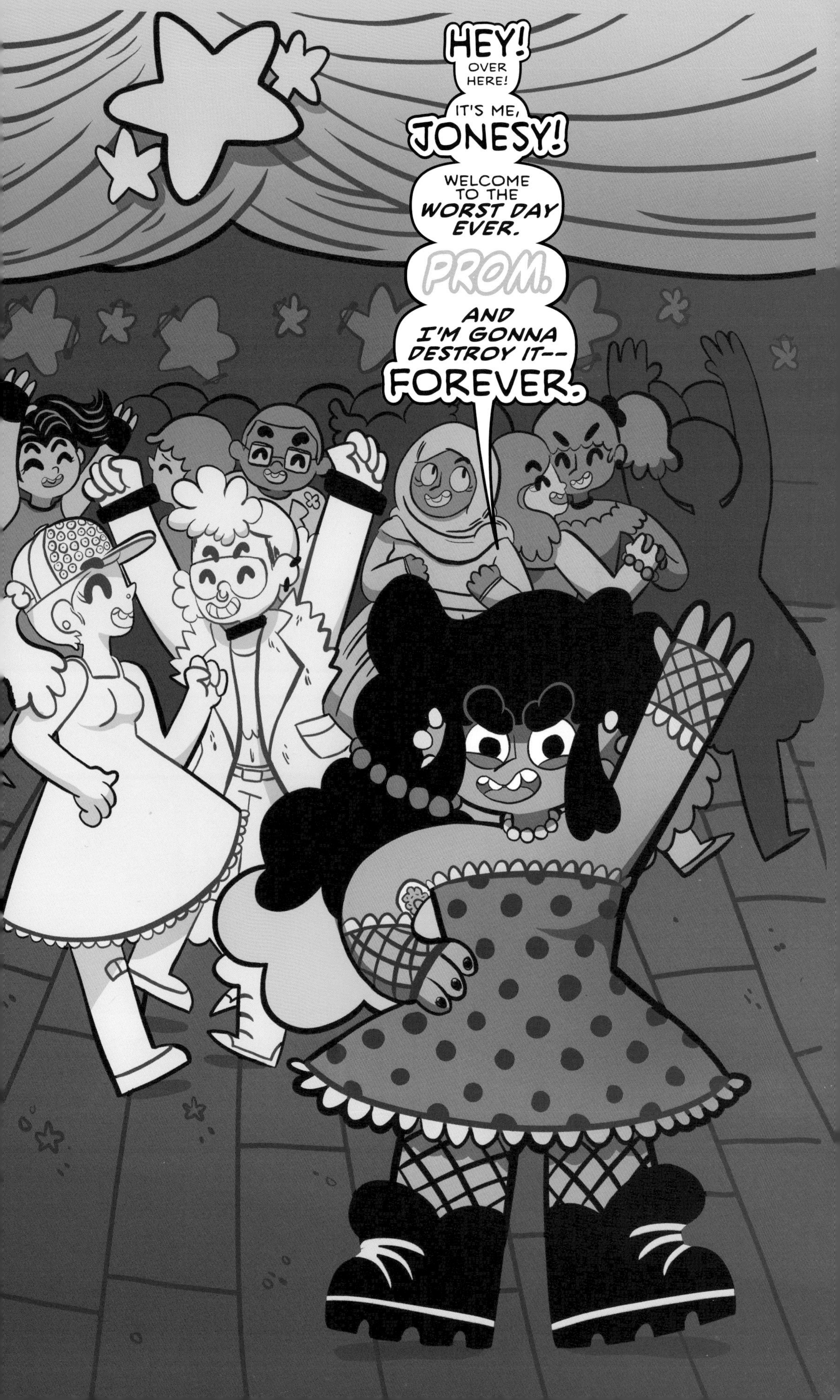
HEY! OVER HERE!
IT'S ME, JONESY!
WELCOME TO THE WORST DAY EVER.
PROM.
AND I'M GONNA DESTROY IT-- FOREVER.

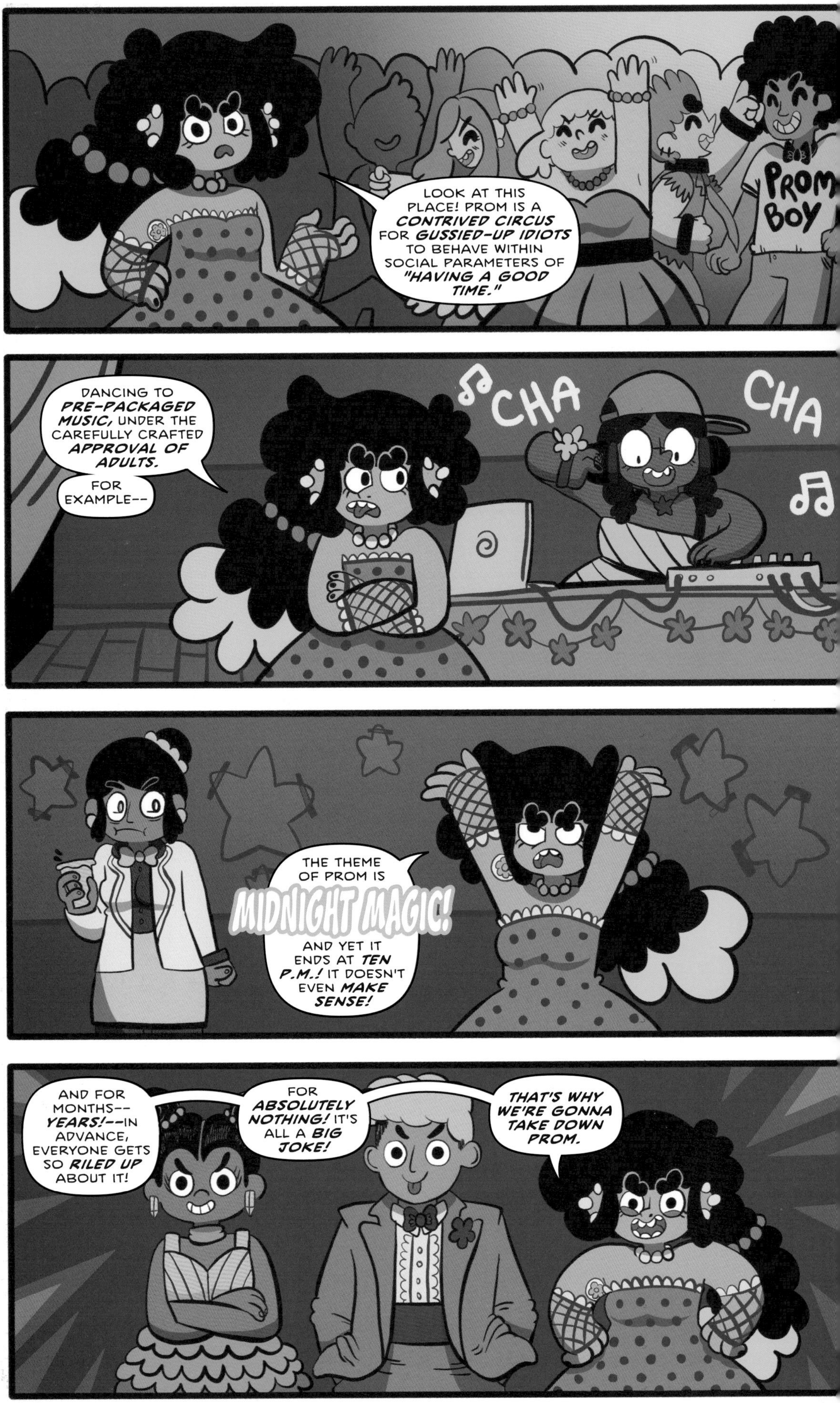

LOOK AT THIS PLACE! PROM IS A CONTRIVED CIRCUS FOR GUSSIED-UP IDIOTS TO BEHAVE WITHIN SOCIAL PARAMETERS OF "HAVING A GOOD TIME."
PROM BOY
DANCING TO PRE-PACKAGED MUSIC, UNDER THE CAREFULLY CRAFTED APPROVAL OF ADULTS.
FOR EXAMPLE--
CHA
CHA
THE THEME OF PROM IS MIDNIGHT MAGIC!
AND YET IT ENDS AT TEN P.M.! IT DOESN'T EVEN MAKE SENSE!
AND FOR MONTHS--YEARS!--IN ADVANCE, EVERYONE GETS SO RILED UP ABOUT IT!
FOR ABSOLUTELY NOTHING! IT'S ALL A BIG JOKE!
THAT'S WHY WE'RE GONNA TAKE DOWN PROM.

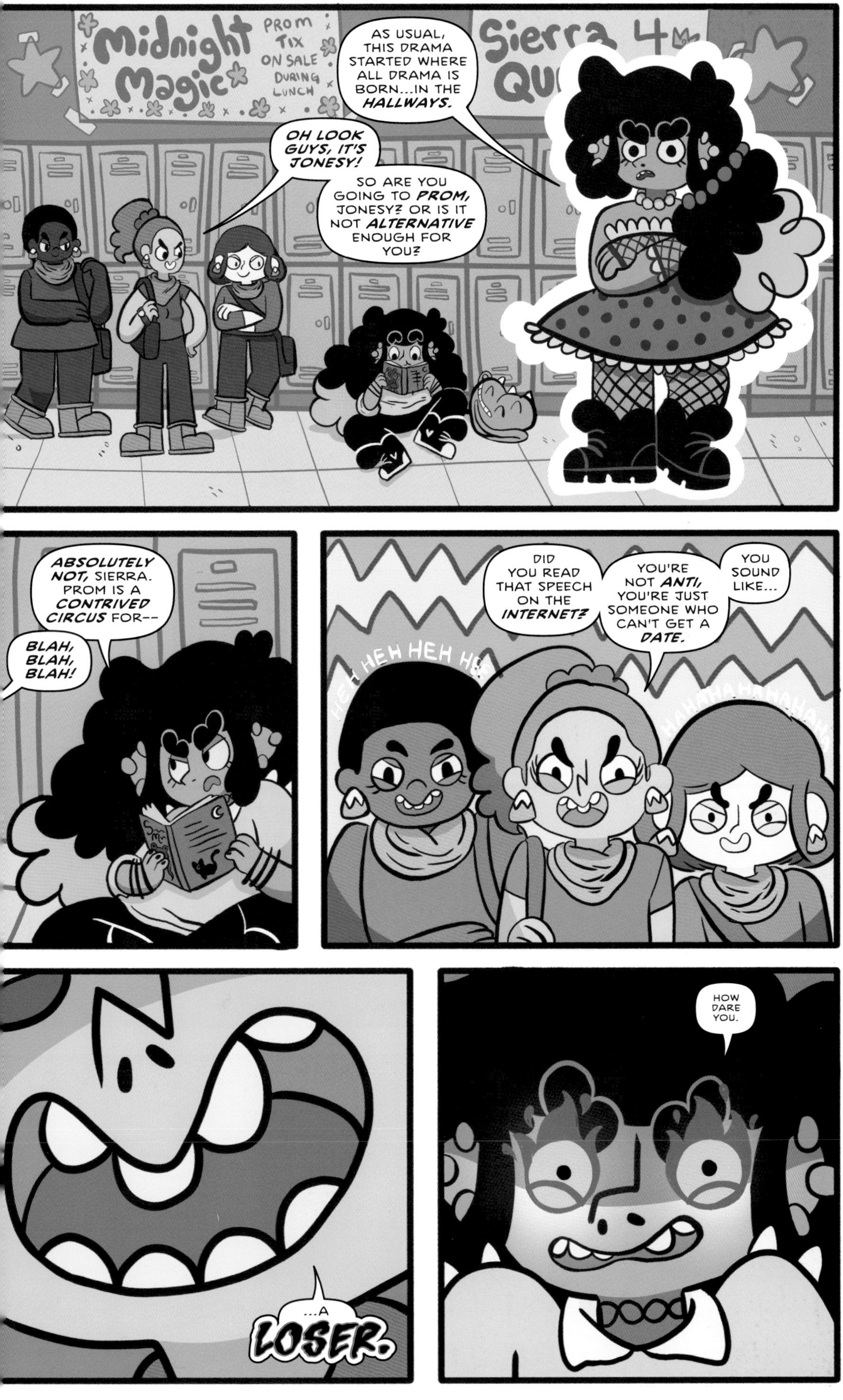
Midnight Magic
PROM TIX ON SALE DURING LUNCH
Sierra 4 Qu
AS USUAL, THIS DRAMA STARTED WHERE ALL DRAMA IS BORN...IN THE *HALLWAYS.*
*OH LOOK GUYS, IT'S JONESY!*
SO ARE YOU GOING TO *PROM,* JONESY? OR IS IT NOT *ALTERNATIVE* ENOUGH FOR YOU?
*ABSOLUTELY NOT,* SIERRA. PROM IS A *CONTRIVED CIRCUS* FOR--
*BLAH, BLAH, BLAH!*
DID YOU READ THAT SPEECH ON THE *INTERNET?*
HEH HEH HEH HEH
YOU'RE NOT *ANTI,* YOU'RE JUST SOMEONE WHO CAN'T GET A *DATE.*
HAHAHAHAHAHAHA
YOU SOUND LIKE...
...A
LOSER.
HOW DARE YOU.

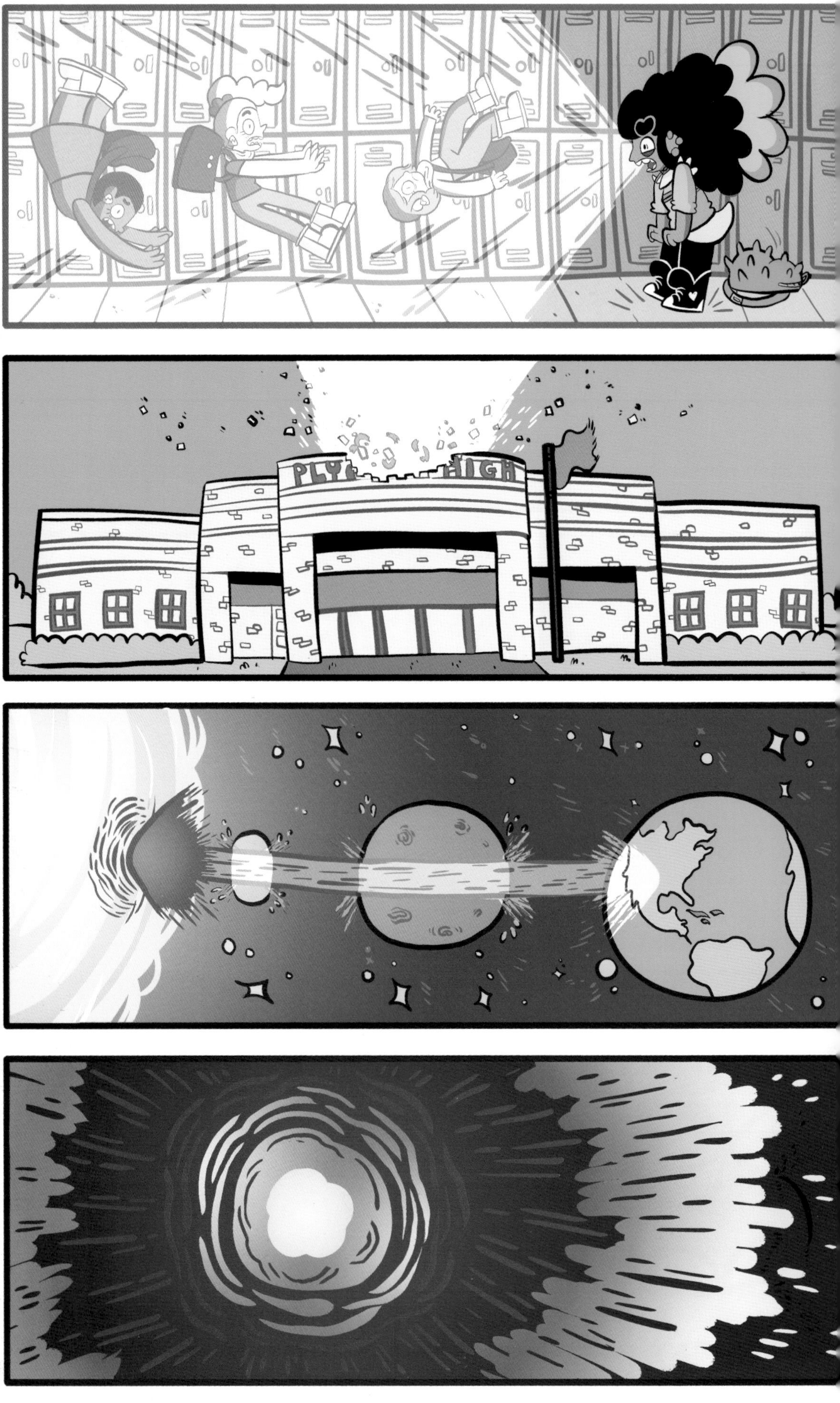
PLY
HIGH

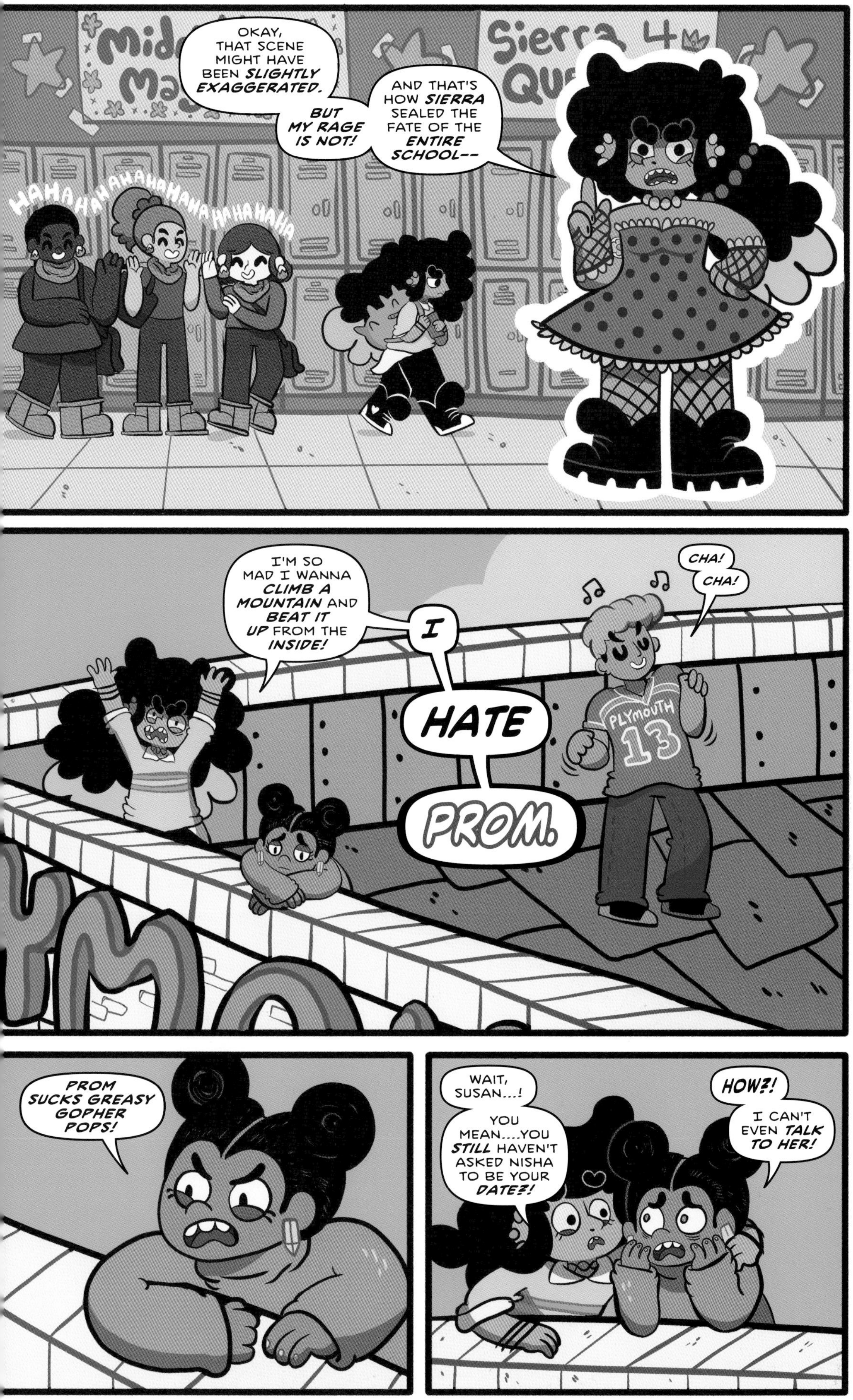
Sierra 4
OKAY, THAT SCENE MIGHT HAVE BEEN SLIGHTLY EXAGGERATED.
BUT MY RAGE IS NOT!
AND THAT'S HOW SIERRA SEALED THE FATE OF THE ENTIRE SCHOOL--
HAHAHAHAHAHAHAHAHAHAHAHAHA
I'M SO MAD I WANNA CLIMB A MOUNTAIN AND BEAT IT UP FROM THE INSIDE!
I
HATE
PROM.
CHA!
CHA!
PLYMOUTH
13
PROM SUCKS GREASY GOPHER POPS!
WAIT, SUSAN...!
YOU MEAN....YOU STILL HAVEN'T ASKED NISHA TO BE YOUR DATE?!
HOW?!
I CAN'T EVEN TALK TO HER!

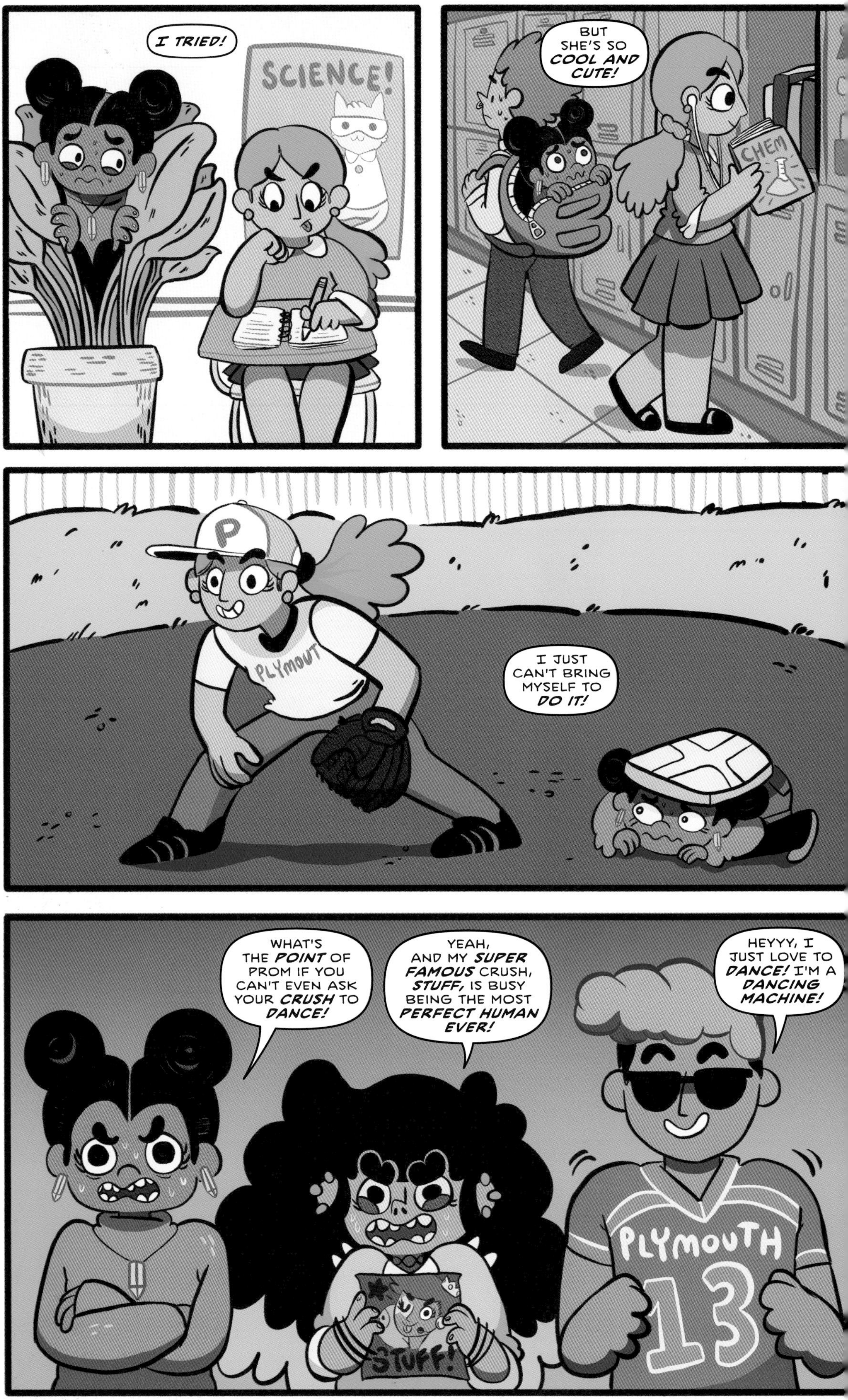

I TRIED!
SCIENCE!
BUT SHE'S SO COOL AND CUTE!
CHEM
PLYMOUT
I JUST CAN'T BRING MYSELF TO DO IT!
WHAT'S THE POINT OF PROM IF YOU CAN'T EVEN ASK YOUR CRUSH TO DANCE!
YEAH, AND MY SUPER FAMOUS CRUSH, STUFF, IS BUSY BEING THE MOST PERFECT HUMAN EVER!
STUFF!
HEYYY, I JUST LOVE TO DANCE! I'M A DANCING MACHINE!
PLYMOUTH 13

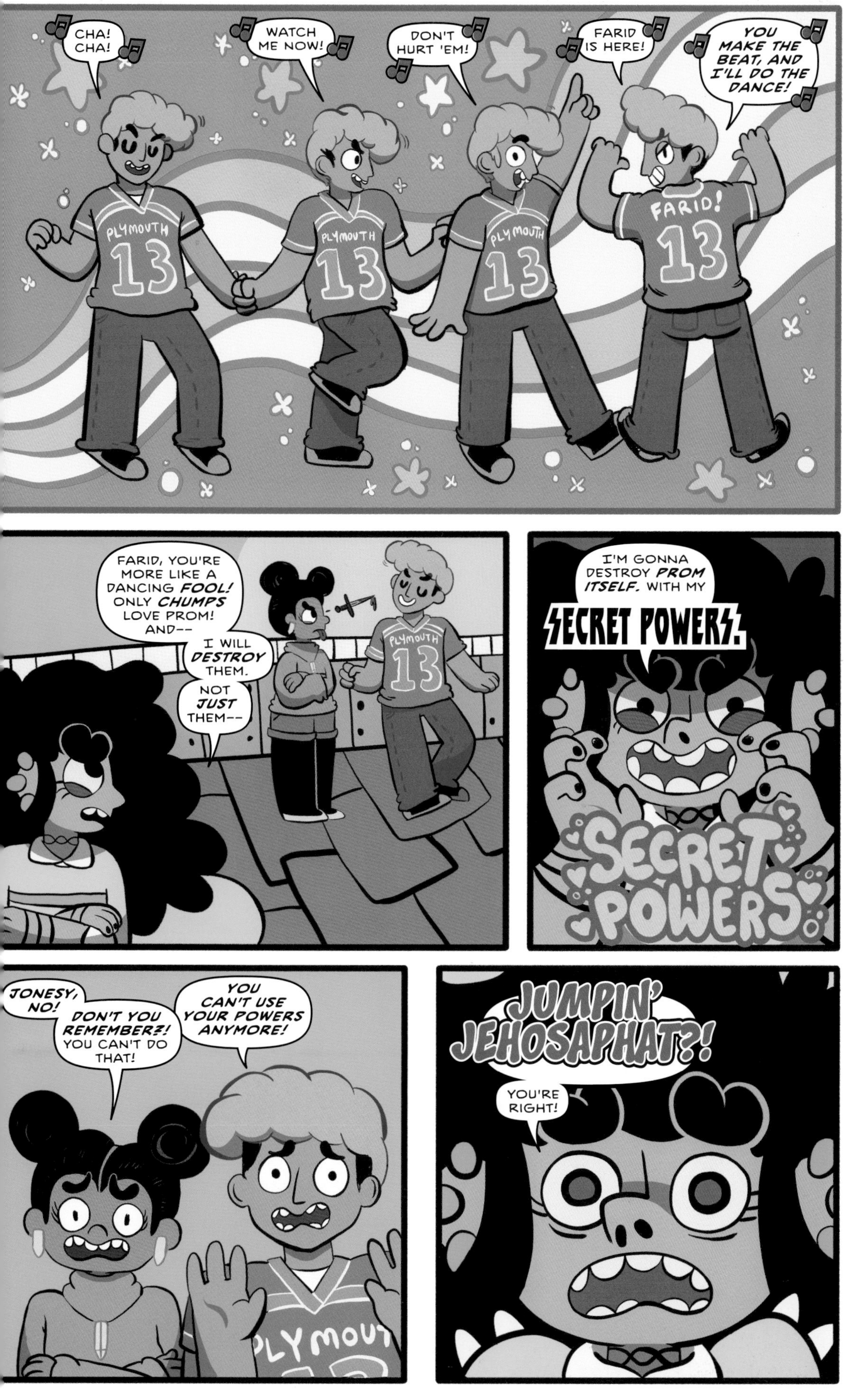
CHA! CHA!
WATCH ME NOW!
DON'T HURT 'EM!
FARID IS HERE!
YOU MAKE THE BEAT, AND I'LL DO THE DANCE!
PLYMOUTH 13
FARID! 13
FARID, YOU'RE MORE LIKE A DANCING FOOL! ONLY CHUMPS LOVE PROM! AND--
I WILL DESTROY THEM.
NOT JUST THEM--
I'M GONNA DESTROY PROM ITSELF. WITH MY
SECRET POWERS.
SECRET POWERS
JONESY, NO!
DON'T YOU REMEMBER?! YOU CAN'T DO THAT!
YOU CAN'T USE YOUR POWERS ANYMORE!
JUMPIN' JEHOSAPHAT?!
YOU'RE RIGHT!

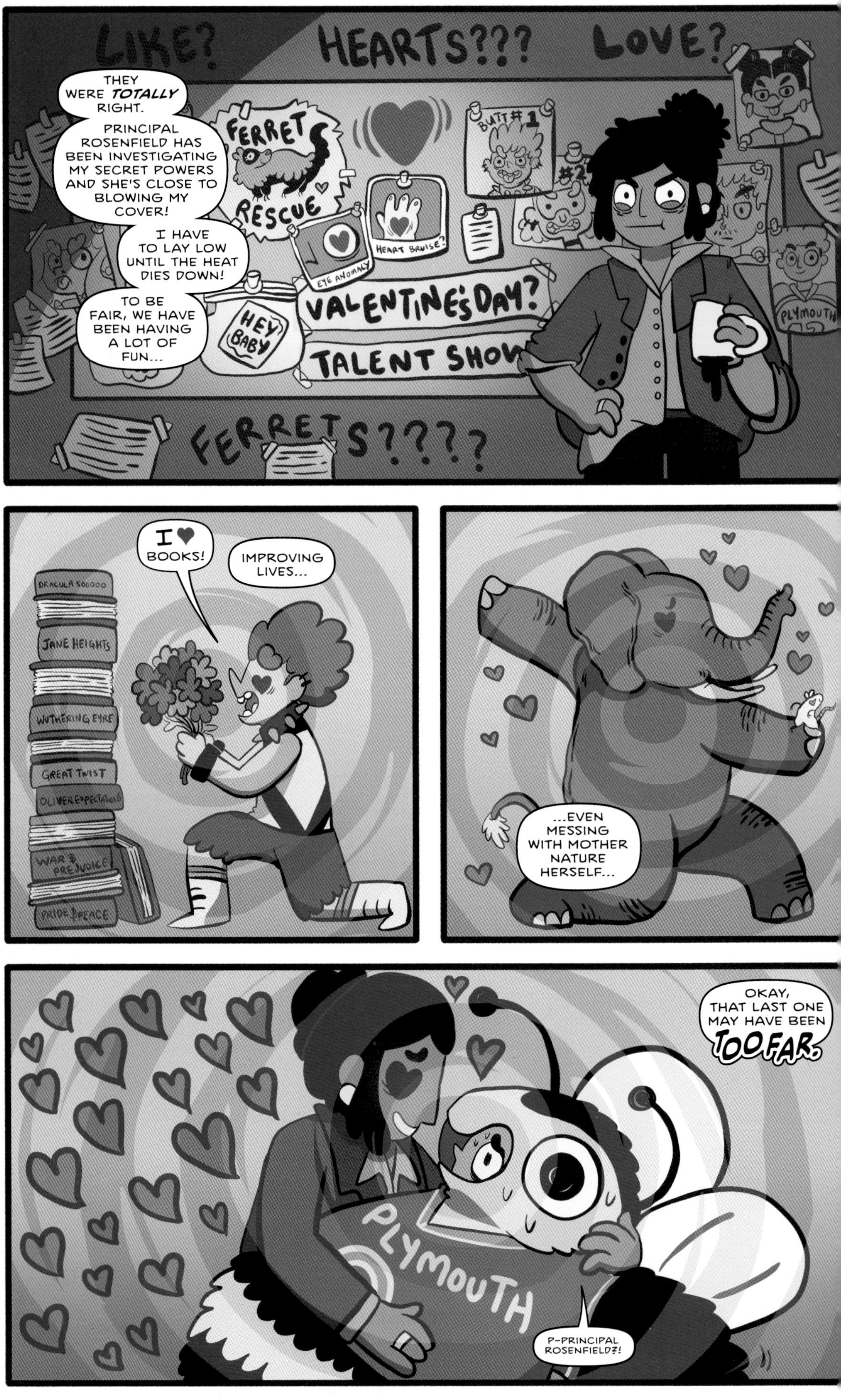
LIKE?
HEARTS???
LOVE?
THEY WERE TOTALLY RIGHT.
PRINCIPAL ROSENFIELD HAS BEEN INVESTIGATING MY SECRET POWERS AND SHE'S CLOSE TO BLOWING MY COVER!
I HAVE TO LAY LOW UNTIL THE HEAT DIES DOWN!
TO BE FAIR, WE HAVE BEEN HAVING A LOT OF FUN...
FERRET RESCUE
HEART BRUISE?
EYE ANOMALY
BUTT #1
#2
HEY BABY
VALENTINE'S DAY?
TALENT SHOW
PLYMOUTH
FERRETS????
I ♥ BOOKS!
IMPROVING LIVES...
DRACULA 500000
JANE HEIGHTS
WUTHERING EYRE
GREAT TWIST
OLIVER EXPECTATIONS
WAR & PREJUDICE
PRIDE & PEACE
...EVEN MESSING WITH MOTHER NATURE HERSELF...
OKAY, THAT LAST ONE MAY HAVE BEEN TOO FAR.
PLYMOUTH
P-PRINCIPAL ROSENFIELD?!

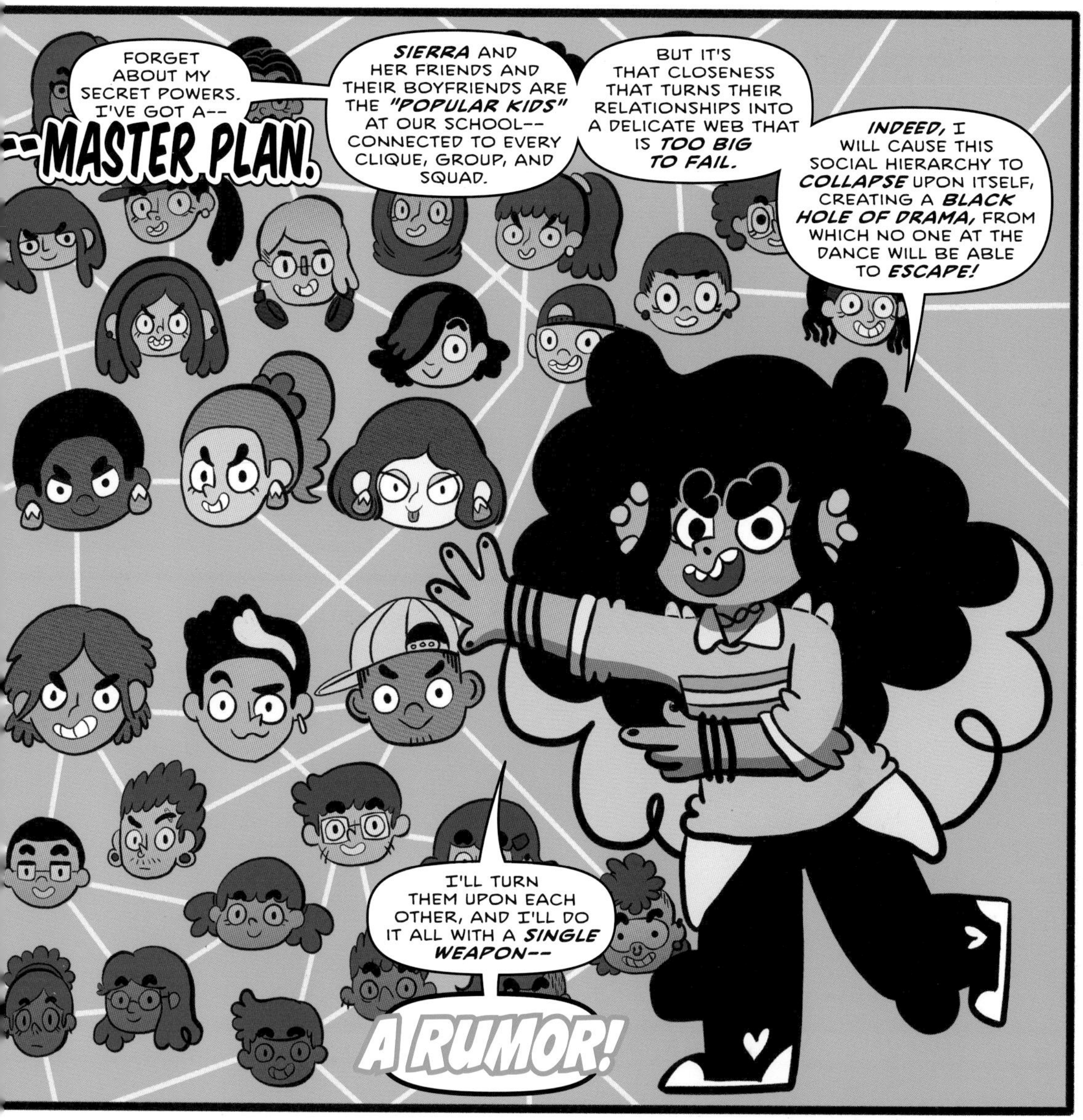
FORGET ABOUT MY SECRET POWERS. I'VE GOT A--
--MASTER PLAN.
SIERRA AND HER FRIENDS AND THEIR BOYFRIENDS ARE THE "POPULAR KIDS" AT OUR SCHOOL-- CONNECTED TO EVERY CLIQUE, GROUP, AND SQUAD.
BUT IT'S THAT CLOSENESS THAT TURNS THEIR RELATIONSHIPS INTO A DELICATE WEB THAT IS TOO BIG TO FAIL.
INDEED, I WILL CAUSE THIS SOCIAL HIERARCHY TO COLLAPSE UPON ITSELF, CREATING A BLACK HOLE OF DRAMA, FROM WHICH NO ONE AT THE DANCE WILL BE ABLE TO ESCAPE!
I'LL TURN THEM UPON EACH OTHER, AND I'LL DO IT ALL WITH A SINGLE WEAPON--
A RUMOR!

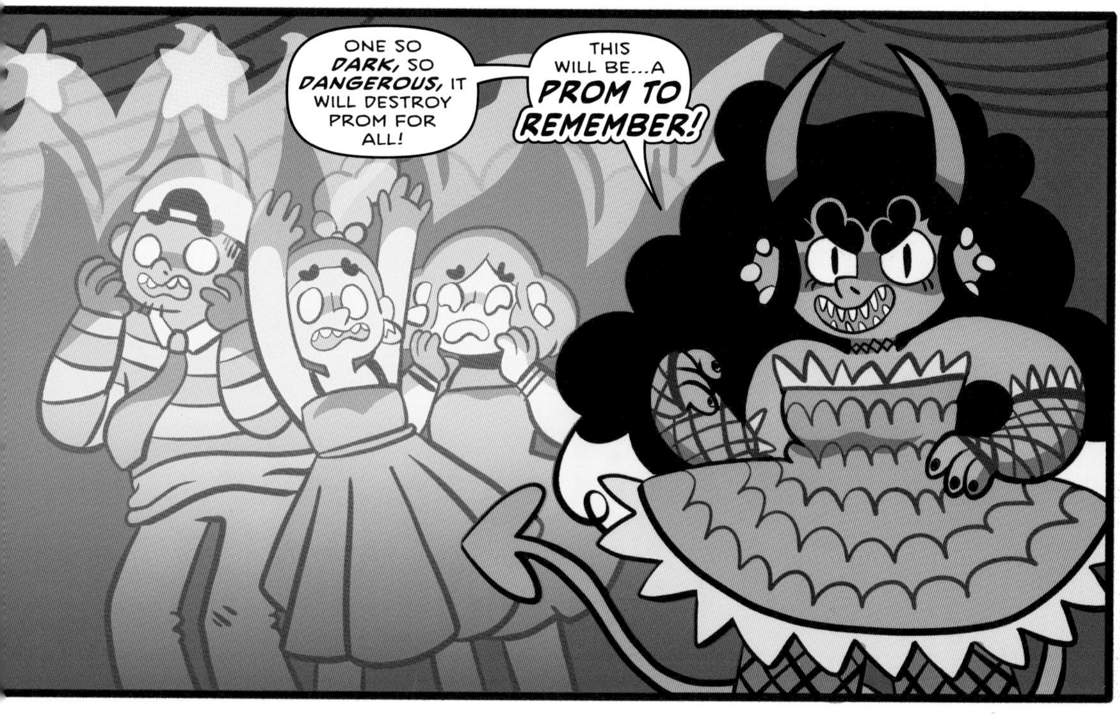
ONE SO DARK, SO DANGEROUS, IT WILL DESTROY PROM FOR ALL!
THIS WILL BE...A PROM TO REMEMBER!

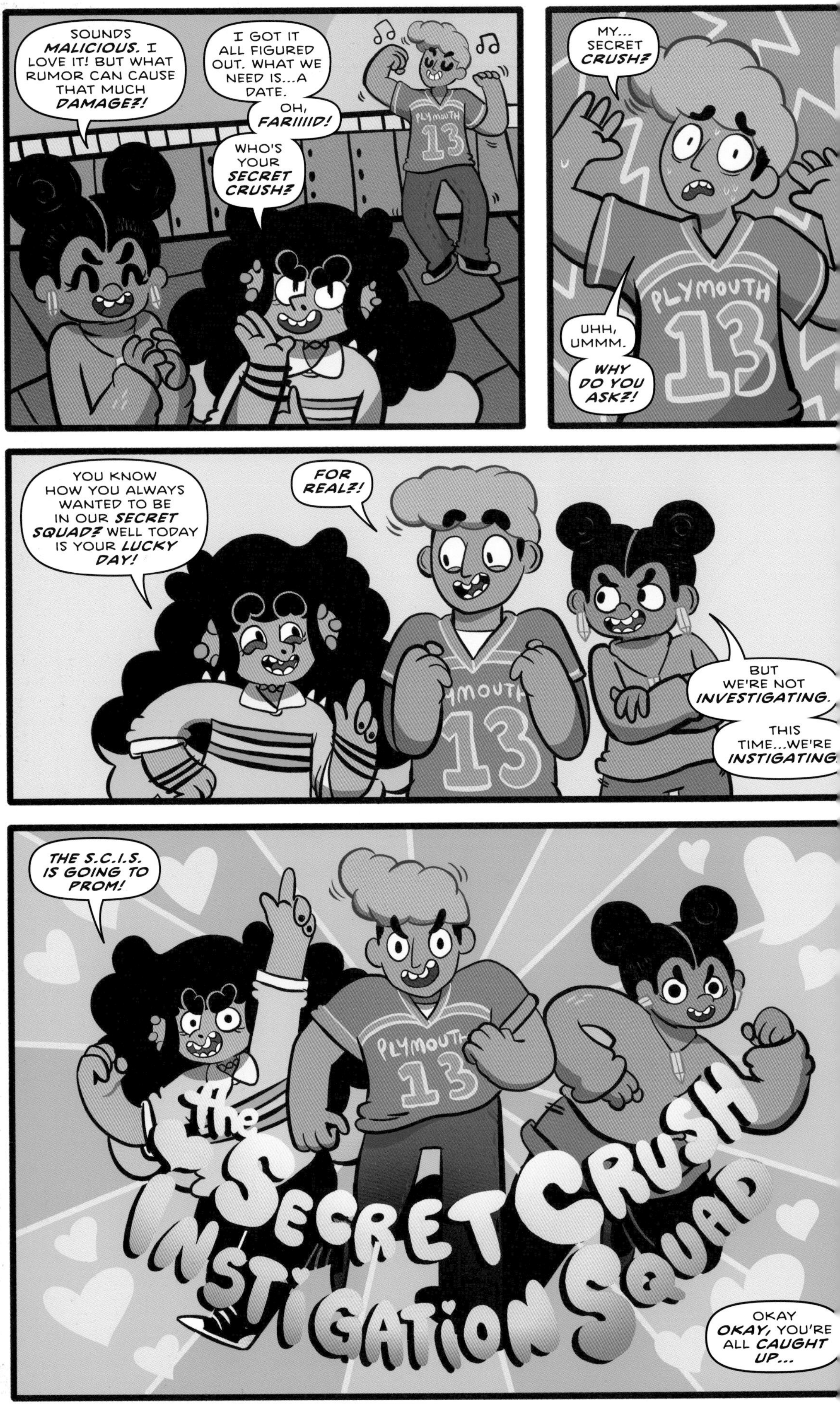
SOUNDS MALICIOUS. I LOVE IT! BUT WHAT RUMOR CAN CAUSE THAT MUCH DAMAGE?!
I GOT IT ALL FIGURED OUT. WHAT WE NEED IS...A DATE.
OH, FARIIIID!
WHO'S YOUR SECRET CRUSH?
PLYMOUTH 13
MY... SECRET CRUSH?
UHH, UMMM.
WHY DO YOU ASK?!
YOU KNOW HOW YOU ALWAYS WANTED TO BE IN OUR SECRET SQUAD? WELL TODAY IS YOUR LUCKY DAY!
FOR REAL?!
BUT WE'RE NOT INVESTIGATING.
THIS TIME...WE'RE INSTIGATING.
THE S.C.I.S. IS GOING TO PROM!
The SECRET CRUSH INSTIGATION SQUAD
OKAY OKAY, YOU'RE ALL CAUGHT UP...

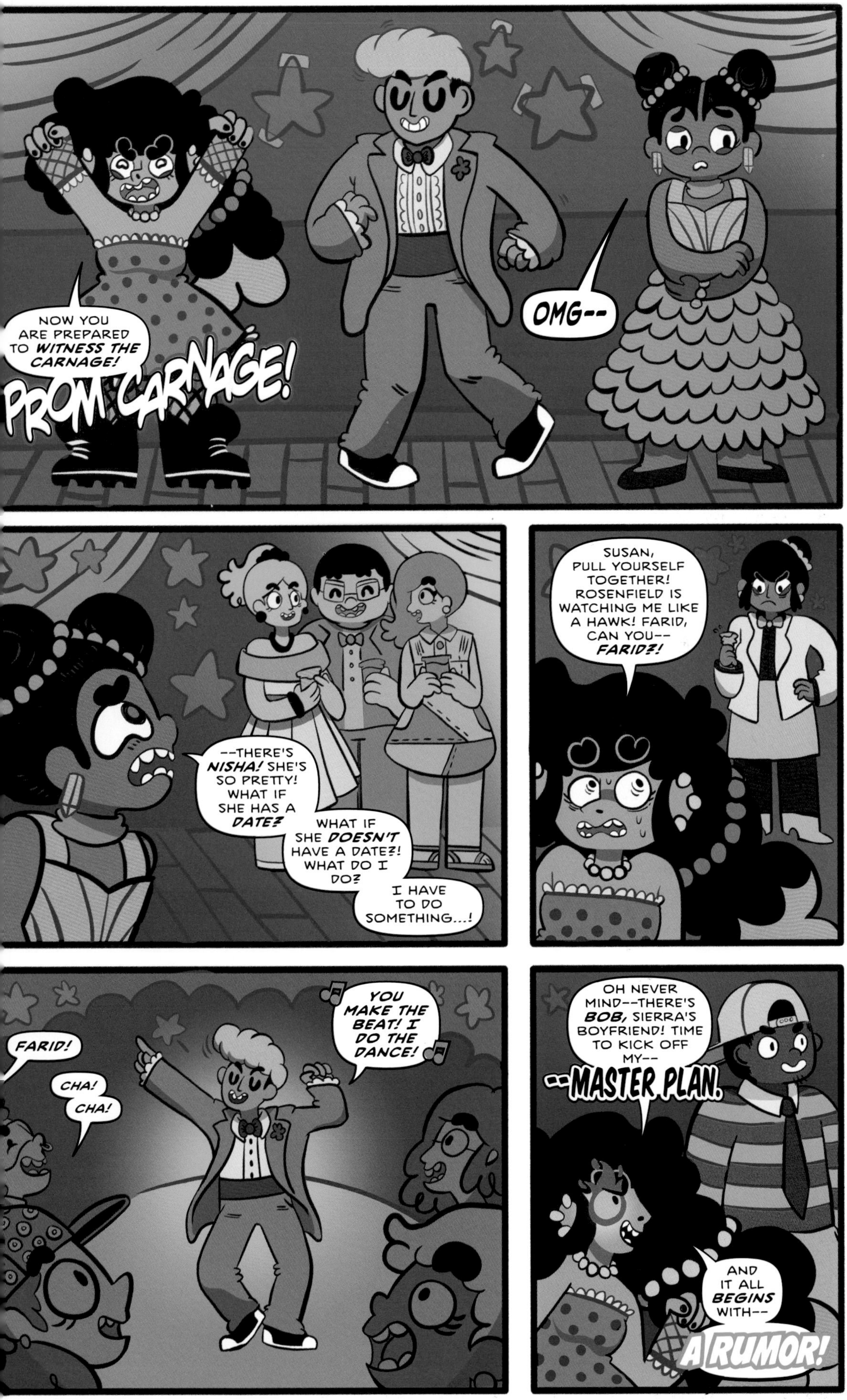
NOW YOU ARE PREPARED TO WITNESS THE CARNAGE!
PROM CARNAGE!
OMG--
--THERE'S NISHA! SHE'S SO PRETTY! WHAT IF SHE HAS A DATE?
WHAT IF SHE DOESN'T HAVE A DATE?! WHAT DO I DO?
I HAVE TO DO SOMETHING...!
SUSAN, PULL YOURSELF TOGETHER! ROSENFIELD IS WATCHING ME LIKE A HAWK! FARID, CAN YOU-- FARID?!
FARID!
CHA!
CHA!
YOU MAKE THE BEAT! I DO THE DANCE!
OH NEVER MIND--THERE'S BOB, SIERRA'S BOYFRIEND! TIME TO KICK OFF MY--
--MASTER PLAN.
AND IT ALL BEGINS WITH--
A RUMOR!

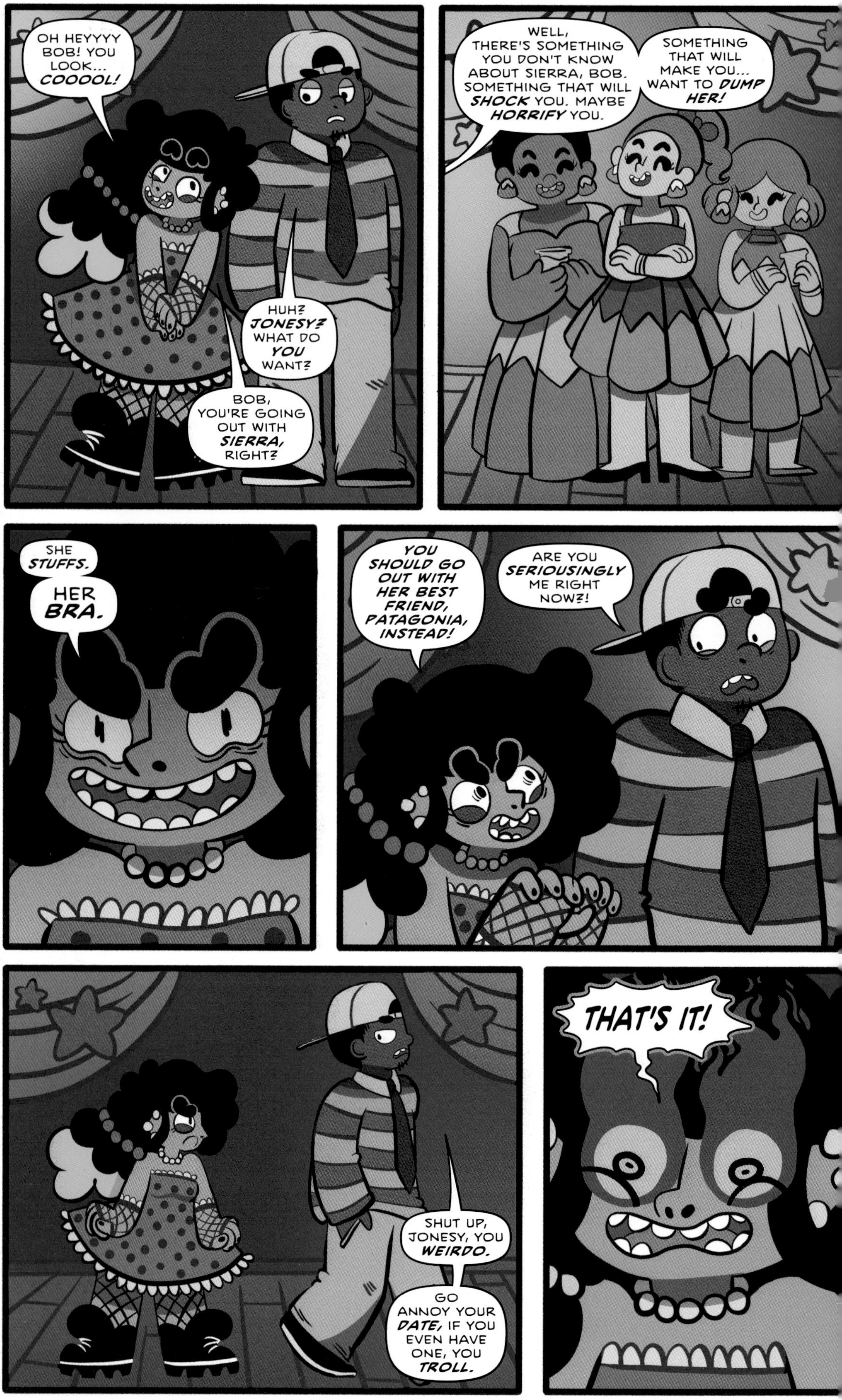

OH HEYYYY BOB! YOU LOOK... COOOOL!
HUH? JONESY? WHAT DO YOU WANT?
BOB, YOU'RE GOING OUT WITH SIERRA, RIGHT?
WELL, THERE'S SOMETHING YOU DON'T KNOW ABOUT SIERRA, BOB. SOMETHING THAT WILL SHOCK YOU. MAYBE HORRIFY YOU.
SOMETHING THAT WILL MAKE YOU... WANT TO DUMP HER!
SHE STUFFS.
HER BRA.
YOU SHOULD GO OUT WITH HER BEST FRIEND, PATAGONIA, INSTEAD!
ARE YOU SERIOUSINGLY ME RIGHT NOW?!
SHUT UP, JONESY, YOU WEIRDO.
GO ANNOY YOUR DATE, IF YOU EVEN HAVE ONE, YOU TROLL.
THAT'S IT!

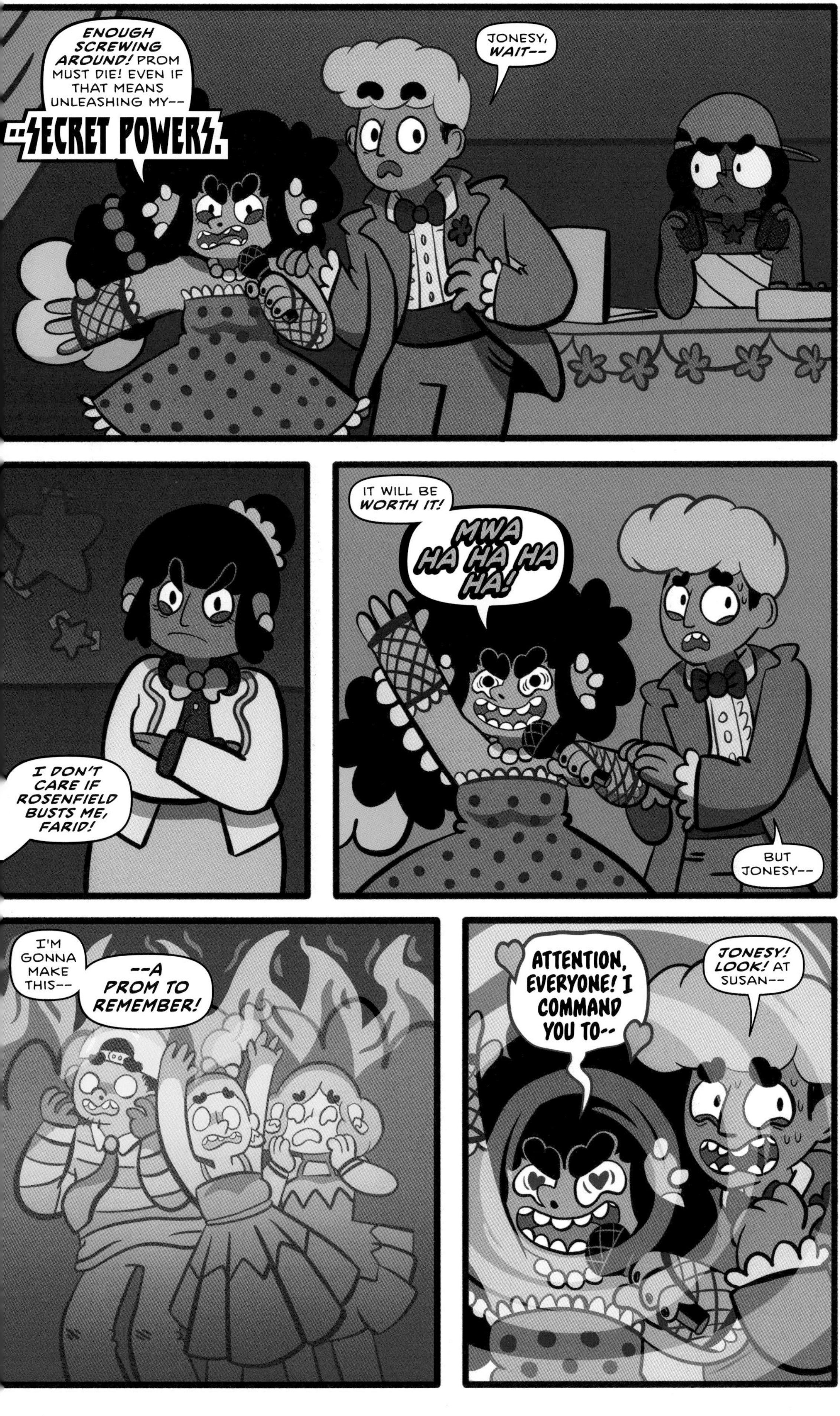
ENOUGH SCREWING AROUND! PROM MUST DIE! EVEN IF THAT MEANS UNLEASHING MY--
--SECRET POWERS.
JONESY, WAIT--
I DON'T CARE IF ROSENFIELD BUSTS ME, FARID!
IT WILL BE WORTH IT!
MWA HA HA HA HA!
BUT JONESY--
I'M GONNA MAKE THIS--
--A PROM TO REMEMBER!
ATTENTION, EVERYONE! I COMMAND YOU TO--
JONESY! LOOK! AT SUSAN--

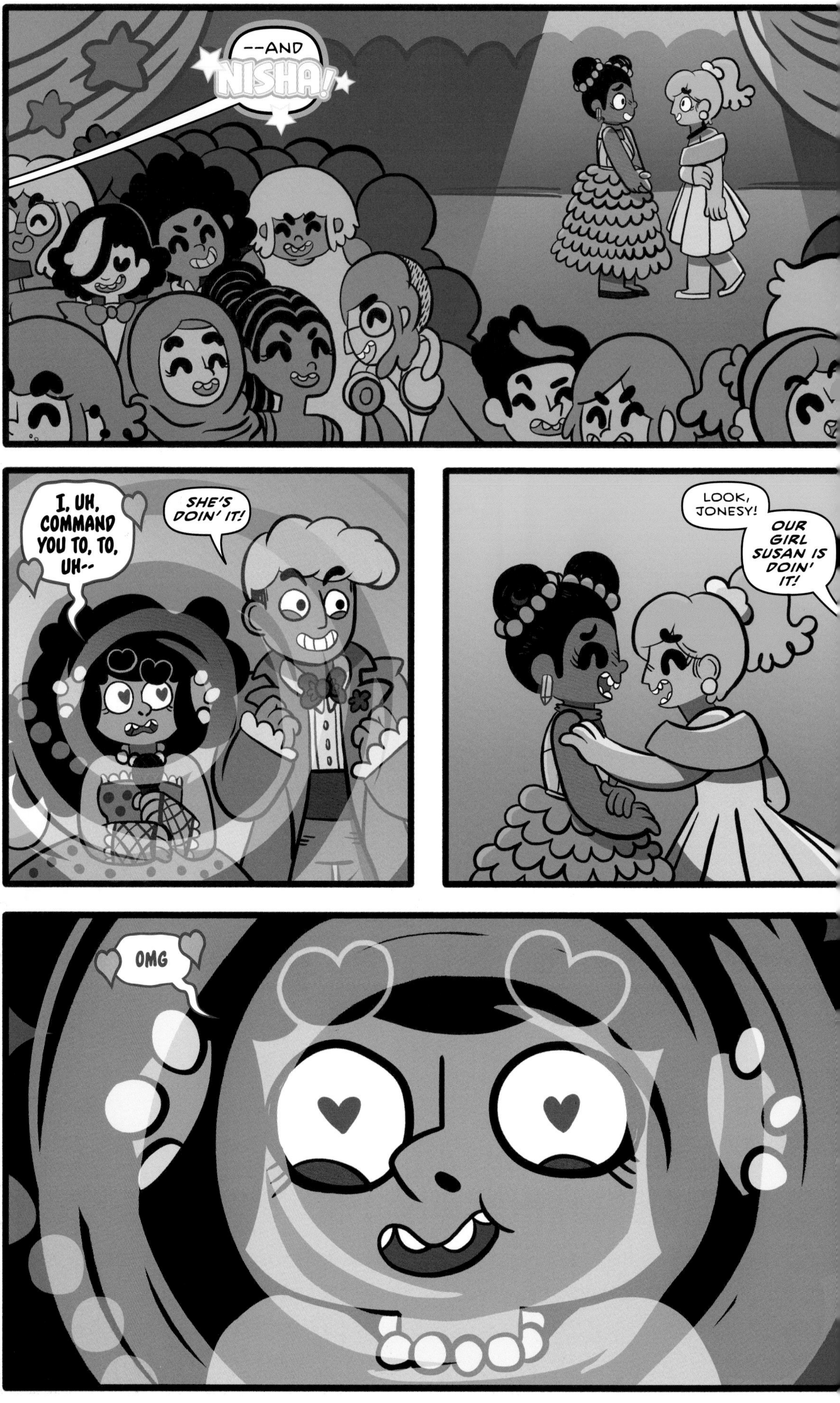
--AND
NISHA!
I, UH, COMMAND YOU TO, TO, UH--
SHE'S DOIN' IT!
LOOK, JONESY!
OUR GIRL SUSAN IS DOIN' IT!
OMG

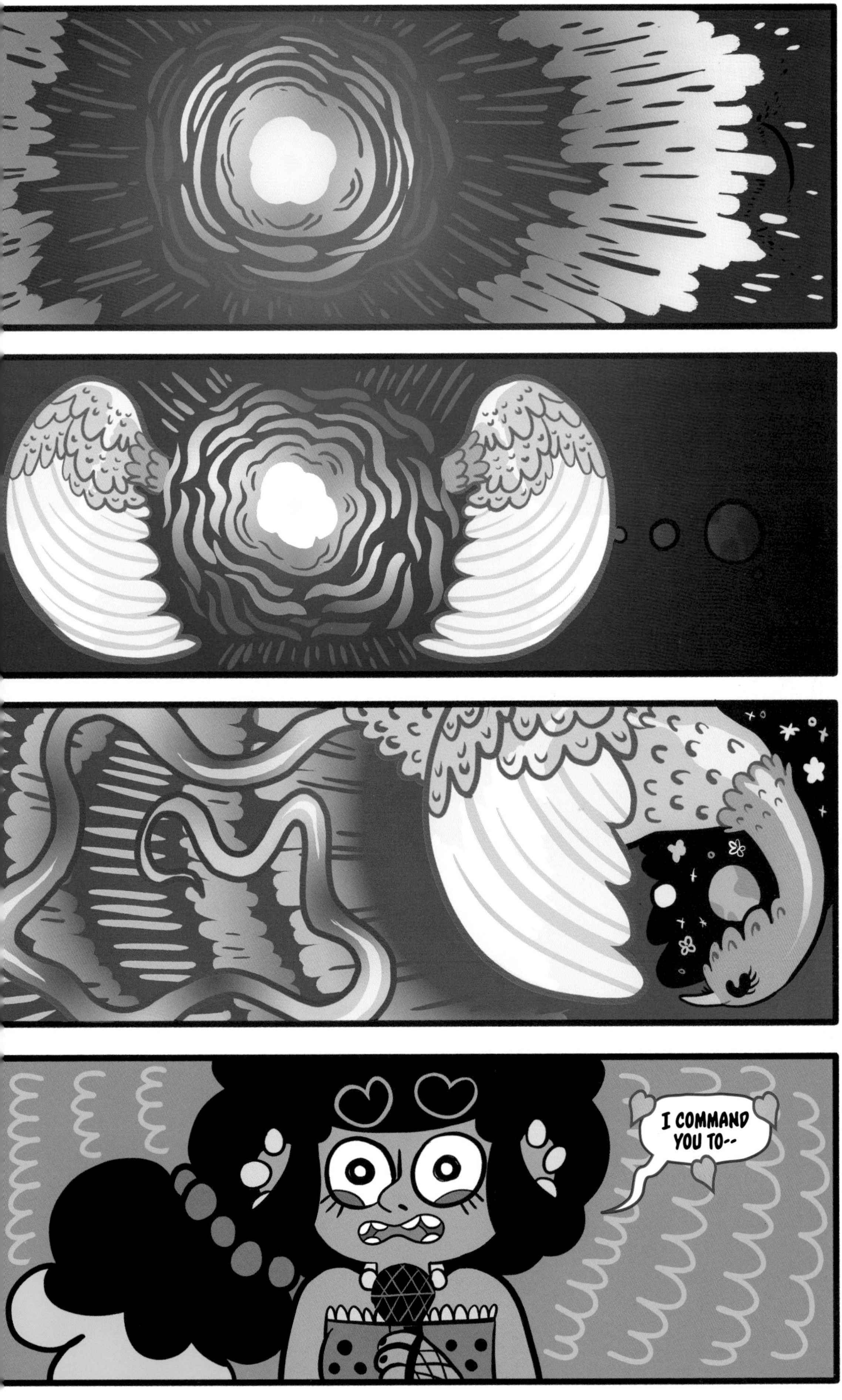
I COMMAND YOU TO--

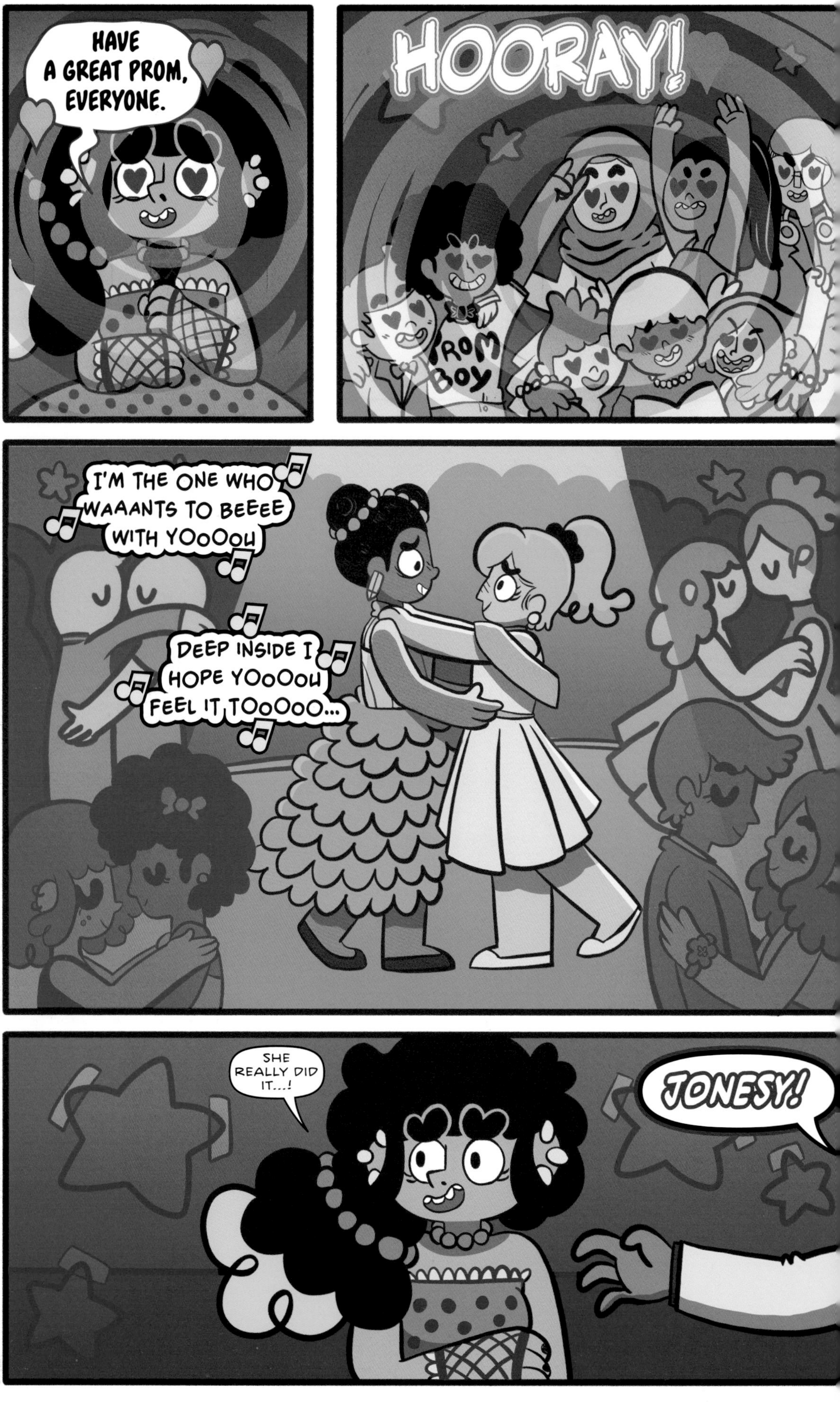
HAVE A GREAT PROM, EVERYONE.
HOORAY!
PROM BOY
I'M THE ONE WHO WAAANTS TO BEEEE WITH YOOOOU
DEEP INSIDE I HOPE YOOOOU FEEL IT TOOOOO...
SHE REALLY DID IT...!
JONESY!

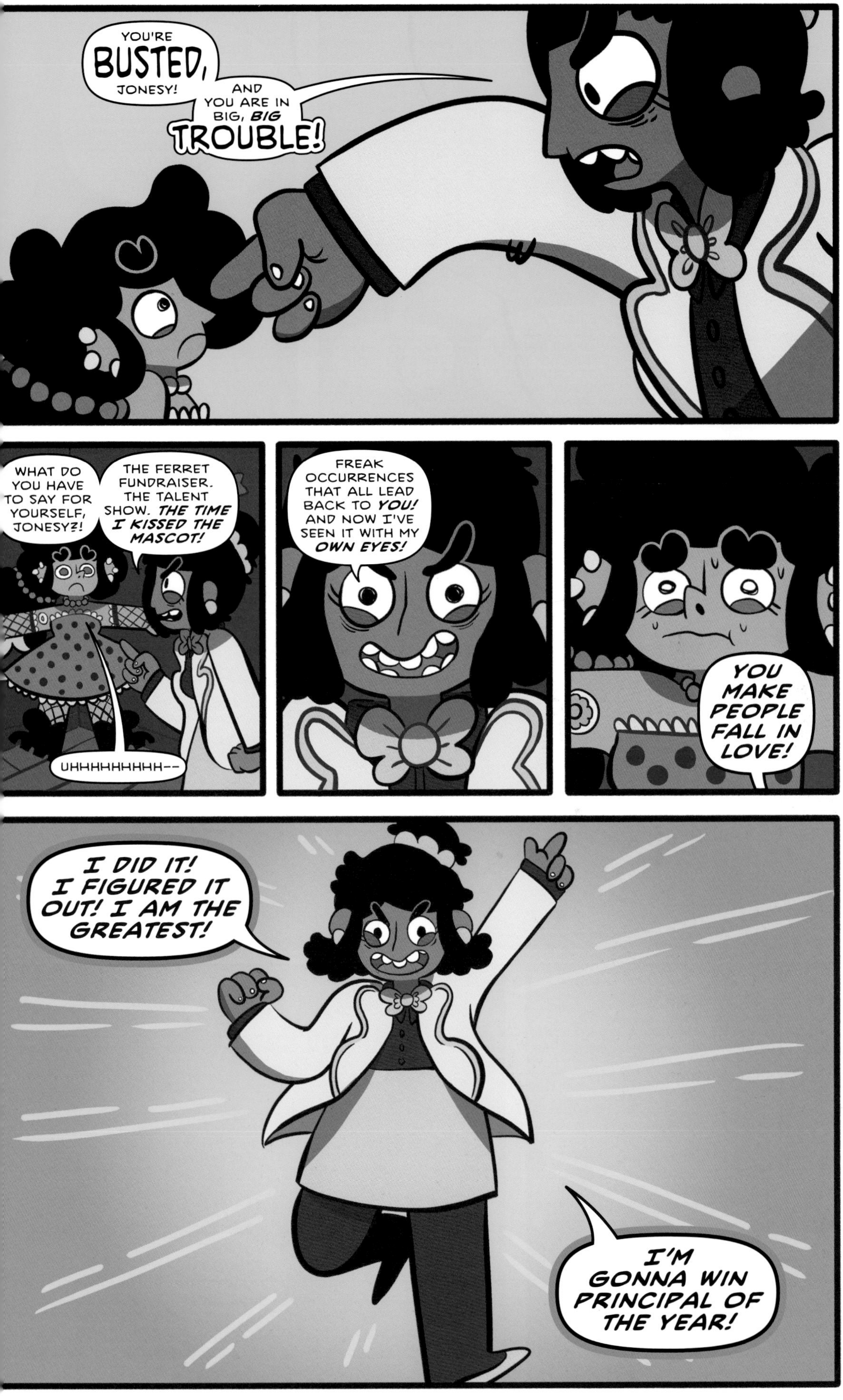
YOU'RE BUSTED, JONESY!
AND YOU ARE IN BIG, BIG TROUBLE!
WHAT DO YOU HAVE TO SAY FOR YOURSELF, JONESY?!
THE FERRET FUNDRAISER. THE TALENT SHOW. THE TIME I KISSED THE MASCOT!
UHHHHHHHHH--
FREAK OCCURRENCES THAT ALL LEAD BACK TO YOU! AND NOW I'VE SEEN IT WITH MY OWN EYES!
YOU MAKE PEOPLE FALL IN LOVE!
I DID IT! I FIGURED IT OUT! I AM THE GREATEST!
I'M GONNA WIN PRINCIPAL OF THE YEAR!

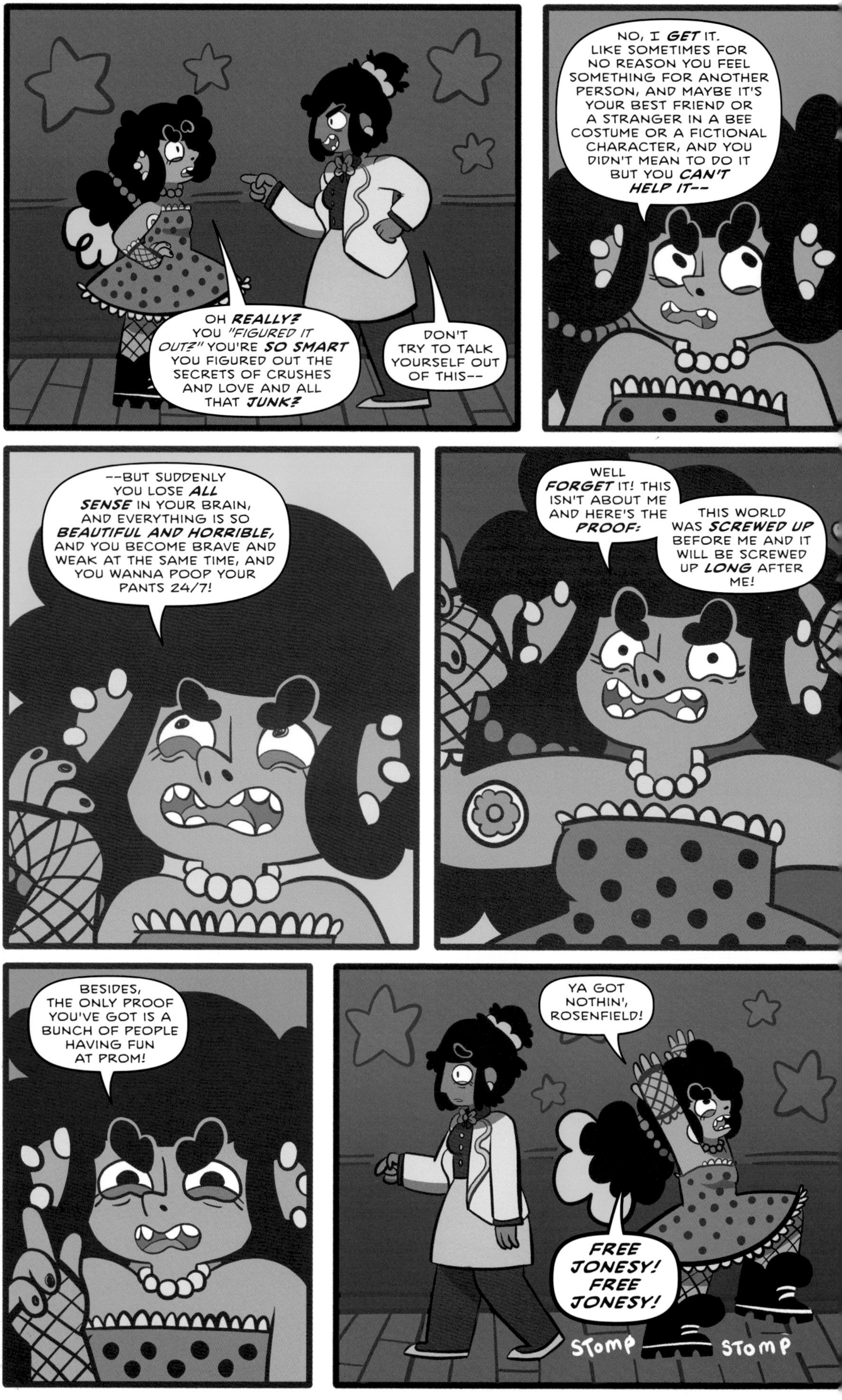

OH REALLY? YOU "FIGURED IT OUT?" YOU'RE SO SMART YOU FIGURED OUT THE SECRETS OF CRUSHES AND LOVE AND ALL THAT JUNK?
DON'T TRY TO TALK YOURSELF OUT OF THIS--
NO, I GET IT. LIKE SOMETIMES FOR NO REASON YOU FEEL SOMETHING FOR ANOTHER PERSON, AND MAYBE IT'S YOUR BEST FRIEND OR A STRANGER IN A BEE COSTUME OR A FICTIONAL CHARACTER, AND YOU DIDN'T MEAN TO DO IT BUT YOU CAN'T HELP IT--
--BUT SUDDENLY YOU LOSE ALL SENSE IN YOUR BRAIN, AND EVERYTHING IS SO BEAUTIFUL AND HORRIBLE, AND YOU BECOME BRAVE AND WEAK AT THE SAME TIME, AND YOU WANNA POOP YOUR PANTS 24/7!
WELL FORGET IT! THIS ISN'T ABOUT ME AND HERE'S THE PROOF:
THIS WORLD WAS SCREWED UP BEFORE ME AND IT WILL BE SCREWED UP LONG AFTER ME!
BESIDES, THE ONLY PROOF YOU'VE GOT IS A BUNCH OF PEOPLE HAVING FUN AT PROM!
YA GOT NOTHIN', ROSENFIELD!
FREE JONESY! FREE JONESY!
STOMP
STOMP

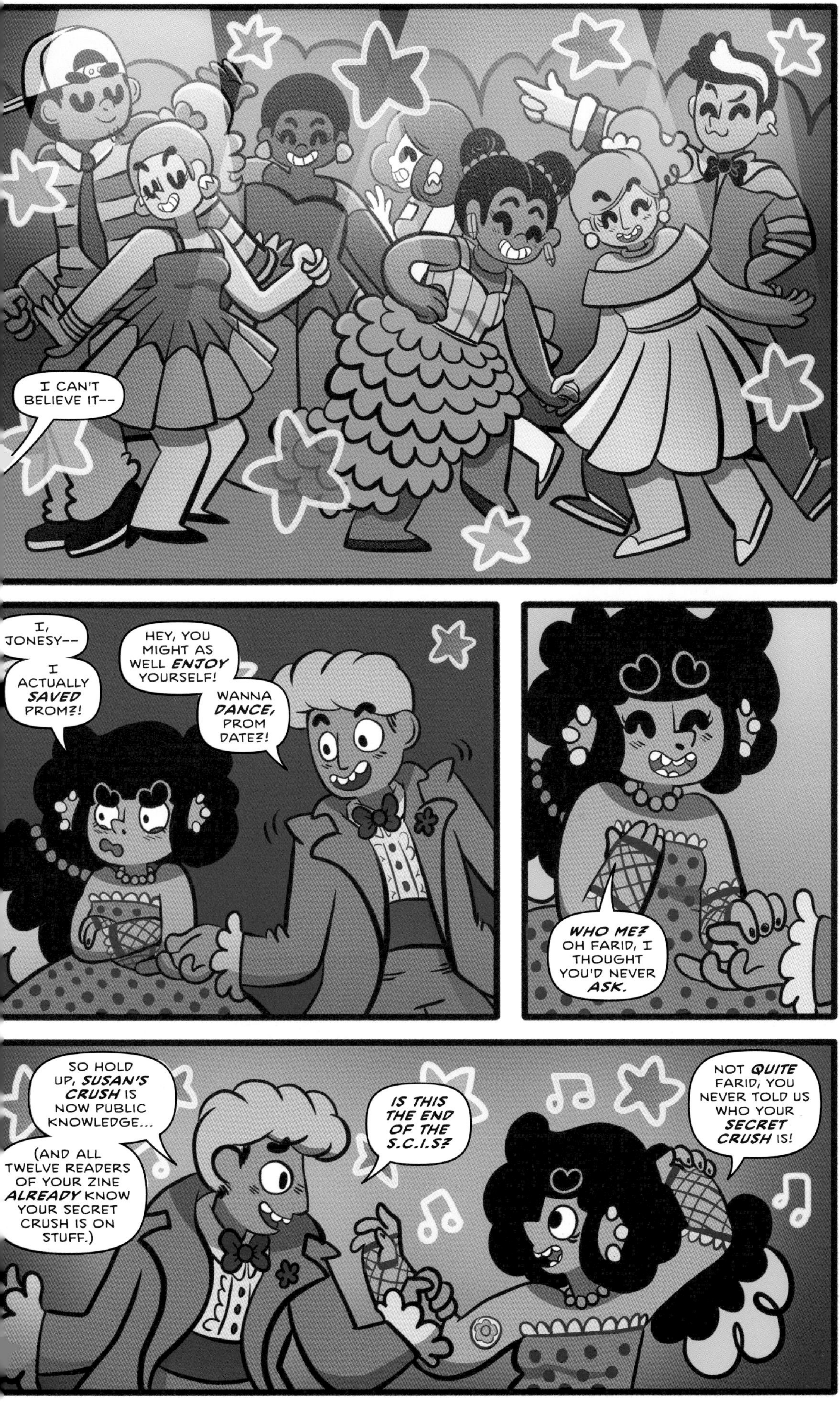
I CAN'T BELIEVE IT--
I, JONESY--
I ACTUALLY *SAVED* PROM?!
HEY, YOU MIGHT AS WELL *ENJOY* YOURSELF!
WANNA *DANCE,* PROM DATE?!
*WHO ME?* OH FARID, I THOUGHT YOU'D NEVER *ASK.*
SO HOLD UP, *SUSAN'S CRUSH* IS NOW PUBLIC KNOWLEDGE...
(AND ALL TWELVE READERS OF YOUR ZINE *ALREADY* KNOW YOUR SECRET CRUSH IS ON STUFF.)
*IS THIS THE END OF THE S.C.I.S?*
NOT *QUITE* FARID, YOU NEVER TOLD US WHO YOUR *SECRET CRUSH* IS!

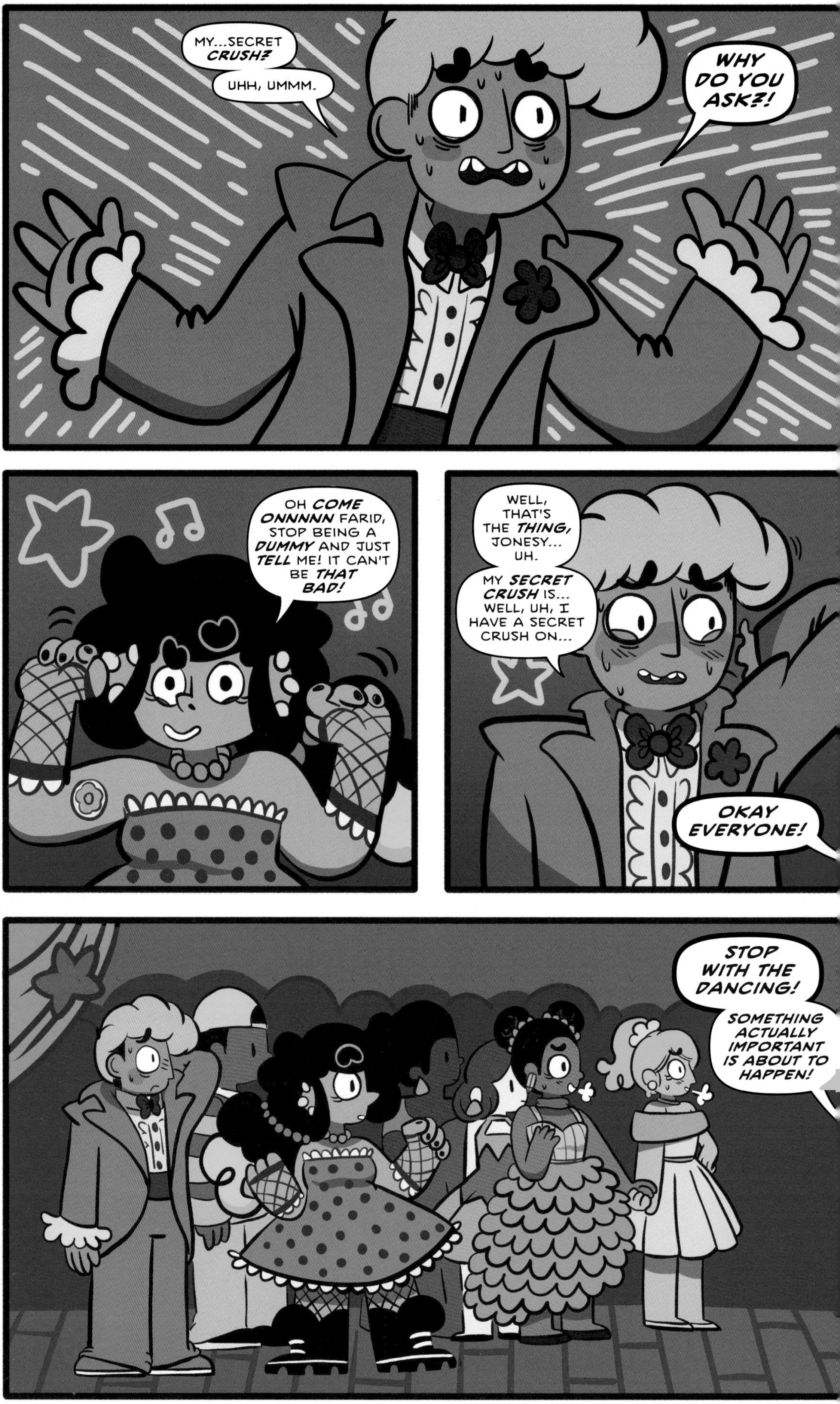

MY...SECRET CRUSH?
UHH, UMMM.
WHY DO YOU ASK?!
OH COME ONNNNN FARID, STOP BEING A DUMMY AND JUST TELL ME! IT CAN'T BE THAT BAD!
WELL, THAT'S THE THING, JONESY... UH.
MY SECRET CRUSH IS... WELL, UH, I HAVE A SECRET CRUSH ON...
OKAY EVERYONE!
STOP WITH THE DANCING!
SOMETHING ACTUALLY IMPORTANT IS ABOUT TO HAPPEN!

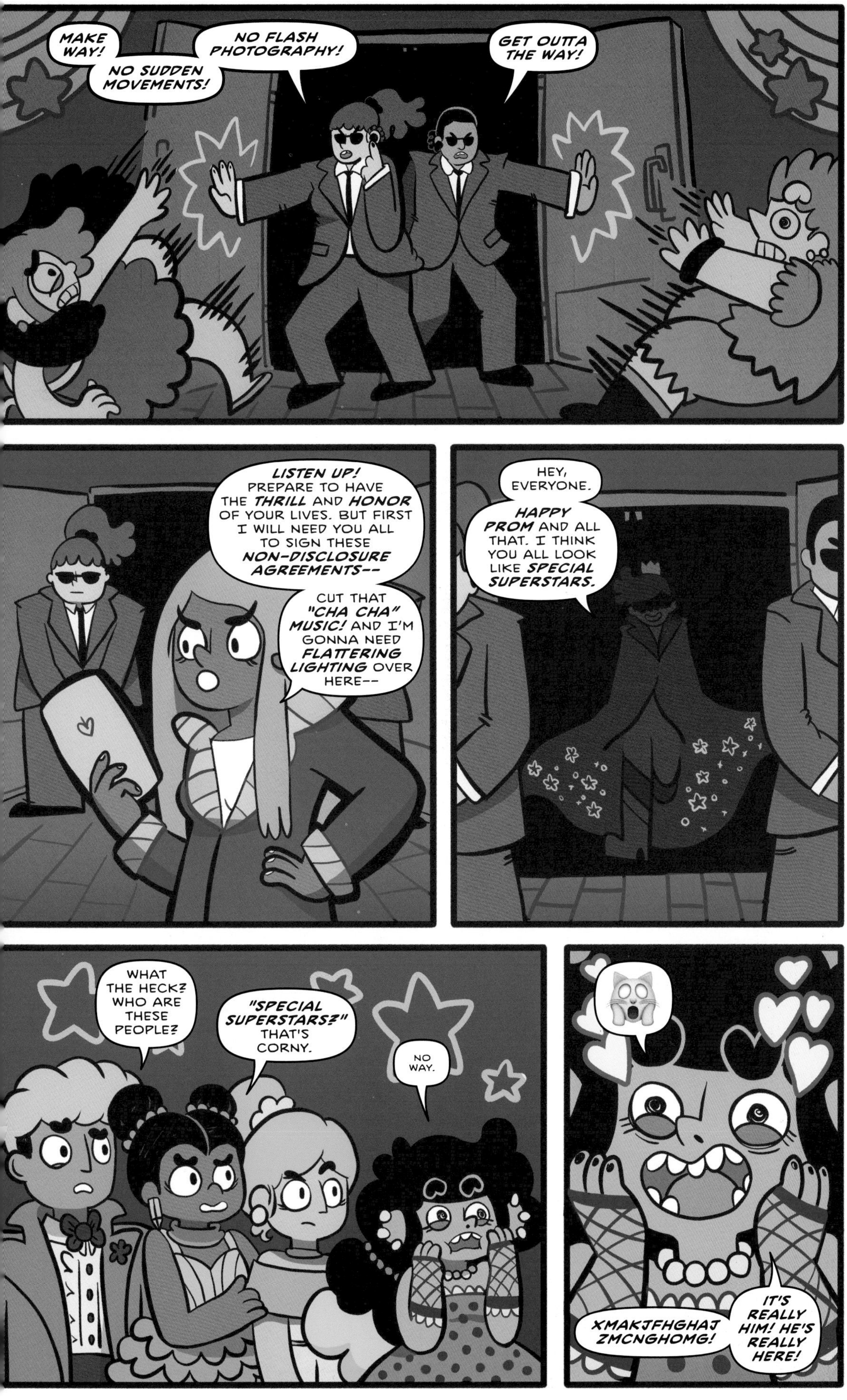
MAKE WAY!
NO SUDDEN MOVEMENTS!
NO FLASH PHOTOGRAPHY!
GET OUTTA THE WAY!
LISTEN UP! PREPARE TO HAVE THE THRILL AND HONOR OF YOUR LIVES. BUT FIRST I WILL NEED YOU ALL TO SIGN THESE NON-DISCLOSURE AGREEMENTS--
CUT THAT "CHA CHA" MUSIC! AND I'M GONNA NEED FLATTERING LIGHTING OVER HERE--
HEY, EVERYONE.
HAPPY PROM AND ALL THAT. I THINK YOU ALL LOOK LIKE SPECIAL SUPERSTARS.
WHAT THE HECK? WHO ARE THESE PEOPLE?
"SPECIAL SUPERSTARS?" THAT'S CORNY.
NO WAY.
XMAKJFHGHAJ ZMCNGHOMG!
IT'S REALLY HIM! HE'S REALLY HERE!

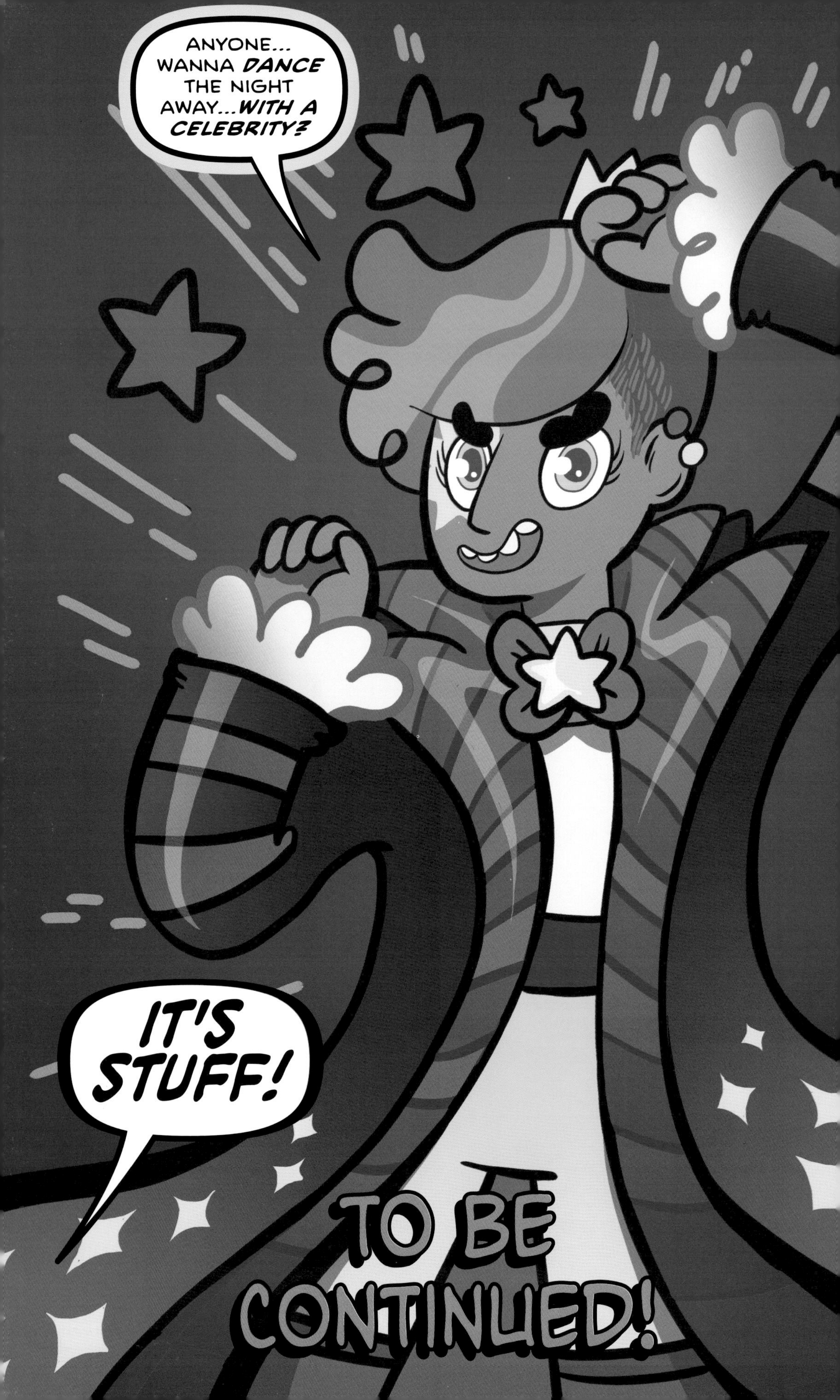
ANYONE... WANNA DANCE THE NIGHT AWAY...WITH A CELEBRITY?
IT'S STUFF!
TO BE CONTINUED!

# COVER GALLERY

ISSUE ONE COVER BY
CAITLIN ROSE BOYLE
COLORS BY MICKEY QUINN

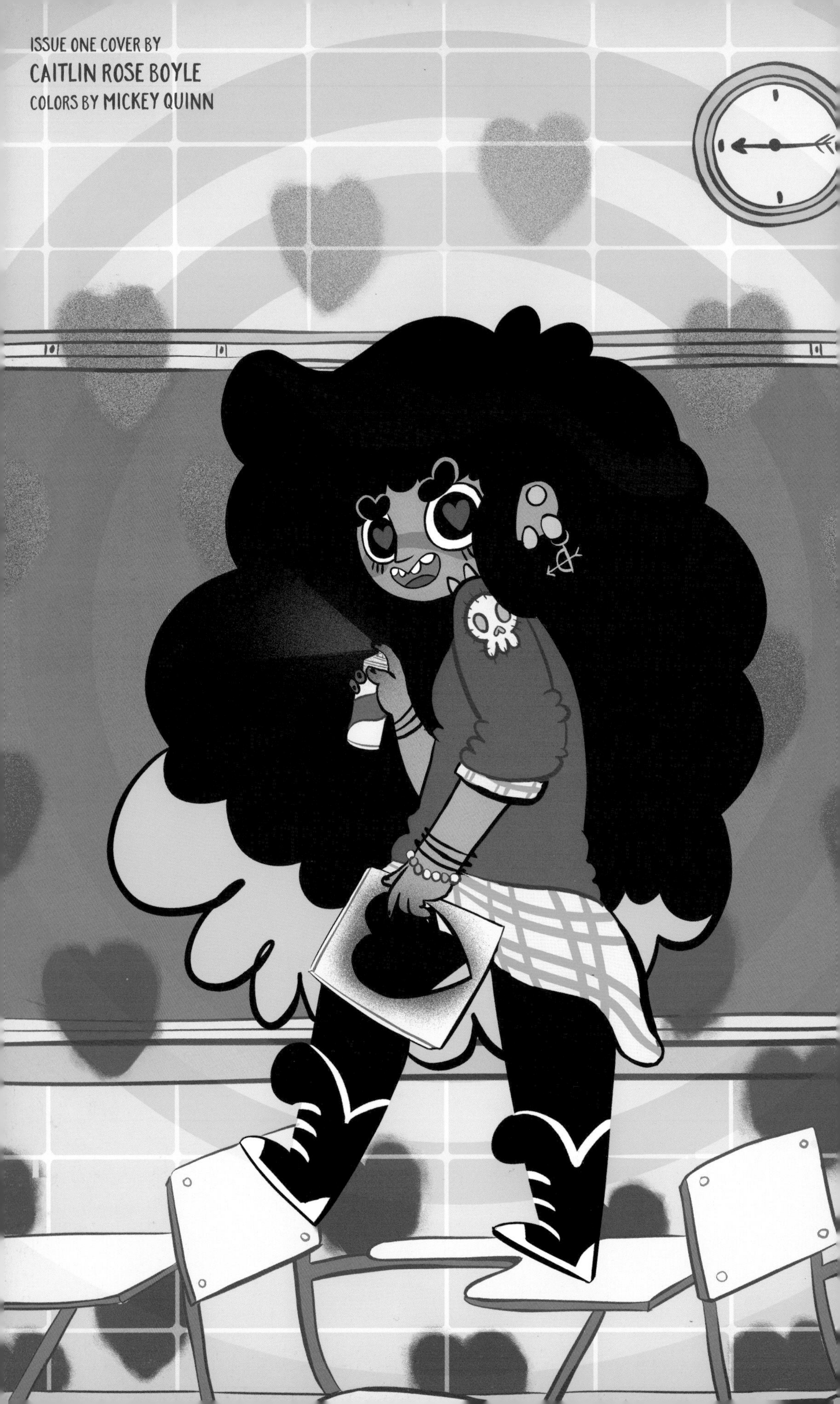

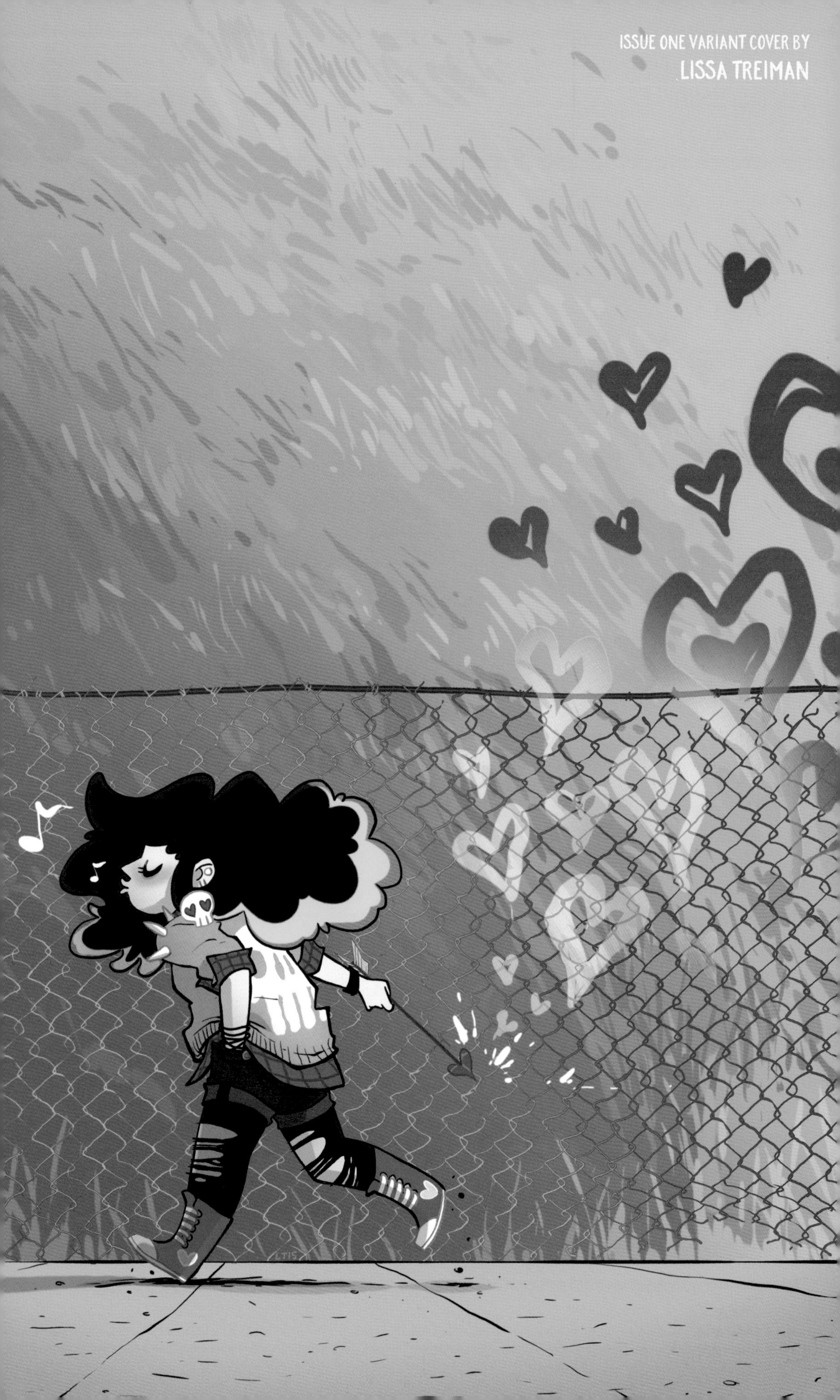

ISSUE ONE VARIANT COVER BY
LISSA TREIMAN

ISSUE ONE UNLOCKED RETAILER VARIANT COVER BY

BRYAN LEE O'MALLEY

& JASON FISCHER

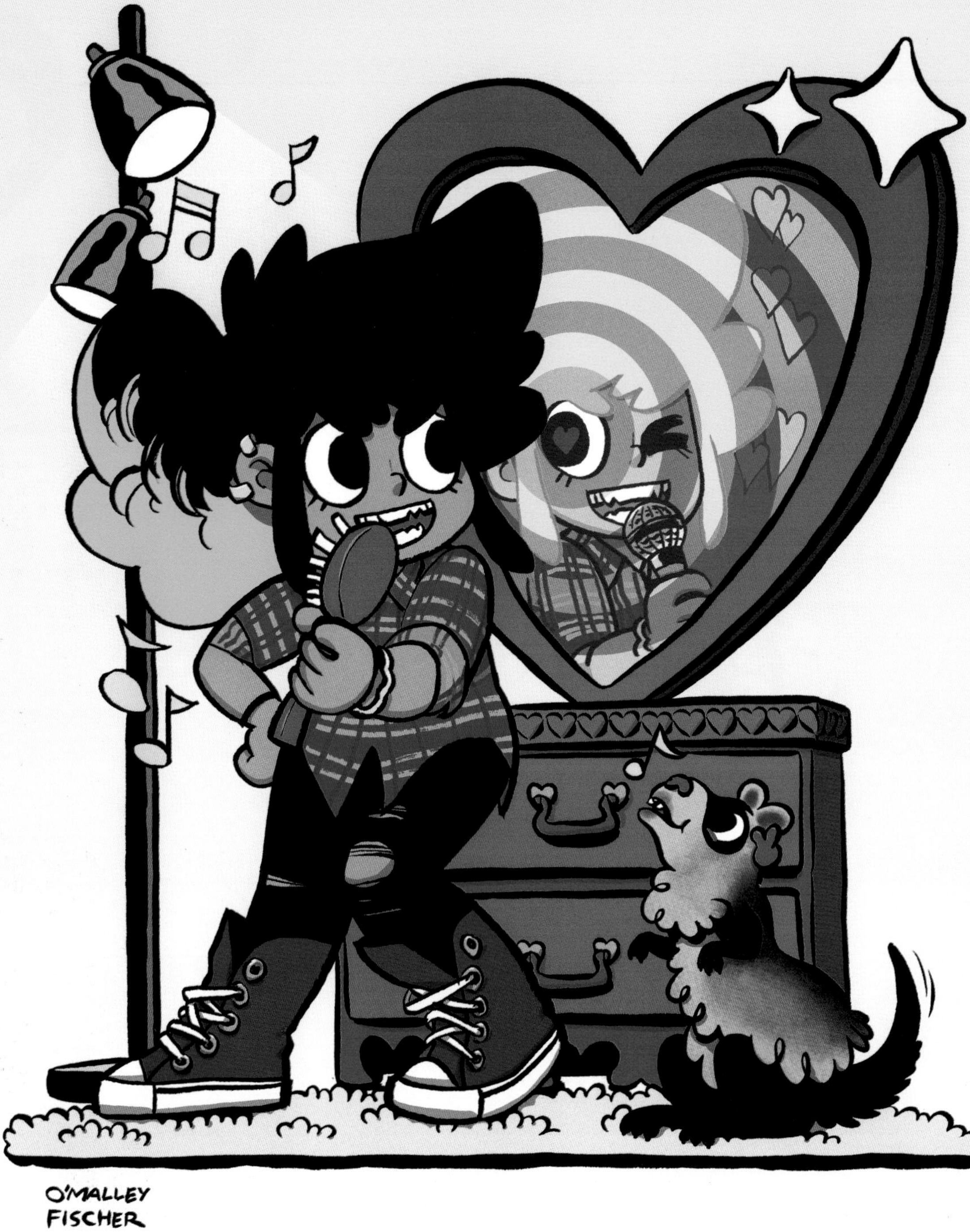
O'MALLEY
FISCHER

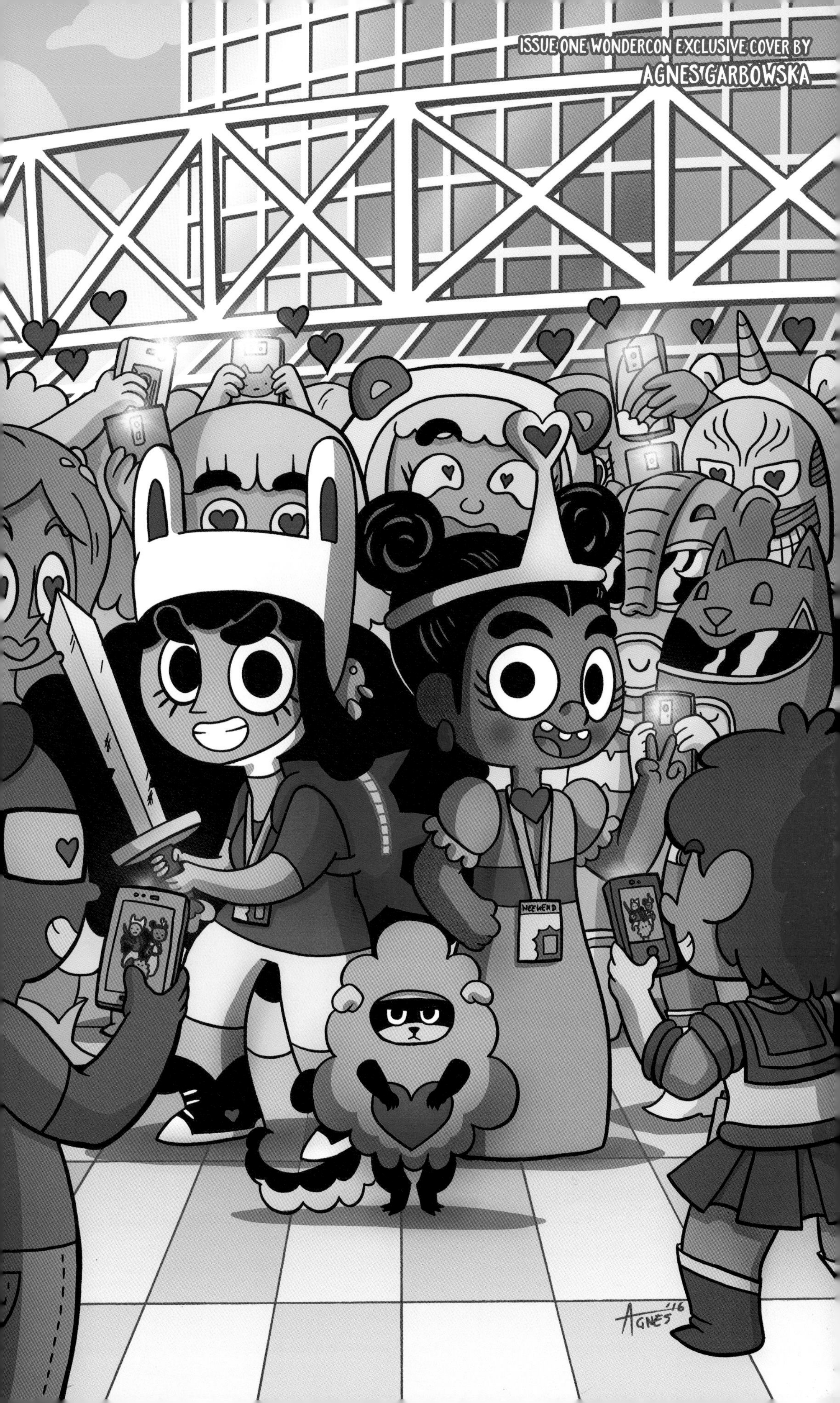
AGNES '16
ISSUE ONE WONDERCON EXCLUSIVE COVER BY
AGNES GARBOWSKA

ISSUE ONE IN-STORE CONVENTION KICK-OFF EXCLUSIVE COVER BY
KENDRA WELLS

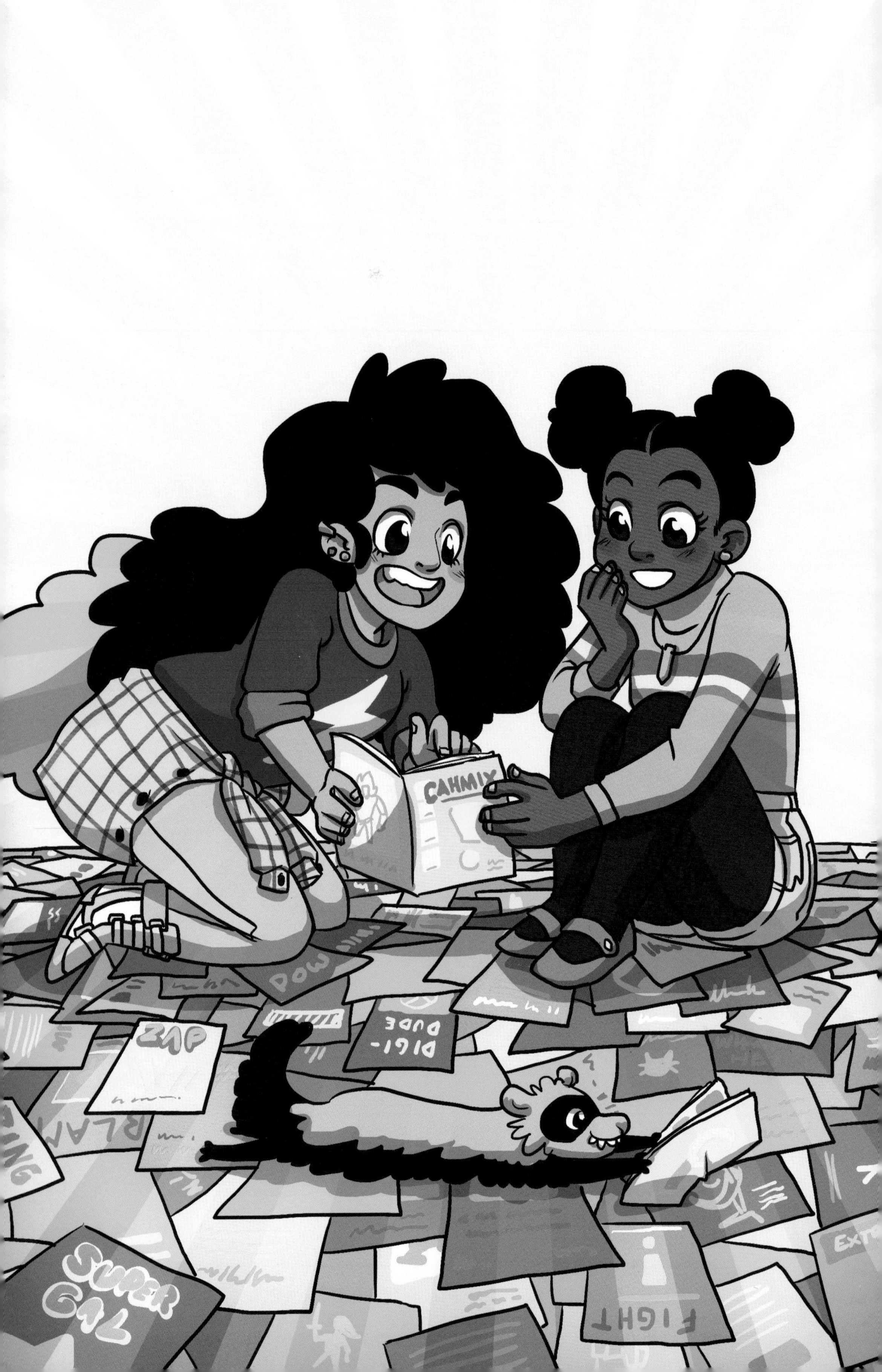
CAHMIX
POW
ZAP
DIGI-DUDE
SUPER GAL
FIGHT

ISSUE TWO COVER BY
CAITLIN ROSE BOYLE
COLORS BY MICKEY QUINN

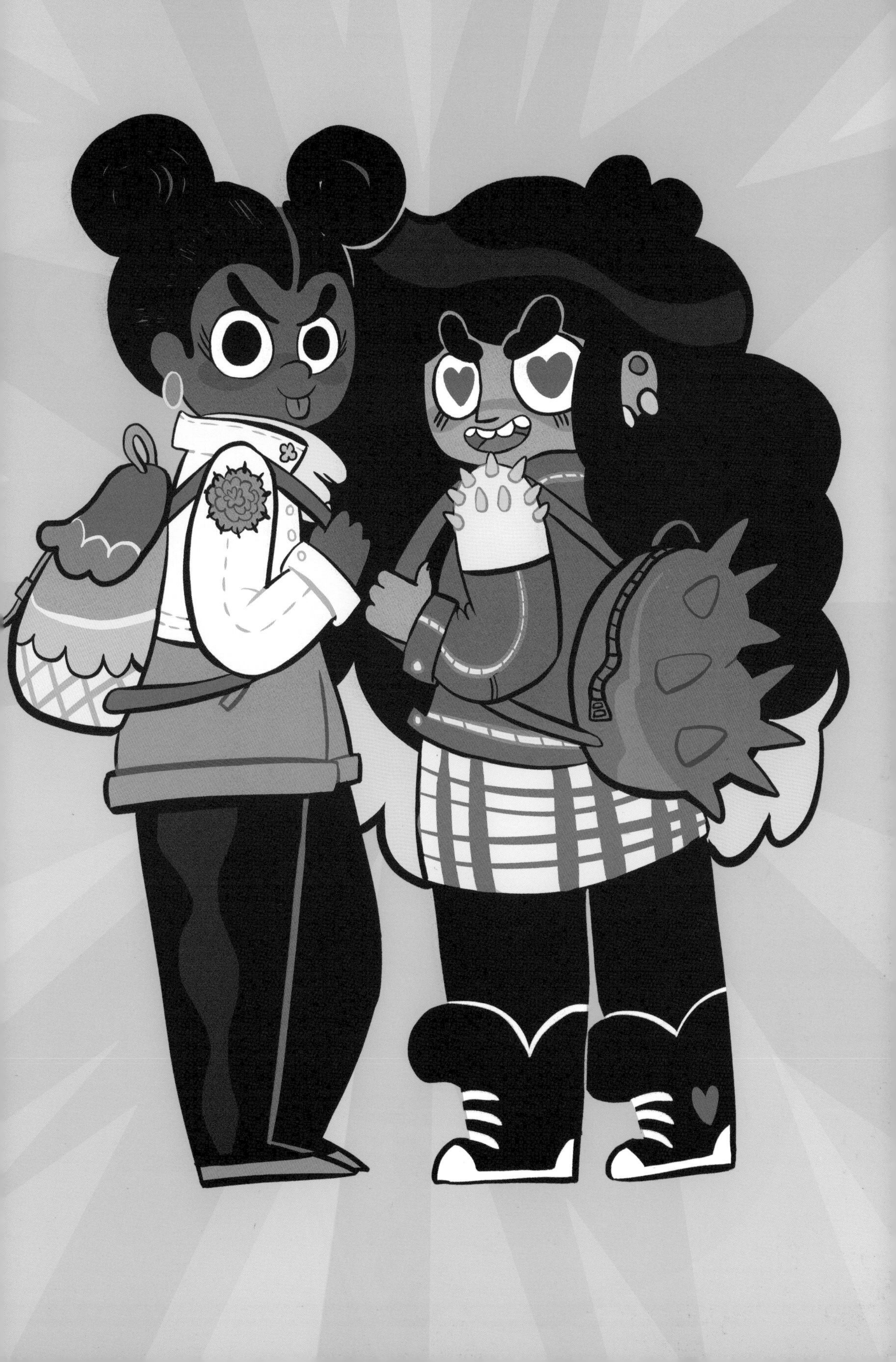

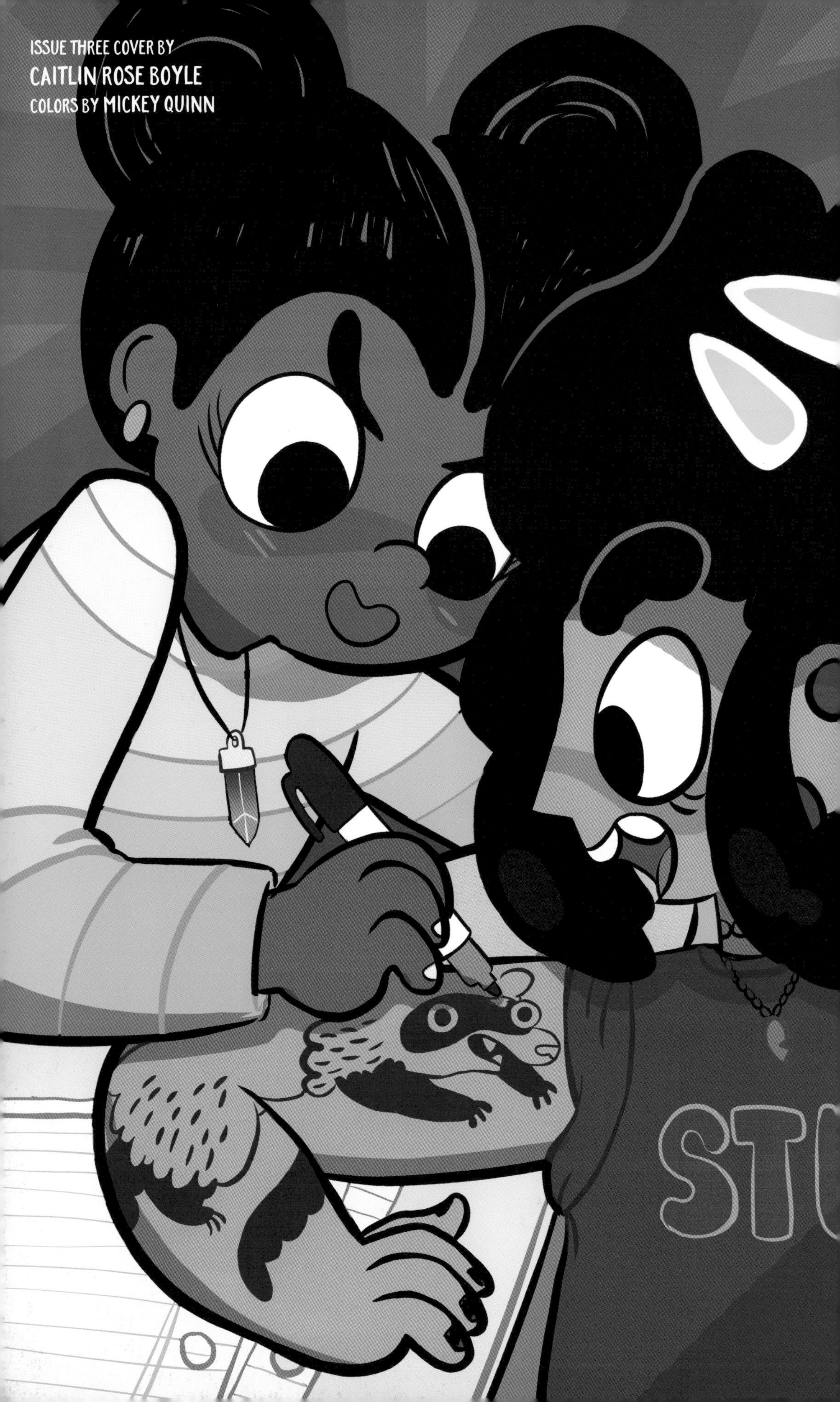

ISSUE THREE COVER BY
CAITLIN ROSE BOYLE
COLORS BY MICKEY QUINN

ISSUE FOUR COVER BY
CAITLIN ROSE BOYLE
COLORS BY MICKEY QUINN

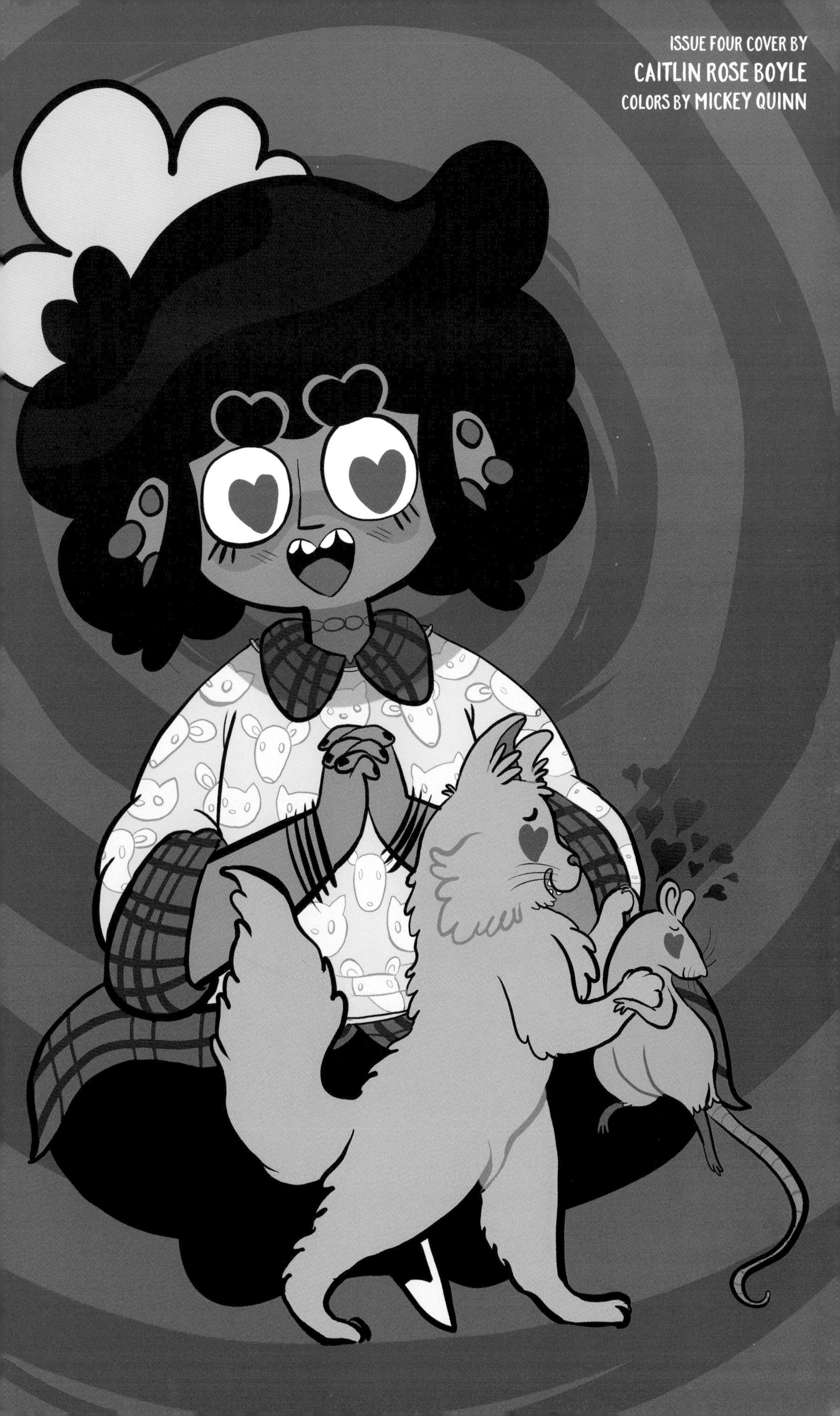

## DEVELOPMENT SKETCHES AND COMMENTARY BY
## CAITLIN ROSE BOYLE

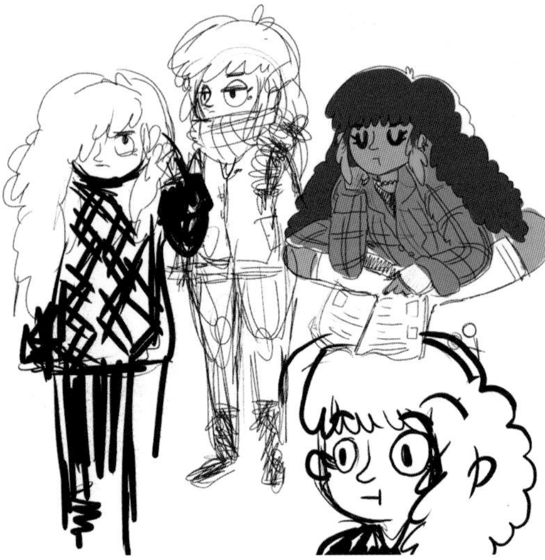

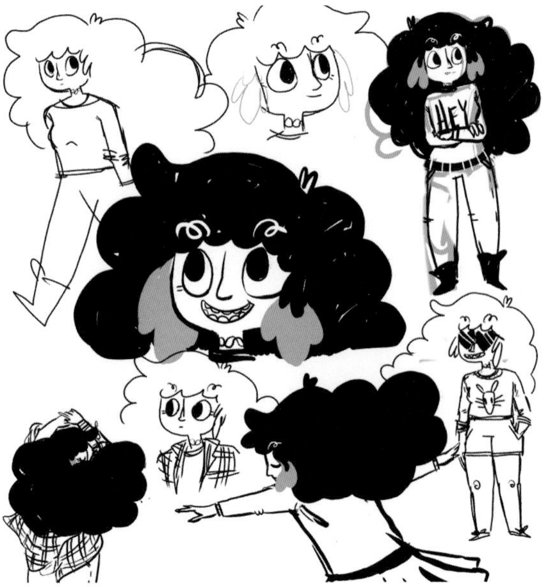
HEY

1

These were my very first JONESY sketches - she's starting to feel like herself down at the bottom right, but she's missing her cartoony sense of fun.

2

Starting to move in the right direction here - instead of dyed tips, she had these dyed tuffs of hair on either side of her face that hid her ears? I'm not sure what I was thinking with that one. She also sported curly eyebrows, instead of her GIANT JELLYBEAN BROWS as I like to think of them.

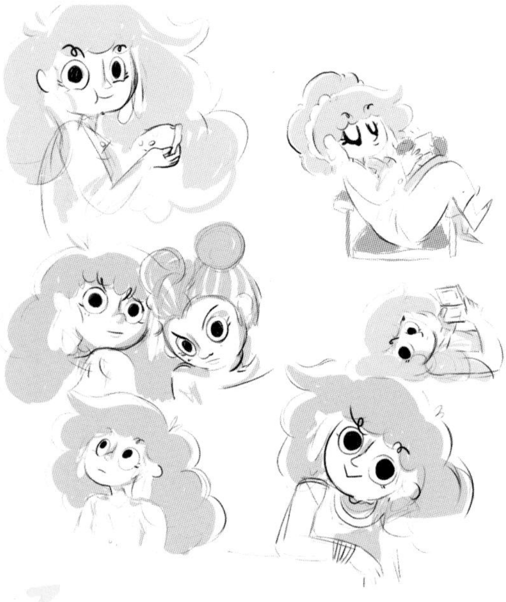

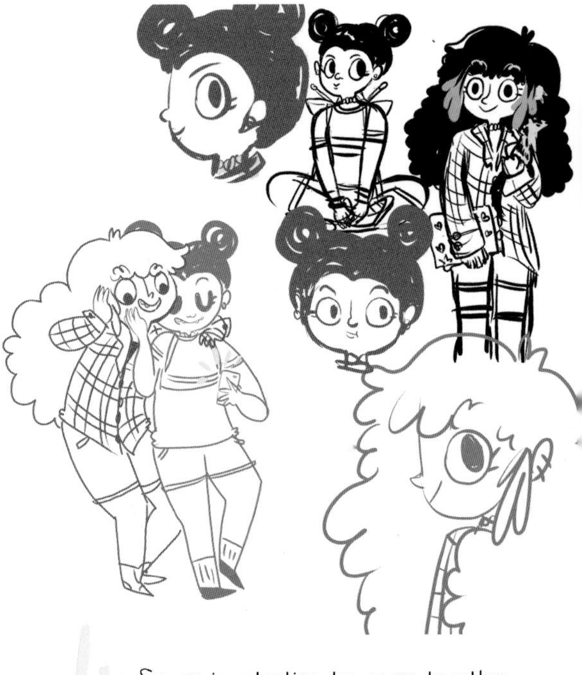

3

I wanted to do a series of sketches of Jonesy just emoting and being a person - she's a little softer here than she is in the comics. The eyebrows and hair are still wrong, but her face is starting to come together.

4

Susan is starting to come together here - Susan is way shorter than Jonesy in a lot of the concept art! I had't figured out her height or her style yet - early Susan looks like she raided Jonesy's closet.

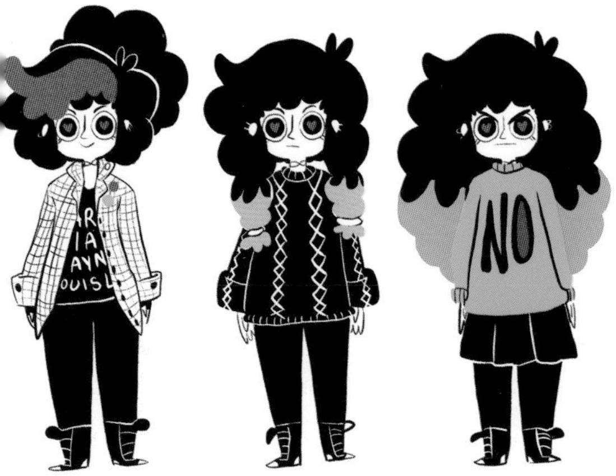
NO

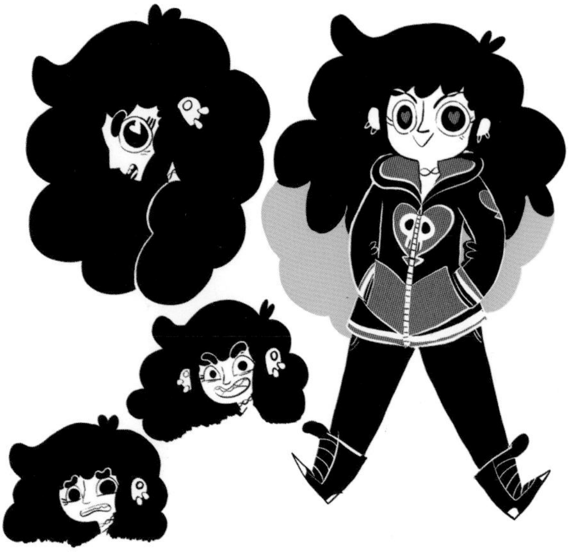

5

Jonesy's style is coming together! These were some hair + outfit options – I still really love middle pigtails Jonesy. The tips of her hair are blue here, but she's getting closer to the jerk we know & love – her ears are finally visible, and her eyebrows are starting to thicken up.

6

Trying out thick eyebrows!!! I love how expressive and MAD they make her look. Jonesy feels everything at like 110%.

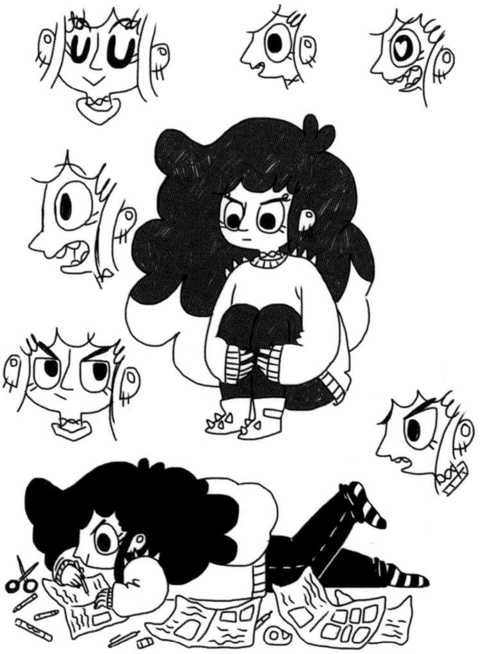

7

This Jonesy is super close to her final form!!! She's got spikes on her shoulders, her ears are getting bigger, and she's hard at work on an issue of HEY BABY, her stuff zine.

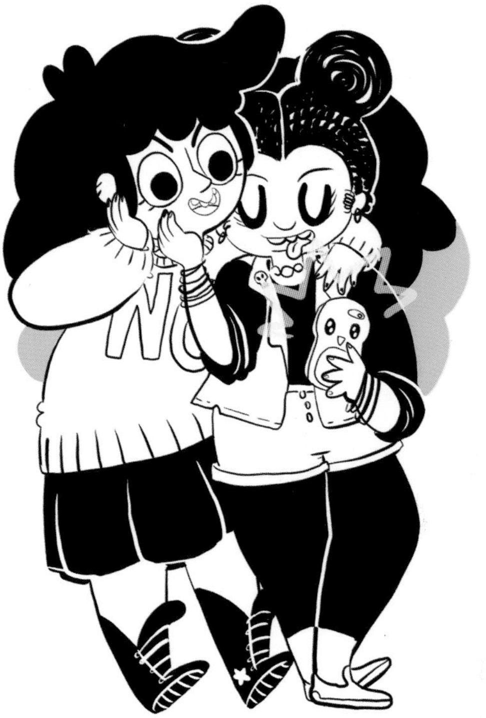

8

Selfies are wonderful, a lot of my early drawings are just the characters taking selfies. I think this is one of the last instances of short Susan? I realized pretty early on that I wanted Jonesy to be this small bundle of attitude, so giving Susan some height was a nice way to visually contrast the two.

# CREATOR
# BIOS

**SAM HUMPHRIES** is a comic book writer. He broke into comics with the self-published runaway hits *Our Love Is Real* and *Sacrifice*. Since then, he has written high profile books such as *Legendary Star-Lord* for Marvel, *Green Lanterns* for DC Comics, and *Citizen Jack* for Image Comics. He lives in Los Angeles with his girlfriend and their cat, El Niño.

**CAITLIN ROSE BOYLE** is a cartoonist. Her work can be found on tumblr, in a handful of fanzines, and in *Chainmail Bikini: The Anthology Of Women Gamers*. She co-created the Short Toon *Buck N' Lou & The Night Crew* for Nickelodeon's 2014 Shorts Program. *Jonesy* is her first comic book series. She grew up in Southern Maryland, but now she lives in Pittsburgh with her boyfriend and enough pokédolls to make up another person if you smushed them all together into one solid humanoid form.

**MICKEY QUINN** got her BFA in Illustration from MICA and since 2011 has written and drawn the online comic-turned-illustrated story *Best Friends Forever* in addition to working as a freelance illustrator, colorist, and storyboard artist. She currently lives in Burbank, working as a storyboard artist at Cartoon Network and colorist for the Image Comics series *Snotgirl* by Leslie Hung and Bryan Lee O'Malley.

**COREY BREEN** has been a professional in the comic book industry for over fifteen years, thirteen of which were for DC Entertainment. As a Sr. Pre-Press Artist, he has contributed art, lettering, color and more to thousands of comic books and other media. Having left DC Entertainment in 2013 to move down to Virginia, Corey is now a superhero in his own right. He is a head designer at a top investment firm company by day, and continues to work in the comic book industry as a freelancer by night. He currently enjoys lettering some of DC and BOOM! Studios' fan favorite books. Corey lives with his loving wife, Kristy, toddler son Tyler, and three cats.

**JEANINE SCHAEFER** has been editing comics for over ten years. She's worked at both Marvel and DC, and her current titles include the upcoming *Motor Crush* and *Prima* from Image Comics. She founded *Girl Comics*, an anthology celebrating the history of women at Marvel, and edited the Eisner-nominated Marvel *Ya Mystic*. She lives in Los Angeles with her husband and tornado/daughter, and sporadically runs a tumblr celebrating the special relationship between nerds and cats.

**SHANNON WATTERS** is an editor at BOOM! Studios and the head of its BOOM! Box and KaBOOM! imprints. She is also the co-creator and co-writer of the Eisner Award-winning comic book series *Lumberjanes*. She lives in Los Angeles with her beautiful Canadian wife and their exceptionally adorable dog.